LOCKDOWN LIFE
The Pandemic Experience for Older Diarists

Nicola Madge

First published in Great Britain in 2026 by

Policy Press, an imprint of
Bristol University Press
University of Bristol
1–9 Old Park Hill
Bristol
BS2 8BB
UK
t: +44 (0)117 374 6645
e: bup-info@bristol.ac.uk

Details of international sales and distribution partners are available at
policy.bristoluniversitypress.co.uk

© Bristol University Press 2026

British Library Cataloguing in Publication Data
A catalogue record for this book is available from the British Library

ISBN 978-1-4473-7252-3 hardcover
ISBN 978-1-4473-7253-0 paperback
ISBN 978-1-4473-7254-7 ePub
ISBN 978-1-4473-7255-4 ePdf

The right of Nicola Madge to be identified as author of this work has been asserted by her in accordance with the Copyright, Designs and Patents Act 1988.

All rights reserved: no part of this publication may be reproduced, stored in a retrieval system, or transmitted in any form or by any means, electronic, mechanical, photocopying, recording, or otherwise without the prior permission of Bristol University Press.

Every reasonable effort has been made to obtain permission to reproduce copyrighted material. If, however, anyone knows of an oversight, please contact the publisher.

The statements and opinions contained within this publication are solely those of the author and not of the University of Bristol or Bristol University Press. The University of Bristol and Bristol University Press disclaim responsibility for any injury to persons or property resulting from any material published in this publication.

Bristol University Press and Policy Press work to counter discrimination on
grounds of gender, race, disability, age and sexuality.

Cover design: Liam Roberts Design
Front cover image: iStock/dusanpetkovic

Bristol University Press' authorised representative in the European Union is:
Easy Access System Europe, Mustamäe tee 50, 10621 Tallinn, Estonia,
Email: gpsr.requests@easproject.com

Contents

About the author		iv
Acknowledgements		v
Foreword by David Kynaston		vi
1	Introduction	1
2	The pandemic arrives	18
3	Unprecedented control	42
4	All in it together?	68
5	The 'new normal'	92
6	Keeping the virus at bay	123
7	Clouds and silver linings	145
8	The gradual return	170
9	Was anything learned?	192
10	Conclusion	211
References		230
Index		244

About the author

Nicola Madge has had a long career in social research and is currently Honorary Professor at Kingston University, London. She has published widely on topics spanning education, disadvantage, health, deliberate self-harm, and young people and religious identity. Most recently she has turned her attention to older people and is the author of *Sixty Somethings: The lives of women who remember the Sixties* (written with Paul Hoggart and published in 2020 by Quartet Books). More information about Nicola can be found at www.nicolamadge.co.uk.

Acknowledgements

First and foremost, thank you to the wonderful diarists who wrote almost a million and a half words on their thoughts and experiences during the pandemic and lockdowns. You kept me busy, informed and entertained during what was an unprecedented event in recent social history. I am sorry that it has not been possible to include more of your diary entries in this book, but I hope that you enjoyed taking part in the project nonetheless. I also hope that I have done justice to what you wrote, and that you recognise the story I have portrayed. The account is, of course, my own responsibility, but I would like to thank those who have helped me along the way. In particular I would like to thank Kevin Stenson who has been a patient but enthusiastic sounding board as the book has progressed, and has made numerous helpful suggestions. I am also appreciative of the useful comments made by the anonymous reviewers of the manuscript, and particularly pleased that David Kynaston agreed to write a Foreword to the book. Last but not least, my thanks go to Policy Press and associates, and especially Emily Ross, Anna Richardson, Sophia Unger and Bahar Muller, for their friendly help and support in bringing this book to fruition.

Foreword

David Kynaston
Historian and author of Austerity Britain

Lockdown Life is a brilliant idea brilliantly executed. Diaries at their best are a uniquely valuable historical source – naked; unmediated; no idea what the future holds – and those memorable months of spring and early summer 2020, as lockdown took hold, might almost have been designed for the diary form. Madge's account via her diarists does not pretend to be comprehensive, being based solely on the record of older people, but it does get us wonderfully close to what those challenging weeks and months *felt* like, from resolving ethical dilemmas of conduct all the way through to watching the changing behaviour of pets. My favourite diary quote, amid stiff competition, is from Frances on 9 April: 'Reading the newspapers at the moment, and watching the news, is like a relationship that's gone sour; you can't do without them, but you can't bear the sight of them.' Exactly, exactly. And my favourite chapter is on 'The "New Normal"', with its instantly resonant section titles: 'The reorganisation of time'; 'Wills and "death stuff"'; 'Keeping occupied'; 'And then there was Zoom'; 'The significance of food'; 'Keeping up appearances'; 'Spending and spending less'. Again, this is spot-on – and all of it so richly, shrewdly and often humorously documented. Historians and sociologists are going to be in debt to Nicola Madge and her diarists for many years to come; while as for the general reader, and despite the inevitably darker and more troubling aspects of this account, I can only reach for an overused but nevertheless meaningful word: enjoy – even if at the same time having fingers firmly crossed that in our lifetimes we do not have to go through anything like the COVID era again.

August 2024

1

Introduction

The COVID-19 pandemic, which reached Britain in early 2020, was an event like no other. It arrived with little warning, led to previously unheard-of restrictions and control within the general population, and transformed everyday lives. The times were imbued with risk and uncertainty.

This book draws on the diary entries of 68 relatively advantaged older men and women, mainly resident in England but also living in Scotland and Wales, written at the time. It describes their experiences and reactions over the next year or so as they abandoned many taken-for-granted behaviours and activities and adopted new patterns of daily life. Their personal accounts are examined within a, mainly, symbolic interactionist framework, but also set within the political and legal context as well as alongside contemporary research and comment.

Setting the scene

On 11 March 2020 the World Health Organization (WHO) declared a pandemic. COVID-19, the official name given on 11 February 2020 to the coronavirus first identified in Wuhan China in late 2019, was sweeping the world and had already claimed over 4,000 lives. It was reported that there were three times as many countries with cases, and 13 times as many cases outside China, as only two weeks previously. Everything was happening very quickly and the British government was set to act. People were urged to stay at home and avoid contact with others not in their immediate family, while stronger measures were in the offing. Matters came to a head on 23 March 2020 when Boris Johnson, then British prime minister, announced a national lockdown in England that was followed, albeit with some minor differences, in Scotland and Wales.[1] This was not a recommendation but a directive backed by legislation.

Although pandemics are nothing new and have been responsible throughout history for more human deaths than wars, natural disasters or any other cause, largely because they are able to reproduce and transmit themselves through animals and humans (Piret and Boivin, 2021), this

---

[1] This study is restricted to the three constituent countries of Great Britain: England, Scotland and Wales.

occurrence was an unprecedented event. Previously, the worst outbreak was undoubtedly the Spanish flu' pandemic that coincided with the end of the First World War in 1918–19. Others have been the Asian flu' pandemic of 1957–58, the Hong Kong flu' pandemic of 1968–69, and the less serious outbreak of swine flu' in 2009–10, These four pandemics led to around 200,000, 33,000, 80,000 and under 500 deaths in Britain, respectively. Two other threatened pandemics which did not materialise in this country were Serious Acute Respiratory Syndrome (SARS) in 2002–03, and Middle East Respiratory Syndrome (MERS) in 2012. COVID-19 has been more serious than all the other pandemics in the past century. It has swept the world, created havoc almost everywhere, and led to large scale illness and death.

This pandemic was a new experience, for Britain and for individual members of its population, in other ways too. Nationally, and quite apart from the widespread risk to health, it was unknown in current lifetimes for the government to dictate to its citizens what they could and could not do. However, these were unusual times and normal service was suspended. As has often happened in the past, ongoing priorities and policies were overtaken by an unanticipated crisis. As Harold Macmillan had reputedly once said when prime minister, 'Events, dear boy, events'. In this case it was the pandemic that had taken control. There was no reliable information on the course it would take, the likely toll on human health and life, or the best strategy to follow, but something had to be done. The real debate had not yet begun. It was a time for quick decisions.

Once the country entered the first lockdown the endless discussion began. How were public health and economic priorities to be balanced, and how were the interests and freedom of individuals and social groups to be set against the needs of the wider collectivity? There were many possible policy directions and, despite the international oversight role of the WHO, countries went their own ways, even if they had a keen interest in policies elsewhere. At one end of the continuum were nations, such as China, instigating strict lockdowns and at the other, notably Sweden, those choosing to impose few restrictions and let life continue as much as possible as before. On the whole, most Western countries opted for a largely risk-averse strategy.

In Britain, the most prominent advisers were public sector professionals, especially medics and epidemiologists. They were often seen to flank the prime minister in the daily public broadcasts and their advice was influential. On the whole they favoured a public health management model whereby relatively stringent restrictions had the aim of minimising severe illness and death and keeping the strain on the NHS to a minimum. This strategy had both proponents and opponents. Jonathan Portes (2020), a professor of economics and public policy, was among those calling for a greater diversity of backgrounds among those advising the government. There were charges that other perspectives, such as social science, were being marginalised. Robert Dingwall (2023a and b), a professor of sociology, has endorsed this view.

There were other keen dissenters, particularly from business and the more precarious sectors of the community. Hospitality, the retail and travel industries, the arts and many other sectors were suffering badly and urged a different approach. There were serious concerns for the economy and the impact on unemployment, hardship, education, and health issues other than COVID-19.

In the event, the public health perspective predominated and Britain was to err on the side of caution. A 'state of exception' (Schmitt, 2014) was decreed and this emergency provided the justification for the immediate introduction of a new set of rules. Until Thursday 24 February 2022, when all COVID-19 legal restrictions in England were removed (the removal of restrictions in Scotland and Wales followed a little later), and the requirement to self-isolate morphed from legal restriction to guidance, there was a changing raft of measures that set limits on freedom. There were three national lockdowns, localised lockdowns, tiers whereby stricter restrictions were in place in some geographical locations than in others, as well as continuing requirements for social distancing, self-isolation and mask wearing. Business was, nonetheless, also accorded some attention, notably with the chancellor's furlough system that paid many salaries for some months, albeit at a reduced rate, and other forms of additional support.

These measures had profound implications for the nation. Individuals were being asked to yield to new powers and dictates, and make sacrifices for the greater good. Thus almost overnight the personal rights of citizens and the autonomy to take their own decisions were undermined. There were changes in acceptable conduct and changes in normative order. A new morality and a new view of criminality were established. This was an unknown experience and not at all in line with the tradition and democratic status of the country. It was hoped the nation would go along with it, but the law was evoked to maximise compliance.

How did the citizens respond? Of course, nobody was any clearer than the government on what would happen next. There was a strong sense of uncertainty in the air and citizens had to contend not only with formal proclamations but also misinformation and disinformation, whether provided in good faith or maliciously, via social media and other sources. There was a lot to make sense of. It was easy enough to comprehend the rapid increase in hospitalisations and deaths, but beyond this there was much that remained unknown. How did one catch the virus, what was its *modus operandum*, how could it be kept at bay, what did many of the new restrictions actually mean, and when could one venture out safely again? It was presumed, or at least hoped, that the restrictions would be a temporary measure, but how long might they last and what could follow? How long would people be prepared to put up with an erosion of their civil liberties, and what would be the sustaining factors? These and many other questions dominated as the pandemic progressed.

And there was no single set of answers. Indeed, it was apparent that the pandemic would not provide the same experience for everyone. Early on, and before the initial lockdown, older adults had been identified, alongside those of any age with specific disabilities and vulnerabilities, as at special risk from the virus. Some months later there was support in some quarters for the Great Barrington Declaration (Kulldorff et al, 2020), published in America in October 2020. This advocated a herd immunity strategy whereby the shielding of the elderly and the vulnerable allowed everybody else to get on with life as normal. It has its proponents but was not fully implemented in any country.

In the event there was no differential treatment according to age in Britain, although the most vulnerable, due to underlying conditions, were ordered to 'shield' themselves. The association between age and risk was nonetheless recognised, perhaps most memorably in September 2020 when Matt Hancock, then health secretary in England, told young people 'Don't kill your gran' as infection rates rose steeply among teenagers and those in their twenties.

There was also recognition that not everybody could be equally protected. The mass of the population could not (comfortably) remain in isolation without 'essential workers'. The majority became dependent on the minority to, for example, bring them food, maintain law and order, run the hospitals and care homes, operate power and sewerage plants, collect the rubbish and catch the rats. There was a very real collective dimension to the new life. The population at large seemed aware of this, giving public acknowledgement to the essential workers keeping the show on the road by clapping in appreciation on Thursday evenings.

And so the show went on amid continuing debate and shifting restrictions. Undoubtedly experiences varied enormously between people of different ages, occupations, ethnicities, geographical locations, cultures and so on. Everyone had their own story to tell.

They saw it happen

This project was instigated to contribute to social history by gathering the accounts, *as it happened*, of 68 older men and women as COVID-19 reached the shores of Britain in 2020. At the outset of the pandemic it was mooted that those aged 70 and above might be singled out for enhanced protection from the virus. The age of participants in this diary project was selected to enable a focus on this group. It was anticipated that their experiences would be very different from both younger groups as well as others of their own age living in more disadvantaged circumstances.

Even if fit and active, members of the target population were likely, in the main, to be retired, and hence unlikely to be in a position of losing a job or having to leave their homes on a regular basis. Consenting to write diaries for a prolonged period also suggested that they would be drawn from an educated section of the community. It was not known how they would react to the pandemic but it was likely that their experiences would be very different from, and complementary to, those of large swathes of the national population. Building a picture of life in any one period is rather like completing a jigsaw and hoping that not too many of the pieces are missing. It was hoped the pandemic diaries written by the seventy somethings might enable at least a piece or two to be slotted into the puzzle.

Social history has always placed a strong reliance on the thoughts and experiences of individuals, whether provided directly through word of mouth, letters, diaries and other writings, or second-hand through poetry, song, art, novels and more formal social enquiry. It is, for instance, well documented that much of the material for Shakespeare's plays was gathered from conversations he overheard in public houses, while Dickens' novels reflected his first-hand experience of poverty and hardship. Much literature indeed contributes to understanding of the times in which authors lived.

In more modern times, opportunities for people from all walks of life to espouse their views, and leave these for posterity, have increased enormously. Literacy has improved manifold, and diaries and autobiographies have proliferated accordingly. The recent rise of the mass media has also led to countless blogs, much messaging incorporating both words and images, and so on and so forth. The current trend towards vox pop and the continuous portrayal of voices from different backgrounds and persuasions on news programmes and chat shows adds to the mix.

The personal diary, within this tsunami of personal perspectives, does nonetheless still retain a special status. Historically it has been invaluable in providing insights into both specific events and everyday life.

The English diarist Samuel Pepys, for instance, contributed more than a million words between 1660 and 1669 (but wrote hardly at all for the last 30 years of his life). Combining eyewitness accounts and his own observations, he provided valuable testament to such events as the Great Plague of London and the Great Fire of London. He also wrote about his own everyday life, charting his daily activities in detail, including his illicit affairs.

Many of the early diarists were persons of relatively high social standing who were educated and literate, and who had time and inclination to chart their observations and feelings. As time has gone by, however, noted diarists have increasingly come from very different backgrounds.

Anne Frank is a good example. Born in Germany of Jewish heritage in 1929, she was living in the Netherlands in 1940 when the country was under German occupation and the family was forced into hiding in her father's workplace. Anne had been given an autograph book for her birthday in 1942 which she used as a diary to record her daily life until the family was arrested and taken to concentration camps in 1944. She died in the Bergen-Belsen camp in March 1945 but her diary was later found by her brother Otto. It has since been published in over 70 languages. The English version, first published in 1952, was entitled *The Diary of a Young Girl* (Frank, 1952).

The encouragement of diary writing by those from all walks of life took a new turn with the birth of the Mass Observation movement founded in 1937 by three one-time students at Cambridge University: Tom Harrisson who was also an anthropologist, Charles Madge, a poet and sociologist (and incidentally the author's uncle), and Humphrey Jennings, a film maker. The aim was to give voice to 'ordinary people' leading 'ordinary lives' through a variety of means such as diaries, interviews and questionnaires. Its first publication, *May the Twelfth: Mass-Observation Day-Surveys 1937 by over two hundred observers* (Jennings and Madge, 1987), presented views on the abdication of Edward VIII to marry Mrs Simpson and the succession of George VI. Interestingly, and giving some justification to the movement, this report exposed the mismatch between what the papers said and the views of the 'man in the street'.

The onset of the Second World War provided an important role for Mass Observation by inviting members of the general public to keep diaries to record their thoughts and experiences over the wartime period. Nella Last, a housewife from Lancashire, was among the 480 diarists to respond to this challenge and she was the most prolific. She wrote copiously (writing some 12 million words) and regularly about her life, and continued throughout the subsequent peace period between 1945 and 1966. Her diaries have since been published (Malcolmson and Malcolmson, 2012) and her life portrayed in the television drama *Housewife 49*. The Mass Observation movement ran until the mid-1960s, largely with the help of a large network of volunteers. It was revived in 1981 when the Mass Observation Archive was set up at the University of Sussex.

The telling of social history continues to rely on the everyday experiences of people from all walks of life. Kynaston has proved himself a master of the art in bringing together a range of evidence, including personal diaries, to help in the understanding of how recent events have shaped both individual lives and the more collective whole. His history of post-war Britain, to date covering the period between 1945 and 1965 (Kynaston, 2007, 2009, 2013, 2014, 2021, 2023), provides an excellent example of how this can be done.

Introduction

According to Trevelyan (1944), who painted a portrait of English family life over six centuries, social history is 'the history of a people with the politics left out'. And as the British historian Cannadine (1985) wrote:

> To Trevelyan … social history encompassed the human as well as the economic relations of different classes, the character of family and household life, the conditions of labour and leisure, the attitude of man towards nature, and the cumulative influence of all these subjects on culture, including religion, architecture, literature, music, learning and thought.

In the present study, key questions focused on how the diarists reacted to the erosion of freedom, the expectations and behaviours they developed in the face of uncertainty and the unknown, and the ease with which they adapted as familiar activities were cancelled and time took on a new meaning. It was hoped that the pandemic diaries drawn upon in this book might uncover lessons to be learned should a similar occurrence happen in the future. As Santayana (1905) wrote: 'Those who cannot remember the past are condemned to repeat it'.

Recruiting the COVID-19 diarists

The *Lockdown Life* project was envisaged as a modern day Mass Observation exercise and needed to get off the ground quickly. It was important to recruit the diarists as speedily as possible to enable the coronavirus pandemic to be charted from the very beginning. The project had been conceived on 19 March 2020 and the author accordingly put together a proposal to distribute to potential contributors. It outlined the purpose of the project as well as what participants would be asked to do. In essence, the expectation was that they would first complete a retrospective diary on events leading up to the lockdown, and then provide entries when they could, but hopefully around three times a week, until an unspecified time (which turned out to be the end of July 2020, four months later). They would also be asked to participate in a small number of subsequent follow-ups.

Recruitment began two days later, on 21 March 2020, and proceeded well. Target participants for the study were men and women of 70 or over and living anywhere in Britain. The only other requirement was that they were willing to keep regular diaries. The aim was to recruit authentic voices rather than a representative sample. Initially, the author wrote to eligible participants from an earlier study she had carried out, as well as anybody else that she knew who might be interested to take part. In turn, these contacts passed the information on to others they knew, and so on. This 'snowballing' was particularly successful as details of the project would be passed only to others who were eligible and might wish to participate.

Just over 70 participants were initially recruited, and 68 were included within the project. In terms of demographic profile, there were 48 women and 20 men in the group. Three had been born in or before 1940, 17 were born between 1941 and 1946, and 48 were born between 1946 and 1950. Thus most diarists were in their 70s, with only three aged 80 or more. Overall, 37 were married, in civil partnerships or cohabiting while 31 were widowed, divorced, separated or otherwise single. At the time of the project, 22 were living alone. Apart from two diarists describing themselves as French or Dutch, everyone said they were British. Although it was not explicitly recorded, it is believed that all were white. Almost all said their health was good or fairly good, with a few mentioning current or past health problems. Ten indicated that they might be particularly vulnerable to the coronavirus.

Almost all the diarists reported themselves to be retired, with just a small number mentioning part-time occupations or other professional activities that they were still involved with. Most were living in houses, with a few in flats, and nobody said that their personal space was inadequate. Indeed, almost everyone said it was good or even excellent. Many were also living in rural or semi-rural locations with gardens and access to green spaces. The vast majority of the diarists were from England, but seven were from Scotland, and one was from Wales. The English contingent was widely distributed although predominantly from the West Midlands, London and the South East, the South West and the East of England. There were no diarists from Northern Ireland.

In summary, the sample was white and middle class. This reflected the targeted age group which, nationally, is far less diverse than younger generations and predominantly white British, the snowballing method of recruitment whereby participants forwarded details of the project to people they knew and who, presumably, were likely to be similar to themselves demographically, and the requirement that anybody taking part was willing and able to keep a diary. It was a specific population sample and not representative of the country as a whole or the age group in particular.

Diarists, who were almost all in their 70s, were maybe more representative of ex-Baby Boomers, as described by Madge and Hoggart (2020) in *Sixty Somethings: The lives of women who remember the Sixties*, than of the totality of their age group. This generation often began life in relatively frugal conditions but was able to take advantage of a booming economy and the growth of the welfare state. They benefited from a good education, and women were much more likely than their mothers to have had careers. The more advantaged of this generation were able to buy their own homes and profit from the boom in house prices. Once retired, often with decent pensions, most could lead comfortable lives, perhaps volunteering and travelling, pursuing their own interests, and helping care for grandchildren. Although said to be privileged by some, they were more likely to say they had been lucky.

Introduction

Recruitment proceeded well and within days the first diary entries had been completed. A handful of diarists said they were keeping diaries when the project began, but most were not. A considerable number, however, reported having kept personal records at some point in their lives. These were often during childhood, the teenage years, holidays, or times of particular stress. Quite often these diaries had subsequently been destroyed. Several diarists explain.

APPLETREE
Friday 19 June 2020

This diary has, for the time being, superseded the usual diary I keep. That one's sporadic ... perhaps three times a month, handwritten, a little more personal, sometimes illustrated with drawings, bits from the newspaper, photos. That one, too, has more about wildlife in it, more family stuff, more comment on what I'm reading and is more sourly judgmental.

ARAMINTA
Thursday 18 June 2020

I did keep a diary for quite a number of years but then I decided to destroy them all as I didn't want anyone to read them once I was dead. These days I normally only keep a diary when I am on holiday.

BEA
Friday 19 June 2020

I have marked significant periods of my life with diaries with mixed success. After reading Anne Frank I started a very pretentious diary of my own which didn't last long. I had three diaries spanning my ages 15/16/17 which are full of teenage angst and which my daughters have read with my permission and found hilarious. My diary for 1968 caused me huge troubles. I packed it in my trunk which was sent on in advance when I left university. My mother unpacked the trunk and read the diary and discovered that I was on the pill. That went down well. ... It never occurred to me that she had no right to read my diary. Since then I have kept diaries on occasions but have destroyed some of them when the moment had passed.

BENCHMAN
Saturday 13 June 2020

This is probably the longest period in my life that I have kept a diary of any kind since I was a teenager. I still have that diary, but it's too embarrassing to read, and anyway I can't understand half the references. What's interesting is that I was writing it during the winter of 1962–63, and yet I make almost no reference to the weather conditions. As a teenager, relationships were much more important than the environment. This diary, by contrast, has lots about the weather and rather less about relationships!

CHARLES
Saturday 27 June 2020

Thank you Nicola for giving me the opportunity of writing a diary, something I have not done since I kept a day to day diary for an entire year in 1963/4!

EVE
Friday 19 June 2020

This is the first time I have written a daily diary since I was a teenager. It's part of my routine now so I may well carry on with it after this project ends. I think it will be a useful record of this odd time to look back on to remind me of how I felt.

HOLLY
Friday 26 June 2020

In answer to Nicola's questions about diary writing: yes, I've often written a diary but don't ever do it continuously. As a child, I always started the year with good intentions but entries usually tailed off sometime in February. The ones that have survived are quite good fun, though. At the age of exactly eight, there is an entry I'm particularly fond of on 21 January. It reads, 'My birthday. I had a bath'.

As an adult, I've sometimes used the diary form to record my thoughts and sort my head out if things were a bit tough. Again, it's not very consistent – I may write every day for a while and then nothing much for a long period after that.

TARANAKI
Friday 19 June 2020

Nicola, you spoke about being a diarist. Yes, I have been. Sadly in 1996/1997 I suffered from clinical depression and part of my therapy was to keep a daily record of how I felt and how much different activities either helped or hindered me. I wrote it for the best part of a year. Finally last year, I threw it away. It was not a happy document ... but very useful.

For the last five years or so I have taken to keeping a journal when we are on holiday. We cruise a lot and frequently do trips lasting two or three months. I love writing the daily entry. It is not a catalogue of I did, I saw, I ate ... but much more about my reactions to the places I see and the people I meet. My husband thoroughly enjoys hearing me read it to him once every few days while we are away. It requires a fair amount of self-discipline but I always buy really nice books to write in and try to keep it neat. I have a new journal for each trip and they are stacked up on the lower shelf of the coffee table in the living room and occasionally I dip in. Of course, they are an excellent aide-memoire.

WILL

Saturday 20 June 2020

I have not been an inveterate diarist though, as I said about a million years ago when starting this exercise, I have done so from time to time, usually during periods of stress (though stress is not something I tend to suffer from) but this usually lasted no more than a week or two. I never kept what I had written after it had served its purpose.

The diary entries

Once enrolled on the project, diarists were asked first to provide some basic demographic information, a pseudonym by which they would be known, and a retrospective diary entry to record their perceptions and reactions since they had first heard of the coronavirus. Beyond this point, they wrote entries and forwarded them to the author according to their own timetables. It was suggested that they forward their entries approximately once a week, which is what most did, but some preferred different timings.

The regular diaries continued until the end of July 2020 and were followed by the two follow-ups the diarists had signed up for, plus a subsequent call for additional information. The first follow-up was one month after the main data collection period, in early September 2020, and collected information on how far the diarists had gone back to 'normal'. Most restrictions had been lifted and a vaccine was on the horizon but not yet available. The second follow-up was not until February 2021. By this time there had been two further lockdowns, bubbles had been introduced, there had been the Christmas 2020 last-minute turnabout, and most diarists had been vaccinated. In addition to the two main follow-ups, diarists were invited to provide further diary entries following the so-called Freedom Day on 19 July 2021 if they so wished. A small number of diarists also provided concluding entries a year later in July and August 2022.

The majority of diarists contributed diary entries at all main stages. Of the 68 members of the sample, 52 provided information throughout the period to the end of July 2020 and a further eight tailed off only in the last month or so. Eight diarists overall provided more limited diary entries. Initial entries had been in March 2020 for 46 diarists, and in April (mainly early April) for a further 21. Only one diarist provided a first entry at the very beginning of May that year. In addition, 52 and 55 diarists responded to the first and second follow-ups, respectively. There were 26 responses to the call for entries detailing reactions to the so-called Freedom Day. Five provided additional comment more than two years after the start of the initial lockdown.

Diarists decided when they wished to write and how they organised their diaries and there was, inevitably, considerable variation among them in terms of the amount written and the regularity of their entries. They also decided whether and how they wished to respond to the specific questions and prompts raised by the author for the retrospective diary and in the weekly updates sent out to all diarists. Some of these weekly questions had been raised by diarists themselves. In addition, there were a number of 'activities' instigated by the author during the course of the diary project. There was, for instance, a call for Lockdown Recipes, which were assembled and circulated to diarists, a Poetry Challenge, with contributions again sent round to all diarists, and an opportunity to provide Desert Island Discs, Books and Films.

Once received, diary entries were read, catalogued and acknowledged. At a later stage, each diarist's entries were collated, and all contributions were analysed by broad theme and indicative content. Summaries were then used to plan the structure of the ensuing report. There was an interest in both commonality and diversity among the participants as well as relevant illustration. The purpose of the project was not to test a specific hypothesis but to provide a grounded account of lockdown life for a group of comfortably-off over 70-year-olds living predominantly in England.

Almost one and a half million words were written by the 68 diarists to record their thoughts, understandings and experiences during the COVID-19 lockdowns and beyond. The diary excerpts that follow are, therefore, but a fraction of what they wrote. Inevitably there is a wealth of interesting, poignant and often humorous information that has, unfortunately, landed up on the cutting room floor.

A unique publication

This book makes an important contribution to the documentation of daily life during the COVID-19 pandemic. Indeed, there is no volume that compares with *Lockdown Life* in looking longitudinally at the experiences and reactions of British men and women during the pandemic, and letting them speak for themselves. And while many projects do not have age restrictions, no other report has focused in similar depth on the circumstances of older people in the community. *Lockdown Life* provides an in-depth account of the reality of the pandemic for older, relatively well-off, men and women that it will not now be possible to replicate. While *Lockdown Life* happily stands alone, it also complements many of the other projects undertaken over the same period.

Inevitably there has been much written about personal perspectives on COVID-19, the lockdowns and the pandemic. There have been newspaper and magazine articles galore, often drawing on the personal views and experiences (typically of only a small number of people), comment from experts of all kinds as well as charities representing particular interest groups, numerous novels exploring emotions and behaviours during lockdown, and an array of surveys from the Office for National Statistics as well as researchers from universities and other organisations charting the nation's reactions as events have unfolded. There have also been the 100 portraits displayed in the National Portrait Gallery as part of the *Hold Still* project spearheaded by the now Princess of Wales. These portraits were selected by over 31,000 submissions from people of all ages across the country. They were all based on a theme related to the lockdown. These initiatives, and many more, have contributed to a picture of what the pandemic has meant to those living through it.

Diaries and personal accounts have also been published. Notable among these is the compilation of diary entries collected by the Mass Observation Archive for the single day of 12 May 2020 (Clarke, 2024), mirroring the 1937 Mass Observation exercise mentioned above. The selection is drawn from the 5,000 responses to a call for diary entries on that day and represents different age groups, genders, geographical regions, and occupations. There have, too, been books with a specifically personal focus. Thus Rachel Clarke (2021) wrote *Breathtaking: The UK's human story of Covid* as a palliative care doctor, Michael Rosen (2021), the former Children's Laureate, was the author of *Many Different Types of Love: A story of life, death and the NHS* as a patient admitted to hospital with COVID-19 towards the beginning of the pandemic, and Sue Julians (2023) wrote *Breakable* on 'Everything I know about health, and how it went wrong' from her perspective as a physiotherapist. Alan Bennett (2022) also made a contribution with his *House Arrest: pandemic diaries* in which he took a typically wry look at his daily life and thoughts between February 2020 and March 2021. More recently, Matt Hancock (with Oakeshott, 2022), health secretary for much of the period of the pandemic, has published his own *Pandemic Diaries: The inside story of Britain's battle against Covid* which documented events from his perspective. This latter volume was more recently complemented by *The Lockdown Files* (The Telegraph, 2023) revealed by Isobel Oakeshott and containing over 100,000 WhatsApp messages between Matt Hancock and other ministers and officials at the height of the COVID-19 pandemic.

Many other projects have also been ongoing. Early in the pandemic, Michael Ward of Swansea University made a call for participants in a study of personal voices to provide entries in any of a number of formats (handwritten or word-processed diaries, blogs, social media posts, photos, videos, memes and other submissions such as songs, poems, shopping lists, dream logs and artwork). In May 2020 an initial report on *Lockdown Diaries: The everyday voices of the coronavirus pandemic* (Ward, 2020) presented the accounts of 164 participants aged between 11 and 87, and from a range of different backgrounds and countries. Additionally, BritainThinks (2020) followed 50 people in Britain for three weeks through written submissions and follow-up focus groups or interviews. An interesting conclusion from this venture was the striking gap between families with young children and older affluent participants. More recently, Helen McCarthy (2024), an historian, has drawn together a wide range of accounts from different sources that bring experiences during the pandemic to life.

Several projects have focused on the more disadvantaged in society. The online publication of *Lockdown Diaries of the Working Class* by Lisa McKenzie and the Working Class Collective (2022), for instance, combined words and artistry in portraying the working-class experience in the early days of the pandemic. Also pertinent is *A Year Like No Other: Life on a low income during COVID-19* by Ruth Patrick and colleagues (2022) which gave voice to low-income parents and carers. The experiences portrayed in these reports contrast sharply with those reported from the present study.

The rest of the book

The present volume examines the experiences, reactions and thoughts of older diarists as they conducted their daily lives during the COVID-19 pandemic and lockdowns. These are set within the context of the changing legislation and edicts, pertinent surveys and research, and relevant comment.

The diary entries are also presented and interpreted within a social scientific framework, and particularly from the perspective of interactionist sociologists, both traditional and present day. The central thesis of this school of thought is that actions are based on subjective understandings of the world and not simply on external circumstances and events. Meanings are socially and interactively produced.

The theoretical perspective of the symbolic interactionists seems particularly relevant to the circumstances of a population in lockdown. Key theorists, such as Goffman (1959), Berger and Luckmann (1966) and Blumer (1969), had been influenced by the American pragmatist philosophical tradition that stressed how knowledge of oneself and the surrounding world is rooted not just in contemplation but in action led by human agency, and how changing situations and contexts are accompanied by pragmatic adaptation (Dewey, 1929; Mead, 1934; James, 1949; Rock, 1979). They took these ideas forward in their empirical work, notably in an examination of the process of adaptation, and the construction of knowledge and understandings of new personal and social circumstances, within the many new populations moving to America in the latter part of the nineteenth century and the early decades of the twentieth century. They pointed to the importance of subjective meanings, derived through face-to-face interactions with people, objects and situations, and exchanged through language and symbols. These meanings, together with personal agency, were key to pragmatic adaptations.

Although the context and timings were very different, the COVID-19 pandemic also led to sudden transformations in daily life. Adaptations had to be made almost overnight amid a climate of uncertainty. Information was scarce and individuals sought their own understandings from what they could glean from their interactions, not only with other people but also with the symbols all around them. These symbols included the portrayals of the situation by politicians, the media and others, as well as their observations on the changing nature of time, space and the environment and the opportunities they presented. Their interpersonal interactions also called for further adaptations not present in the studies conducted by the early symbolic interactionists in which face-to-face interaction had been paramount. The pandemic limited opportunities for physical meetings and necessitated new forms of interaction.

The following chapters accordingly examine patterns of interaction among the diarists in a context where not only they, but also the government, institutions and everyone else, were facing uncertainty in unknown territory. How did they construct the new life-world and how did they react and behave? Of particular interest is whether diarists simply followed the rules newly imposed upon them, or if they behaved pragmatically and in accordance with their social construction of the new setting and their own wishes and needs. According to Menand, quoted by Hannem (2021), pragmatism is 'an account of the way people think, the way they come up with ideas, form beliefs, and reach decisions'. Here, and in the context of the pandemic, pragmatic adaptation is taken to refer to behaviours that are problem-solving and imbued with personal agency.

Following this introduction, Chapter 2 begins with the arrival of the pandemic in Britain. Although realisation of the seriousness of the pandemic as a social problem was gradual (Blumer, 1969), its legitimation through legislation progressed rapidly. Uncertainties abounded and diarists and others gained what knowledge they had through their interpretation of signs and symbols (Berger and Luckmann, 1966) rather than from direct evidence of illness and death. Immediate cancellations and adaptations became necessary as lockdowns were mandated and life became very different. A breakdown in symbolic order had been enforced and the taken-for-granted world (Schutz, 1945) was in abeyance.

Unprecedented change and unprecedented control, in which governments worldwide ostensibly embarked on managing and minimising risk (Giddens, 1991; Beck, 1992), were the new social order. Chapter 3 examines the reasons why the imposed restrictions were, in the main, respected and complied with. First and foremost, the situation was imbued with uncertainty, and diarists did not want to become ill. A link between media exposure and public fear has been stressed by social interactionists (Best, 2021), and the symbolism of Boris Johnson, then prime minister of England, contracting the virus, as well as the often graphic and grave language and symbols of the extensive news coverage at the time, no doubt reinforced public anxiety and fear. Conformity to the new social order was also reinforced by the police who could be seen as rule enforcers (Becker, 1963), by the diarists' own children and families, and by the new morality and judgementality encouraged by the pandemic.

A frequent message, often voiced to encourage compliance with restrictions, was that everybody was in the situation together. As outlined in Chapter 4, this was only seen as partly true by the diarists. It had some currency in that nobody was free of risk from the virus, and the nation was subject to universal rules and restrictions. Nonetheless, diarists felt singled out on account of their age, but also considered themselves relatively privileged in comparison with many others, such as the many varieties of essential worker, and children and young people unable to pursue their careers and education. They themselves were cushioned from illness and adversity unlike many other population groups. Although, in this sense, they felt they were a group apart, they did feel an affinity, and often a heightened affinity, with family, friends and, particularly, neighbours and local communities. There was increased social cohesion, at least locally and at least temporarily (Putnam, 2000). Pets could also be important. Shared humour was another factor that encouraged a sense of togetherness.

The pandemic overturned the taken-for-granted world (Schutz, 1945) and called for a reconceptualisation of daily life. Chapter 5 considers this 'new normal'. Time was reorganised, new routines were established, and activities changed. Homes and gardens gained a new significance, as did the sourcing, preparation and eating of food. Of especial importance was the increased reliance on Zoom and other technologies enabling close interactions with family, friends and others to be maintained, and the emergence of the 'terminal self' (Gottschalk, 2021). There was, perhaps, a lesser or changed significance of personal appearance, although keeping healthy remained important. Spending patterns were also modified.

Despite an ability to minimise the risk of contracting COVID-19 by staying at home much of the time, diarists were confronted with uncertainty in many aspects of their new lives. They might, for instance, be unsure about how to manage encounters with others when out for daily walks or occasional forays to shops, and they might question the tenacity of the invisible virus on gateposts, food and other deliveries. It was up to each individual to employ personal agency in constructing their own social world and deciding on their own actions in these respects (Hannem, 2021). Chapter 6 examines how diarists dealt with requirements to socially distance, wear masks, and take other precautions to avoid illness. It also discusses the impact of these measures on life more generally, including the operation of medical services and funerals. Pragmatic adaptation, as defined in this context, rather than unquestioning compliance, was in evidence.

While there were undeniably grey clouds overhead, these could have silver linings. Chapter 7 outlines how the diarists experienced disappointments and anxieties but also saw the positives in the situation. In a sense they experienced some cognitive dissonance (Festinger, 1957) between their own lives and the suffering they were reminded of around them. Their personal relationships were generally good, they had found ways to keep in touch with family, friends and others, they had become 'environmental citizens' (Puddephatt, 2021) through their increased interactions with the natural environment, and celebrations had turned out to be better than expected. Nonetheless there were uncertainties to contend with, things that were missed, and many fears and concerns. It was a time of mixed emotions.

Diarists, along with the majority of the country, had for the most part gone along with the coronavirus restrictions. They had abandoned many aspects of their taken-for-granted world and adapted with pragmatism and stoicism. Was the reverse process to be as easy? Chapter 8 looks at the short-term evidence and uncovers a mix of reactions. There was variance in the speed with which diarists were willing to resume close proximity to others, and in the continuation of fear and anxiety. And while the availability of vaccines gave cause for optimism, it did not change behaviour overnight. Many diarists expected the pandemic to make permanent changes to their lives.

COVID-19 presented the world with a global crisis quite unlike anything that had gone before. Has anything been learned? Many judgements and recommendations will emerge from the ongoing formal inquiry, but these are outside the scope of this volume. Chapter 9, however, outlines some of the key messages for discussion and debate that emerged from the experiences and views of the diarists. These include the mandate for the legal restrictions that accompanied the pandemic and the necessity of lockdowns, and the broader range of evidence and opinion to be taken into account should another similar situation arise. Beyond this there is a call for honest and transparent information, clear instructions on what is expected of citizens, sensitivity and pragmatism when it comes to the enforcement of regulations, and the availability of the internet for all. There is also discussion of the significance of national mood, the need to direct scarce resources to where they are most needed, and the importance of older people as a national resource. Being prepared in case there is a 'next time' is fundamental.

Chapter 10 sums up the earlier chapters. The diary project identified the pandemic as a social problem characterised by uncertainty and constant change. It dominated society, imposed restrictions and required the general population to adapt quickly. The diarists reacted pragmatically, doing what they could to stay safe as well as interacting with technology, time, space and food in new ways. Altruism was also in evidence. Everybody's experience was different and the diarists, while not wanting to be singled out simply on account of their age, numbered themselves among the more advantaged. There were lessons to be learned should a similar event occur.

This final chapter also considers the value of writing diaries during periods such as the pandemic, and their importance in contributing to social history. How will it all be remembered?

2

The pandemic arrives

Boris Johnson, then British prime minister, made a formal pronouncement to the British population at 8.30 pm on Monday 23 March 2020, mirrored by announcements from Nicola Sturgeon, First Minister of Scotland and Mark Drayford, First Minister of Wales. A national UK-wide lockdown was about to commence. COVID-19 posed a real threat and urgent and severe action was required.

This announcement was not unexpected and was really a confirmation rather than a surprise. There was evidence from around the world that the pandemic was accelerating and, although at that point Italy had suffered more deaths than any other country, rates were increasing almost everywhere. The WHO reported how it had taken 67 days to reach the first 100,000 reported cases, but only 11 days to reach the second 100,000 cases and a further four to reach the third 100,000 cases. In the United Kingdom, and according to the Department of Health and Social Care, 6,650 people had by this time tested positive for COVID-19, 77,295 had tested negative, and 335 patients had died from the virus. The mortality rate had increased six-fold in the previous week. On 16 March an Imperial College COVID-19 team had warned that around a quarter of a million people would die in Britain unless more draconian measures were adopted.

The new ruling followed some two weeks of build up that saw British daily lives curtailed. Matters had become more serious on Friday 20 March when stronger measures[1] on social distancing were brought in and all cafes, pubs, bars, restaurants, gyms, leisure centres, nightclubs, theatres and cinemas were required to close. People should work from home where possible. At the same time an economic rescue plan, including furlough payments for retained workers and the deferment of VAT payments, had been announced to combat the impact on individuals and businesses. Nurseries and schools were also to close on this day, except for some children of key workers. GCSE and A-level examinations were cancelled and pupils would instead receive calculated grades.

---

[1] There were some differences in restrictions and timings between England, Scotland and Wales as the pandemic progressed. However, as the diarists were predominantly living in England, the reporting of measures throughout this book largely focuses on those existing in that country.

First inklings

Although COVID-19 was rapidly taking over the world, it had at first seemed safely distant. Then the first UK cases were confirmed at the end of January 2020 when two Chinese nationals became ill in York. One week later a British businessman, recently returned from Singapore, was diagnosed positive in Brighton, and in early March it was reported that an 'older patient' had died from COVID-19 contracted in Britain. From then on the numbers of hospitalisations and deaths rose rapidly.

For most diarists, realisation of the seriousness of the pandemic was a gradual process that had begun earlier in 2020. The symbolic interactionist Blumer (1971) believed that all adaptation is a process and outlined how social problems develop through five stages. The first two stages of the pandemic, which followed closely one upon the other, were the emergence of the problem and its legitimation. Many diarists wrote about how they were aware of the coronavirus before it hit British shores but how they had not fully interpreted and understood the threats. Daily life had not at first been unduly affected. Over time, however, more information became available and much of it was close to home. The pandemic had arrived. It was a reality.

BENCHMAN
Retrospective: Wednesday 25 March 2020
I suppose that it was on 12 February that coronavirus first came up on my radar as something of which I ought to be aware. ... From then on the topic became increasingly prominent in the news but it did not prevent me meeting retired colleagues for a regular coffee morning on 6 March, or from attending a reunion dinner at a Chinese restaurant that evening. There were 70 attending the dinner, although around 100 had been expected. Most people were shaking hands regardless.

CHARLES
Retrospective: Wednesday 25 March 2020
During January and February it all still seemed a long way away. A trip to see family in the United Arab Emirates in mid-February was postponed and rebooked for the end of March, not because of COVID 19 but because some of the family had chicken-pox.

Then we heard that a businessman who had visited Singapore for a conference had gone skiing in the French Alps and passed it on to several other people who were there. Others on the return flight to the UK with him were also infected. After that all the news seemed to centre round cruise ships, mainly one off Yokohama. It still seemed far away. I just felt sorry for those stuck in a ship's cabin with no fresh air and limited exercise.

Italy was suddenly badly hit. Many people were dying. France was beginning to suffer and now so were we in the UK. In the first and second weeks in March we were in London, visiting close family in two major hospitals. I began to feel vulnerable.

FRANCES
Retrospective: Sunday 29 March 2020

I have found it quite difficult to pinpoint the day I first realised that the corona virus was going to be an all-absorbing experience. In January, when we first saw the pictures of locked-down Wuhan, it felt pretty distant. I remember being mildly horrified – but almost as we were by the aerial pictures of the Uighers in their re-education camps a few months previously. So it wasn't 'Oh dear, there's a pandemic coming our way soon', more 'another example of the way an authoritarian autocracy behaves'.

I am a political news junkie. Through February I'm sorry to say that I viewed the development of the epidemic in terms of how it might affect the politics of post Brexit, and the 2020 US election. But then around the beginning of March it began to dawn on me that this might actually affect me and my family. From then on I did periodical mental checks on the location and state of health of my nearest and dearest and started feeling somewhat worried.

Indeed, and when news of the coronavirus first broke, there was some scepticism as to its severity and likely impact in Britain. It was a matter of interest but not necessarily one of personal concern. But that was all soon to change as signs and symbols of the pandemic became hard to ignore. The virus itself could not be seen, but there were images and reports of illness and hospitalisations aplenty that signalled the deadliness of the virus. Thus it was not long before the arrival of the virus was legitimated and Blumer's third stage, the mobilisation of action, began.

EVE
Retrospective: Wednesday 25 March 2020

My attitudes have definitely changed since I first heard about the coronavirus because I was rather sceptical at the beginning about its seriousness. I changed my mind though once I saw the figures from Italy and realised how quickly it was spreading and the number of deaths.

GATZOU
Retrospective: Tuesday 7 April 2020

My friend's son is an epidemiologist and she is a hypochondriac so we have had several warnings of doom. The last one was the Aviary flu. It never happened but she had 'bought' masks and all sorts from America and it never materialised … fraud. Neither did the epidemic. So, when she started on the Chinese virus which was going to arrive any time soon and we should get two months' worth of food because we would not be able to go out, just like the Chinese, the three of us laughed silently. (We are a group of four French women living in GB.) It was March the 5th, our last pizza evening. Then I read a bit more about China. Then there was the first case in France in the Alps brought by a British man working in Singapore and in France on a skiing holiday. …

The 16th of March was the last time I had an 'almost' normal day. … I suddenly realised the seriousness of it all.

JULES
Retrospective: Monday 30 March 2020

I remember hearing about the possibility of a pandemic and my first reaction was 'here we go again', remembering the SARS and Bird flu so-called pandemics which didn't really impact on my life at all. In February I was preparing to go to Iceland for a short holiday and didn't give it much thought. I now feel very lucky to have had that holiday. I returned on March 3rd and still not much was happening in the way of advice or information.

The first thing I remember was people on the media saying don't panic buy, which I always take as a signal that everyone will, and that was when the toilet paper panic started. I was due to play in a concert on March 11th: it did take place but with a very much reduced audience. I played in another on March 14th and had another arranged for March 15th – the first casualty of the pandemic for me as it was cancelled. So the 14th was the last time I was with a group of people.

SWEETPEA
Retrospective: Saturday 28 March 2020

It was a faraway disease that got closer and closer to home. I suppose I just had to take it more and more seriously. However, as I don't know anyone who has it, nor anybody in the NHS who is having to deal with it, it's not very real in my life. This does not mean I don't take the advice of experts seriously.

WARRENER
Retrospective: Friday 17 April 2020

From 5 to 8 March my wife and I were on one of our twice-yearly youth hostel weekends with a group of about 35 friends, in Portland (Dorset, not Oregon). Already the signs were ominous. Although everything was open, the hotel restaurant where we had our traditional Sunday lunch before heading home had just installed a hand-sanitising station at the entrance. One of the group had emailed us all a few days before pointing out that as a group we might be quite vulnerable, suggesting that if any of us felt unwell we just didn't go and that we needed to follow advice re handwashing, touching, kissing, etc. rigorously, especially if we were travelling via public transport. We scoffed at her over-caution. Now it seems highly prescient.

WILL
Retrospective: Saturday 4 April 2020

It was in early January that I first became aware of coronavirus. I'm not sure if it had a name at that stage. Initially I remember little news coverage until the actions in China to introduce what then seemed like draconian measures in locking down whole cities and then the whole of Wuhan province. It seemed like something happening a long way from here that didn't occupy much of my conscious thoughts. But by the end of the month it seemed that the virus was spreading, with the WHO and national governments becoming more concerned.

Things began to change quite markedly from around 10 March. ... We were by that time aware that matters were becoming really serious as restaurants, pubs and theatres closed, closely followed by most retail outlets. Self-isolation and social distancing were being taken seriously and we agreed with our cleaner that Monday cleaning would stop from 23 March for social distancing purposes and as her children were going to be off school until who knows when.

By the time of the first lockdown, and the enactment of Blumer's fourth and fifth stages in the development of a social problem, namely the formulation and implementation of an official plan, there was little doubt about the reality of COVID-19 and the omnipresence of the virus. Until the formality of the first lockdown, diarists had been weighing up the evidence, making their own judgements about the risks of the largely intangible dangers, and acting accordingly. Long before it was formally mandated, many had already decided to isolate themselves to reduce the risk of illness.

Confirmation

The International Federation of Red Cross and Red Crescent Societies (nd) classify disasters as 'serious disruptions to the functioning of a community that exceed its capacity to cope using its own resources. Disasters can be caused by natural, man-made and technological hazards, as well as various factors that influence the exposure and vulnerability of a community'. The pandemic was, however, unlike an earthquake, a tsunami or a war. It was largely invisible and, in its early stages, was understood only through symbols and communications (Blumer, 1969), such as what was learned from the news, the government, personal observation and interactions with others.

Final confirmation came with the new legislation and the first national lockdown. Giddens' (1984) structuration thesis emphasises how a proper sociological view should always consider macro or micro levels of society in conjunction with one another. Actions at one level necessarily have repercussions elsewhere. Thus the initial lockdown and restrictions affected people not only as individuals but also as members of both their nation states and local communities. Closures and instructions to remain at home had implications not only for personal health but also for business and the economy, schooling and employment. From the outset, diarists were aware of these wider effects, again usually vicariously rather than directly. They rapidly gained a symbolic understanding of what was happening.

Indeed, it was not necessary to know that Boris had spoken, that there were new laws in place, or that many aspects of most people's lives had changed beyond recognition, to gather that things were different. There had also been dramatic environmental transformation. Even if venturing out only for the recommended hour a day to exercise, it was evident that the world outside had become almost unrecognisable. All European airlines had grounded most of their planes and largely ceased flying during March and April 2020 in response to the travel restrictions most countries had imposed. Apart from those providing essential services, people were spending most of their time at home. Cars sat in garages or on the road hardly used, and all forms of public transport, including buses and trains, were severely curtailed. Non-essential travel was banned.

ANNA
Thursday 26 March 2020
No planes. No vapour trails. Blue skies. Bees in the garden. Correction – one vapour trail about 5 pm.

OLIVE
Wednesday 25 March 2020
From my front room, I watch completely empty buses pass the window in both directions every ten minutes or so day and evening. The bus service to and from town is excellent, but the public have now been advised not to use public transport, so this can't surely carry on. The repercussions for future public transport may be significant.

PETER
Thursday 26 March 2020
Wonderful clear sunshine. The air around here has improved hugely over the last couple of weeks. Almost no planes overhead on their way to Leeds Bradford. Far fewer cars. Some little git on a motor trail bike raced past

yesterday – twice. Riding with impunity and making a dreadful noise. But lots of offers to get food in for us poor old folks!

Fewer shops, too, were open for business, as only those classified as 'essential' were allowed to remain open for the first three months following lockdown. Some towns became eerily empty. And even with people able to go out for exercise every day, and children and young people at home rather than at school, college or university, there were few people out and about. The parks were not being used as much as they might – perhaps because playground facilities were often out of bounds.

CARACTACUS
Wednesday 25 March 2020

My morning walk takes me along the town's main street from the Vaughan Road junction to the Lion Lane junction, and I can thus observe what the shops are doing. The Royal Fountain is shut (I saw this on Saturday, when the route of my walk is slightly different). The King's Arms is still offering a collect/deliver lunch service. Londis and Select & Save are open. The fish and chip shop (tweely renamed 'Mimi's Plaice' last year) is now delivery only, free delivery, pay by credit card. The café, which had to move into the old butcher's shop from its original premises on the south side of the High Street a few months ago as the building in which it was situated was declared dangerous, is open, presumably for bread etc. sales. Only one person allowed in the shop at a time.

CHARLES
Thursday 2 April 2020

I went for a walk on our local hill this afternoon, via the town centre. It really is a ghost town. Two shops open. M&S and Sainsburys. A few people walking about. Virtually no traffic, but I was nearly run over by a local bus which I was surprised to see still running. It brings people in from the surrounding villages, so for them perhaps a lifeline to buy food and get medicines.

On the hill I saw several people. Ones, twos and threes mainly, many with dogs, some with young children. The pattern for the children seems to be home schooling in the morning and a walk in the afternoon.

EVE
Thursday 9 April 2020

This morning we went into the nearest town to visit the supermarket and get some fish. ... There was a very different atmosphere in town compared with this village [where we live] and it felt more like Edinburgh with people not acknowledging each other and keeping their heads down. The town also looked really run down. Normally it would be buzzing with tourists at this time of year, with the shops and hotels newly painted, so it was sad to see how neglected it looked.

GRACE
Friday 20 March 2020

What we all thought were necessary places to go are now closed down. Shops shuttered, bars bare, coffee shops closed, gyms inactive. Prowling shoppers search the aisles of supermarkets for goods they would never have looked at before … could that jar of beetroot be a well disguised toilet roll!

LOUISE
Monday 30 March 2020

There was hardly anybody about. Two dog walkers, two cyclists, one jogger and a couple of shoppers returning home. We are very law-abiding round here.

The hospitality industry was another to suffer. Hotels, bed and breakfast accommodation, holiday cottages, pubs and restaurants were all closed. Some provided take-away food and drink but their closure, combined with the banning of non-essential travel, had a massive impact on the tourist industry. Amber looked back at the transformation of the Lake District during this period.

AMBER
Thursday 23 April 2020

In the early days of the virus, when we were being told to maintain social distancing, the tourism machine was still in full flow. Lake Windermere was busy with passenger boats, the Pierhead at Bowness and Waterhead teeming with visitors, ice-cream parlours, cafes, hotel and self-catering places, all doing good trade with the prospect of a lucrative summer ahead. Behind all this busy business were the secondary businesses that supply the tourism trade, they too were anticipating a good summer.

And then came the lockdown. For a few days, life seemed normal, the penny had not quite dropped, but the daily news finally got through the disbelief and, almost overnight, the Lake District closed down. No boats, no coaches, shops shuttered, roads almost empty – it was as if a huge hush had descended on the lakes, mountains, fellsides, forests, and into that space came birdsong, lambs bleating and wind rustling the trees.

Almost overnight there had been greater change than in most people's lifetimes. Legal restrictions on behaviour had been introduced, and the great outdoors had responded accordingly.

Making quick decisions

According to Mead (1934), sudden change prompts quick decisions and actions. For most diarists this was simply to stay at home as directed. The alternatives were limited. The law prohibited moving house apart from in unavoidable circumstances, and in any case the housing market had ground almost to a halt with home viewings disallowed and estate agents closed for almost two months. Not only were households not allowed to move home, but anyone with a second home was forbidden from visiting it.

Although most diarists were settled in their homes, a few had options and needed to make quick decisions about where they would live for the foreseeable future. Sometimes the pragmatic decision was not where to live but with whom. The lockdown legislation stated that the only people one could mix with were those in the same household, making it important to decide carefully on arrangements. For instance, was it better to leave behind the familiarity of one's own home in order to have company for the foreseeable future? Or should living arrangements change to ensure the possibility of supporting others through the crisis? There was a brief window of opportunity for such pragmatic decision-making.

Among the diarists, there were, accordingly, a few who decided to live with a partner on a more permanent basis than previously. Eve, Jacca, and Jimmy and Topper, fell within this category.

EVE
Monday 30 March 2020

It was a lovely spring day today as I looked out of the window so that was very cheering. My partner had been self-isolating in his house in rural Scotland but came out of quarantine on Friday and so drove over to stay in my flat on Saturday. It has made for a somewhat different regime for me, for example more time over breakfast and less time reading *The Guardian* on my iPhone. I have also spent more time cooking, as it's much nicer to cook for someone else than just myself.

JACCA
Sunday 26 April 2020

[My partner and I] had made the decision some years ago not to live together as we both like time apart. But we were faced with potentially weeks of lockdown together. But the advantages of having company, of having someone who cares and can comfort and be comforted, the ability to share tasks and to process together thoughts and feelings about the situation has far outweighed the desire to have time alone. We are lucky to have the space to accommodate our periods of alone time. I am very aware of those who are faced with living in a small space with no garden and competing needs.

JIMMY
Retrospective: Monday 30 March 2020
The main changes are that I'm no longer living in London but with my partner in the country. I've had to postpone my academic work and no longer have access to the swimming pool or the park. It has been easy both practically and emotionally.

TOPPER
Retrospective: Thursday 9 April 2020
[My partner and I] realised that it would be sensible to sit out the pandemic in Dorset so on the Wednesday we went up to London to collect his medicaments and alert his GP. We also tried to find his relevant passwords so he could continue studying down in Dorset. He had his last walks in Kensington Gardens and swims in the local pool.

The lockdown also delayed Bea's son's move away from home, and prompted Persia's mother and brother to stay living with her for the duration.

BEA
Retrospective: Tuesday 31 March 2020
I walked up to the allotment with my son, to strim the path and do some digging. He is doing some repairs to the shed. He has been with us for five weeks having moved down from Lancashire to take up a job in the dockyard. He should have been moving tomorrow to a rented flat. But with the 'lockdown', moving is forbidden.

PERSIA
Retrospective: Thursday 26 March 2020
My life has changed dramatically as I have gone from just looking after myself to looking after a 96-year-old mother and a brother who has come over recently from Italy where he has been treated for prostate and bone cancer and has no doctor or care plan in England. ... We went into splendid isolation ten days earlier than the official date.

A few considered flight. April discussed this possibility.

APRIL
Retrospective: Thursday 16 April 2020
I spent a couple of weeks worrying whether to stay at home in London or accept the hospitality of friends in the country. My son and his two sons and

> his wife live a few doors away. He decided they would stay in their home and so I too decided to stay here near them. I was anxious about this decision. My instinct was to flee the big city for fresh country air. I remembered hearing that during the plague in 1665 the landed gentry fled to the country and mostly survived, while the poor stayed in London and died. I've often wondered why people stay and don't flee the oncoming tragedy which, in retrospect, is so obviously upon them. The comforts of home are hard to abandon but I always thought I'd be one of the clever ones and run for the hills. But I didn't. Will I live to regret it or perhaps regret it and just die?

Status passages (Glaser and Strauss, 1971), that change identity and involve movement from one part of the social structure to another, were also suspended or conducted in a different form. Weddings were a prime example of such a casualty with wedding venues required to remain closed from March until July 2020. Bridebook estimated that the pandemic had a direct impact on around two thirds of planned weddings in 2020, through postponements, cancellations or difficulties with travel (Hampson, 2020). Several diarists indeed mentioned how their children's planned marriages were on hold, usually with no alternative fixed plans. Bea, however, reported an amusing story of a couple that were quick off the mark and thus able to beat the restrictions.

> **BEA**
> *Monday 23 March 2020*
> I heard that a friend had had a 'shot gun' wedding during the afternoon. It was arranged so quickly that the bride wore jeans and a tee shirt. It had been scheduled for the 24th.

Places of worship were restricted by law in their use during the early stages of the pandemic, with many services being conducted online. Funerals, however, as important status passages, were allowed to go ahead (see Chapter 6), although with only specified persons in attendance. Key religious festivals, many of which typically occur in April, such as Easter, Passover, Ramadan and Vaisakhi, could not be celebrated in places of worship during 2020.

Caught in the transition

On Monday 23 March 2020, the day that lockdown was announced, Dominic Raab in his capacity as foreign secretary advised all Britons on holiday or working abroad to return home as soon as possible. Any delay ran the risk of becoming stranded. It was suggested that around a million British people might be out of the country at the time.

Several diarists were among this million or had imminent plans to travel abroad. They were caught in the transition, often having to change their arrangements at very short notice.

BARKLEY
Retrospective: Wednesday 25 March 2020

The most immediate impact on our lives was the cancellation of a three-week long holiday in south-east Asia. We were due to fly to Malaysia on Thursday 19 March to visit my son, his partner and their two children. ... On Sunday 15 March, after a week in the UK when the seriousness of the coronavirus threat was becoming more and more apparent, my wife and I became increasingly concerned about going abroad at such a time. We were worried about increasing our chances of contracting the virus and also whether our travel arrangements would be affected. I contacted the travel company we booked the trip with, and one of their reps assured us it was perfectly OK to continue with our plans, not to worry and go off and have a good time! The following day I had a lengthy text chat with my son in Malaysia. ... He was very concerned about our well being and safety if we flew out. After a brief chat with my wife, we decided that even if we lost all the money we had paid out on the holiday (around £4,500 for the two of us), it would be stupid to go ahead with it and our only choice was to unilaterally cancel. About an hour after my final text chat with my son, he contacted me again to say that the Malaysian government had imposed a total ban on foreigners entering the country from 18–31 March, which meant we couldn't have gone anyway.

HELGA
Retrospective: Monday 27 April 2020

On 30th January 2020 we began a six-week holiday – two weeks in Thailand and then on to Australia for a further four weeks. At the time, the coronavirus was well established in China and there had been confirmed cases in Thailand and in Australia too, but as we left home we were more concerned about the bushfire situation there.

We arrived in Bangkok and were met at a very busy airport by our son who, like many others there, was wearing a face mask. There were Chinese tourists everywhere, some leaving, others arriving. Our original plan had been to wait at the airport, to have a coffee perhaps, so as to avoid the rush hour traffic but now this didn't seem such a good idea and we got out of there as quickly as possible. A week later we were back at the airport for a short flight to Koh Samui and the difference in the number of people there was startling. ... Yet another week later and we were back there again for our flight to Sydney. There were even fewer people around now as so many flights had been cancelled.

The next two weeks in Australia were worry free as far as the virus was concerned. It seemed a long way away – until the great toilet paper panic began and cases in Australia began increasing. ... On 5th March we flew from Sydney to Melbourne for the last week of our holiday. The airport was crowded, and so was our plane. If it had been possible we might well have flown home then and there but we had another week of our holiday left. And while we were in St Kilda we were near the beach, the sun was shining and, although some shelves in the supermarket were getting bare, the virus didn't seem too much of a threat – even when, the day before we left, we heard that Tom Hanks and his wife had the virus up in Queensland!

Our journey home was a bit unreal. We were flying with Thai Airways and the cabin crew were all masked throughout the flights. We had a four-hour wait at Bangkok airport and, although the airport itself was eerily empty, the business lounge was fuller than we've ever seen it. When we boarded the plane, however, there were only eight of us in business class. There were more cabin crew than passengers.

The relief we felt when we arrived home early on 13th March was quickly dispelled when later that morning we went to Tesco to stock up our empty fridge and freezer. There were so many bare shelves, but it was the very long queues at every cashout that was really alarming. The next day both our daughters and our granddaughter came round to welcome us home – and we had no idea then that that would be last time they would come into the house for the duration.

JESSIE
Retrospective: Monday 13 April 2020

Our middle son was 40 in March and he had planned a family skiing weekend in France to celebrate. He had booked a chalet just for the family. The week before his birthday there were already lots of concerns about whether it was OK to go or not – at the time flights etc. were still going and there had not been any advice about not going away. After a lot of deliberation we all decided to go, given that we would all be staying in one house not in a hotel. Our oldest son decided not to come as he would have had to do lots of travelling on trains, which he felt was not going to be safe. In the event we had a wonderful weekend where the main concern was whether we would be locked down in the chalet because of a snow avalanche – not the virus. On Sunday 15th March the ski slopes were shut down in France but we were due to return to London so this did not affect us but left us concerned for all the workers on the ski slopes who were then out of work.

WARRENER
Saturday 28 March 2020

We'd been due to spend the Easter weekend in Ireland, with us flying FlyBE from Birmingham. On 5 March, the day we travelled to Portland, FlyBE went bust. Ho hum, we switched to Ryanair, which means going from a different, less convenient, airport – Luton or East Mids. Sunday 15th March, the day after we returned from France, we sat down to a marathon keyboard session to book the flights. Success! To be followed almost immediately by the descending Covid-19 lockdown and disappearing prospect of an Easter trip anywhere. Much talk of cancelling, check insurance policies, researching the credit card laws. Unnecessary as on 24th March the email arrived from Ryanair cancelling the flight and offering a refund. Same day we cancelled the apartment booking and had a very sympathetic message from the owner saying they'd waive the cancellation fee. Turns out we made a £10 profit on that as the euro had gone up between the booking and the refund! The only problem we've got is that East Mids Airport is refusing to refund the £45 we paid in advance for car parking because we paid through Ryanair. We'll see about that! Reflecting on how the pandemic will be wrecking the economy of places like Westport, maybe knocking the stuffing out of them, for a while at least.

These changes to plans were, in the main, met with acceptance and stoicism. The nature and operation of the COVID-19 virus was as yet unknown, and caution was the best option.

Cancellations, cancellations, cancellations

Adaptation was a keyword for the pandemic, and cancellations of many varieties were a consequence. These affected not only planned holidays and social events, professional and work activities, meeting family and friends, but also sporting and exercise activities, health, beautician and therapeutic appointments, regular help from cleaners and others, taking part in classes, book groups, concerts and choirs, theatre bookings, church services, festivals and so forth. For some it could also mean a loss of earnings. There was a very sudden change to the taken-for-granted world.

ARAMINTA
Retrospective: Thursday 26 March 2020

My life has changed dramatically. I normally spend about two evenings a week doing Scottish country dancing, one evening at my choir, also the church choir. I normally go walking with a group once a fortnight. I normally act as a volunteer guide at Glasgow Cathedral once a week. And I attend church on Sundays. All of these activities are cancelled.

All social contacts such as lunch with friends are cancelled. Also trips away are cancelled. There are few things that I have personally had to cancel, they are cancelled by the organisers.

AUSTEN

Retrospective: Thursday 26 March 2020

I have lost so many daily activities it has been much more difficult for me. I belonged to two choirs, two weekly and two monthly walking groups, and the local U3A which meant every Tuesday afternoon I was at either the general meetings, the book group, the local history group or a monthly listen to music group.

    I had also been visiting a friend who has deteriorating Parkinson's on a weekly basis and daren't do that, so I know she is getting very low. We keep in touch by email.

BARKLEY

Retrospective: Wednesday 25 March 2020

Other changes in daily life include … not doing any guiding work [as part-time tourist guide] just as the season should have been about to get under way. This will mean a loss of earnings for me, but as I receive a state pension, a teacher's pension and a small private pension I should be able to cope, unlike younger guides who are totally dependent on work for their income.

BONIVARD

Retrospective: Saturday 25 April 2020

Events which have been cancelled or postponed include a Van Morrison concert, two AGMs, committee meetings, the Guildhall gold medal concert, and very likely the Lords Test against the West Indies. The important events will take place later this year.

CARACTACUS

Monday 16 March 2020

For the past couple of weeks, we have seen a series of announcements of cancellations of various events, forms of travel, etc., including our cruise from Amsterdam to Budapest (which was to have started on 30 April), and two speaking engagements for which I had been booked – Chester on April 8, and Milton Keynes on 16 May.

EDGAR

Retrospective: Saturday 4 April 2020

There are however cancellations in the offing, mainly in connection with music courses. The first is in July, a chamber music weekend which I and a friend have been organising for over 20 years with over 40 people attending. So far the venue has cancelled everything up to the end of May. Next comes a woodwind week which my wife and I have been attending for eight years.

Then there is a weekend in September and my wife has booked something in November. The first two must be doubtful.

HUMPHREY
Thursday 2 April 2020

Our friend died just after her 98th birthday. She had run out of road and it was nothing to do with CV. I was very sorry that we were going to miss her funeral because the date had been fixed for a day when we were going to be in New York. When that trip was cancelled, I thought well at least we will be able to drive to her funeral but when I contacted her son he told me that even the family could not attend. So at the last, the only mourners allowed were the undertaker, the priest, her son and a bugler to sound the last post. Very fitting for a lady who came from a military family and who, on her ninetieth birthday, made her first parachute jump in aid of Help for Heroes.

MABEL
Thursday 2 April 2020

My brother's birthday. He would have been here but obviously his trip had been cancelled. We'd bought him a birthday present from Kew Gardens, some bamboo socks with bicycles on them and two blocks of flavoured dark chocolate, so I sent him a photo of them instead. He said they'd probably last until he was able to visit unless somebody, in the meanwhile, liked dark chocolate or had cold feet.

OLIVE
Wednesday 25 March 2020

Like others, my diary has become a mess of scored out entries. To provide a bit more context about my life: I am involved with two professional journals. One had been planning a seminar in Edinburgh on Friday – cancelled; the other, an annual planning meeting in London – cancelled. I was invited to be a guest speaker at an event in London in early May – cancelled, and was preparing a panel for an international conference in Dublin in June – cancelled. I am also involved in the organisation of a local book festival, to be held in October. Organising meetings have been cancelled for the foreseeable future.

OTTOLIE
Retrospective: Wednesday 25 March 2020

It's been hard for me making the changes, but I am trying not to give in to self-pity. My first book for children was published on 2nd March. This was what I wanted to do all my life, but circumstances prevented me from focusing – divorce resulted in a very meagre income and I had to work hard as my much loved parents became more frail. I looked after my mother in her very old age which also was a great privilege. Since then, I found a lovely agent and a publisher and it has been truly wonderful to do what I love. However, all the launches, school talks and festival talks have been cancelled.

Alongside social and family events, hospital and other health care appointments were cancelled too. The British Medical Association (BMA, 2020) reported how the three months from April to June 2020 saw a drastic cutback in core NHS services due to the pandemic. In England alone they estimated that elective admissions were down by up to 1.5 million patients, first outpatient attendances down by up to 2.6 million, urgent cancer referrals down by more than a quarter of a million, and referrals for first cancer treatments down by some 40,000 patients. In addition, face-to-face meetings with GPs had been drastically cut, albeit with an increase in video and telephone consultations. Dental practices were also closed apart from emergencies.

Cancellations of appointments early on during lockdown, as well as uncertainty about future health care, were mentioned by several diarists. The following entries are illustrative. Strathspey reported a string of cancelled appointments.

CHARLES
Saturday 4 April 2020

Yesterday for the first time I got really stressed.

I was due to see the rheumatology consultant next Monday. I suspected they would ring and change it to a phone consultation. I last saw the consultant in November, so I really needed this appointment. At 11.00 my mobile rang, but fumbling to get it out of my pocket I rejected the call by mistake. 'Number withheld' so I could not call them back. Same with the home phone, no way to call them back and say I had rejected the call by mistake. Idiot!

I rang the hospital and eventually got through and explained. They emailed the rheumatology department and someone rang me, but only to say the appointment was cancelled. No please not that, I really do need to talk to someone about my medication. They gave me a number to ring. A nurse who could answer my questions would be there from 11.30 until 1.00. I rang at 11.31 and got the engaged tone, no queuing system, just engaged. I tried again, still engaged. I was really stressed by now. Feeling abandoned by the NHS. No prospect of being able to talk to someone, or anyone about my condition.

JOJO
Thursday 19 March 2020

I went to Warwick Hospital to keep my ENT appointment for my ear infection. All fine and was signed off but referred to Audiology department for replacement hearing aids as my Spec Savers ones are useless. No idea if/when I'll get the appointment though. The hospital car park was only about half full (very rare!) and it was very quiet in Outpatients as so many people are already staying at home apparently. I was in and out in half an hour.

MABEL
Friday 20 March 2020

Dentist phoned me first thing and we agreed to cancel my appointment for the afternoon. She was no longer allowed to clean teeth or use a drill, two things that I might have gone to see her for.

STRATHSPEY
Retrospective: Tuesday 17 March 2020 to Friday 17 April 2020

Tuesday 17 March: Grandson's pre-planned surgery cancelled for foreseeable future.

Friday 20 March: Phone call from optician to say new specs ready for collection – I decide that this is not essential and can wait for a couple of weeks.

Monday 23 March: At my last dental hospital appointment I was told to contact them in four weeks – waiting on technician and give him ammunition to hurry them up. Tried phoning all three numbers that I had – no response. Phoned switchboard, transferred to department, rang and rang and rang. …

Tuesday 24 March: Second grandson has surgery planned for after his exams – also cancelled indefinitely.

Tuesday 31 March: Received letter from GP, appointment with haematology clinic cancelled. Make appointment with GP in six months' time.

Tuesday 31 March: Received letter from hospital, bone density scan cancelled – got to get a new referral from GP before will reschedule.

Thursday 2 April: Telephone call cancelling my appointment with my cancer specialist next week.

Monday 6 April: Got a telephone call from my cancer consultant. He explained why appointments cancelled – it is more dangerous to bring us into hospital than to leave treatment just now. We had a good long chat and as always, he was very patient and reassuring. Biggest disappointment was that I wasn't expecting the call and so I was not prepared as I would have been if I had been able to attend my hospital appointment.

Wednesday 15 April: Telephone call from speech therapist explaining why we couldn't have face-to-face meeting, good useful chat, will get in touch again in June.

Thursday 16 April: Alarmed by a metal post [12 mm long] dislodging itself from my gum, as I was dozing off to sleep, almost swallowed it. On investigation a second post was also missing. When did that happen? Why hadn't I noticed? What were the repercussions?

>   *Friday 17 April*: Phoned dental hospital. Asked lots of question and told they would get back to me.
>   One hour later a consultant phoned me back. Not to go into hospital just to be rigorous about cleaning wound – fortunate that I had not inhaled it [them]. That would have been much more serious.
>   Had a sore throat for a couple of days. Was it coronavirus? Had the metal pin lodged in my throat? I will never know.

>   WARRENER
>   *Saturday 28 March 2020*
> The GP surgery texted on 23rd asking me to ring for a review. Bit of a faff as the receptionist didn't know what kind of review and arranged for a doc to ring the next day. They didn't, so I rang and asked why not. Claimed they'd tried and fixed for another try the next day. Turned out to be a meds review as I'd suspected. We agreed I'd need a blood test to see if statin dose was still right and that would have to wait till after the pandemic. Brief chat about how much pressure they're under. Not much it seems, and he sounded relaxed. I reckon they're finding it much more efficient to run mainly on phone appointments and not having the surgery bothered by time-wasters. But also maybe people who should be going to their GP aren't.

These and other changes to everyday occurrences represented a breakdown in symbolic order (Berger and Luckmann, 1966) where taken-for-granted aspects of daily life (Schutz, 1945) were no longer present. The changing of the rules necessitated a new social order and the renegotiation of the processual arrangements for day-to-day living (Strauss, 1978). Later chapters outline the pragmatic adaptations that were subsequently made.

Onwards and upwards

By the time of the first lockdown in March 2020, diarists were generally resigned to the changes in their lives. They had cancelled their meetings and events, and were hunkering down to await further developments. In the main they accepted the seriousness of the situation. They had observed the rapid change of circumstances and were adapting their behaviour and beliefs to their evolving understandings (Giddens, 1984). The aim was to avoid illness but to carry on as much as possible as before. On the whole, they approached the next phase with a good measure of stoicism.

Stoicism, which dates back to around 300 BC in ancient Greece, has much in common with the tenets of symbolic interactionism. Both disciplines posit that individuals react to personal perceptions and interpretation of events rather than the events themselves. Stoicism further recognises that there are aspects of daily life where individuals have control and other aspects where they do not, and that Stoics worry only about the things they can do something about. In *The Little Book of Stoicism*, Salzgeber (2019) described ten practical mindsets adopted by Stoics that reinforce the message that it is the reactions to events that are important in determining a 'calm and wise life'. Among these mindsets are 'Don't Get Disturbed and Buy Tranquillity Instead', 'See the Opportunity in Challenging Situations', 'Choose Courage and Calm over Anger' and 'Love Whatever Happens'. Time would tell, but many diarists appeared to display these characteristics in the early weeks of the pandemic.

ANNA
Retrospective: Thursday 26 March 2020
Practically, apart from endless waits at hospital switchboards, [it's] not [been] too difficult [to make changes]. ... Emotionally, I'm really bad at disappointment so at least I've had a long run in for holidays. I had withdrawn from choir tour even before it was cancelled. But some sort of boarding-school stiff-upper-lip these-things-happen-to-us emotional self-censorship kicks in.

AUSTEN
Retrospective: Thursday 26 March 2020
I just keep thinking of my mother in WW2 who coped with all this on her own with two young children and a husband fighting abroad, so I can't really grumble.

FRANCIA
Retrospective: Monday 30 March 2020
Buoyant. I feel determined to fight this crisis! I am determined to stay optimistic in the hope that the situation will clear, although I think we are in for the long haul.

JACCA
Sunday 26 April 2020
Lockdown initially felt like a survival challenge. In a way I have been preparing for this all my life. It might have been a post war ration thing or a love of adventure travel books that laid the foundations of a mentality excited by the thought of having to find survival strategies. This in a way was my very own adventure trip down the Grand Canyon on a raft or up Everest, but all was to happen within the comfort of my own home, with a decent bed, a comfortable chair and a stunning view. But never forgetting the backdrop of fear of infection, anxiety about the future, worry about my loved ones, the horror of people being very very ill and increasing numbers of deaths.

ROSEMARY
Retrospective: Thursday 2 April 2020
People began to say 'Looking forward to seeing you again on the other side'. I took this to mean earthly get-togethers.

For a considerable number, the 'Love What Happens' seemed particularly relevant. The practical reality that they could stay at home and away from risk, and would not lose jobs and income, was acknowledged. So far as they were concerned, they were among the luckier ones.

CHARLES
Friday 27 March 2020
I love being able to spend almost all day in the garden! After my cleaning chore, which actually I quite enjoy, the day is mine to do as I want. Far from suffering, I am enjoying being locked down.

ELEANOR
Retrospective: Wednesday 8 April 2020
I am in the luckiest of situations so am secretly beginning to enjoy the situation. No appointments to keep, time to myself, time to tackle those long-postponed jobs in the house and garden, and the marvel of modern communication technology to keep in touch with family and friends.

TOPPER
Monday 30 March 2020
There was a feeling of cheerfulness in that, apart from social distancing, my life would continue along normal lines. I collected my nephew's dog and my neighbour's and took them up to the local Woodland Trust property for a lovely walk where the first bluebells were starting to show.

There were, nonetheless, also diary entries that reflected the worry and anxiety that were also inherent in a situation imbued with uncertainty. Personal mood was subject to flux, and part of the adaptation shown by diarists was to the unknown reality of the 'new normal'.

ARAMINTA
Retrospective: Thursday 26 March 2020
I am most worried about depression. I will need to keep busy. I am worried about members of my family who are inclined to be depressed, and I am worried that families cooped up together may experience difficulties.

The pandemic arrives

BARKLEY
Retrospective: Wednesday 25 March 2020

We've adapted pretty well to these changes, but what I have noticed is a big jump in my anxiety levels. My mood fluctuates during the day, but I seem to have permanent butterflies in my stomach. I'm waking up earlier and find I'm not able to go back to sleep. I'm worried about getting the virus and, if I do, will I survive or will I endure a horrible and painful death with no medical attention. Starting with my wife (who will be 70 in October) I'm worried about my family getting the virus.

HOLGATE
Retrospective: Wednesday 8 April 2020

My mood is generally positive, nevertheless there is always the fear of catching the virus. I'm not panicking although I'm more aware of my mortality.

OTTOLIE
Retrospective: Wednesday 25 March 2020

The first day of isolation I wept, not just for me, but for the world. I was so surprised that some friends didn't share this terrified feeling. I talked it through with my dearest friend, and he helped me to see it in perspective. Now happy and calm, being contemplative, doing a little ballet now and then (weird sight), but underneath frightened for the world with this existential threat. I have noticed that the air is cleaner already and the little stream at the end of my cottage garden is crystal clear.

PERSIA
Retrospective: Thursday 26 March 2020

I am feeling worried and stressed for my 'lodgers' and daren't risk going out myself in case I become a carrier. As a result, definitely feeling sorry for myself and must buck up!

PETER
Retrospective: Thursday 26 March 2020

It's a hard one to admit, but I fear dying away from my beautiful family. Many people are already having to go through that. I can't help thinking that we've all brought this on ourselves by treating our planet so badly. It's not God's judgement, it's our lack of judgement.

TARANAKI
Retrospective: Tuesday 24 March 2020

Ok, but I have a constant nagging feeling in the pit of my stomach.

Cognitive adaptation, as described by psychologists, also progresses in stages as shock and disorientation give way to greater acceptance. At the early stages of the formal restrictions there was, accordingly, a sense of disbelief expressed by some diarists who described an air of unreality about the pandemic and the situation it had created. This was beyond experience and called for a change of mindset.

JANWIG
Sunday 29 March 2020

It's been an unimaginably long month. Usually once January is over the year races. Not this one. We returned from our amazing holiday in Chile and Argentina on 7th March. Since then, the world has completely changed. Margaret Atwood didn't go this far in her dystopian imagination. No one would have dared. Closed borders. Businesses going down like flies. Unemployment soaring – not to mention deaths. And we are in lockdown.

Sun has shone continuously since Monday's announcement by BJ. It's felt doubly ironic watching the birds and flowers spring into spring life while we close our lives down. Reassuring though.

JIMMY
Thursday 2 April 2020

I can remember World War 2. It is different now in that life seemed normal then, but seems unreal now.

KATJA
Thursday 26 March 2020

We are about a fortnight in now since this devastating virus hit the UK, the effect on the population has been bewildering. The first few days it seemed as if everybody lived in suspense and it did not seem real, but as the population realised the gravity of the situation action started, neighbourhoods became proactive and organised WhatsApp for individuals to access, and provided a lifeline for the housebound.

PEN
Retrospective: Monday 30 March 2020

The irony of all this is that way back, late at night after a jar or two (and probably a few cigarettes) we used to joke with the children and their partners/spouses that, come the Apocalypse, we could all muddle through together here. There is even a stream which would be clean enough to drink if you boiled it. And sometimes it now feels as though it has come true.

Some diarists also asked if the pandemic signalled the end of normal daily life as it had been known.

The pandemic arrives

CAMPBELL
Retrospective: Wednesday 25 March 2020
It's funny how over the last two weeks, starting with the weekend of March 14–15 everything seemed – sometimes even at the time – to be the *last*: the last visit to the cinema, the last rides on the tube, the last dinner at a friend's house; even (perhaps, but not, I fear bankably) the last funeral.

And would priorities change?

GRACE
Sunday 22 March 2020
Mother's Day: The phrase 'I would like to spend more time with my family' may go out of fashion soon!

Was there anything that could still be taken for granted?

Summary

There was a gradual, but quite brief, period between the time that most diarists became aware of the severity of COVID-19 and its arrival in Britain. There had been news of a pandemic taking hold in China, but at first there was not too much concern that it would come to Britain. However, once the first case was announced in this country, it did not take long before hospitalisations and deaths were rising rapidly. The consequent legislation and lockdown meant that rapid decisions and changes of plan were suddenly called for, as life as it had been known became different for the foreseeable future. Some diarists had to decide where to live, others had to hasten back from distant shores, and almost all were faced with a plethora of cancellations from holidays to voluntary or paid occupations to medical appointments. Diarists witnessed the unusual peace in the largely traffic-free physical environment and quickly began to respond to the new social order. They embarked on a process of adaptation to the uncertainties of the 'new normal', often with a good measure of stoicism.

The new legislation and requirement to remain at home most of the time was without parallel in the diarists' lifetimes and put their taken-for-granted world on hold. The next chapter discusses how they reacted to the call for unprecedented control over their lives.

3

Unprecedented control

The Coronavirus Act 2020 became law on Wednesday 25 March when it cleared the House of Lords without amendment. Its sweeping emergency powers placed previously unknown restrictions on the general public. Leaving the house was allowed only for specified reasons, such as to buy food, to take exercise for an hour a day, to seek medical assistance, or to go to work for those classed as 'essential workers'. All shops selling non-essential items were to close, non-essential travel was forbidden, gatherings of two or more people from different households were to be banned, and public events including weddings, but not funerals, were outlawed. Social distancing, defined as remaining at least two metres away from anybody not in the same household, was to be observed at all times.

This was unheard-of and change was immediate. Something might be normal one day, but against the law the next. In the name of the collective good, the government had exercised unprecedented powers and legislation to effect huge changes in everyday life. Citizens were now being required to ask questions such as 'Where can I go?', 'How long can I take?', 'What do I do when I get to the shop?', 'Can I touch the gatepost?' and 'Who am I allowed to see?'.

Managing the crisis

Britain was in the throes of a social crisis. There were, however, preconditions for the reactions of the government. As already outlined, advanced societies are these days beset with pessimism and focused on the management and minimisation of risk (Giddens, 1991; Beck, 1992). Agents of control do their best to turn uncertainties into actuarial knowable risks. Examples might be threat levels for acts of terrorism, the likelihood of side-effects from medications, the risk of torrential storms, or the putative cost of strikes. The pandemic, however, arrived with little warning and much uncertainty and was not amenable to such predictions. There was little pre-existing knowledge about it, or how best to deal with it, but decisions had to be taken quickly. We do not know the full story, but the voices clamouring for lockdowns and restrictions won the day.

An enforcement model was adopted that prescribed the new social order and severely reduced personal agency. This was a specific conception of a good society, linked to a public health model of social policy, that favoured state control. It was at odds with some other models both adopted and proposed. It differed, for example, from countries such as Sweden that took a much more libertarian approach that limited the power of the state and, to a great extent, charged citizens with managing their own risk – although less extreme than, for example, New Zealand that imposed long-standing and severe restrictions. It also resisted the recommendation of the Great Barrington Declaration (Kulldorff et al, 2020). This was written and signed by an international group of infectious disease epidemiologists and public health scientists of different political persuasions on 4 October 2020 and called for 'focused protection'. It was concerned with the impact on public health, including 'lower childhood vaccination rates, worsening cardiovascular disease outcomes, fewer cancer screenings and deteriorating mental health – leading to greater excess mortality in years to come, with the working class and younger members of society carrying the heaviest burden. Keeping students out of school is a grave injustice.' The recommendation was to protect those at greatest risk from the virus, namely the old and the infirm, but to let those less vulnerable go about their lives as normal and build up immunity to the virus.

These differing approaches, characterised by the balance between external control and individual agency, to some extent mirror Durkheim's (1997) description of the collective conscience and the distinction between mechanical and organic solidarity. Mechanical solidarity is based on enforcement of uniformity of beliefs, such as in theocratic societies, while organic solidarity develops in complex urban industrialised societies with greater cultural and demographic diversity, and a measure of democracy effecting checks and balances on the power of governments and elites. Whereas individuals are strongly controlled in the former, they are able to employ greater volition and independence in the latter.

Although Britain fell somewhere between the extremes, the new regime was unusual and contrary to previous times in many ways. First and foremost, it removed a considerable amount of individual agency from everyday actions. The Coronavirus Act 2020 introduced lockdowns and restrictions and forbade citizens to determine, and act upon, their own perceptions of personal risk. Rather than presenting evidence on the existence of risk, there was a new instruction to avoid it. Britain is a country often seen as a global beacon of freedom and democracy, and this policy constituted a sea change.

An additional change that characterised the restrictions ushered in by the pandemic was that normal channels of support were often absent. Generally speaking, crises lead people to seek comfort and support from their closest friends and families. This changed with the new legislation as face-to-face contact became restricted to those living in the same household. Nonetheless, as documented in later chapters, diarists did find ways and means to maintain closeness with loved ones.

To sum up, these mandated changes and measures transformed, almost overnight, a democratic state of mobile risk-taking citizens to something very different. Britain was in unexplored territory, and it was unknown how the general population would react. So far as the diarists were concerned, and as witnessed by their accounts in the following chapters, there was a good deal of compliance with the prevailing restrictions. There are a number of reasons why this might have been the case.

Survival amid uncertainty

Perhaps first and foremost, a survival instinct came into play. Understandably, nobody wanted to contract a virus that was creating chaos worldwide. However, very little was known about the pandemic. It was not like threats such as earthquakes, floods or wars that have tangible forms. The coronavirus was invisible. There was uncertainty all around and no credible knowledge as to its likely career or the precise risks involved. As the psychologist Barber (2020) suggested, it had to be imagined that the virus was everywhere if it were to be avoided. With this uncertainty, the most sensible adaptation at this stage was to stay out of the way and, hopefully, stay safe. This is what most diarists decided to do.

ATHELSTANA
Retrospective: Thursday 26 March 2020
Being in the 'vulnerable' age group (so qualify for food/chemist deliveries), having my own home, being relatively healthy and being in a comfortable position with a regular pension I have not got too many worries. I feel luckier than many. Just sit it out.

JIMMY
Retrospective: Friday 1 May 2020
I have no plan other than sitting it out. The silver lining is that I am with my partner all the time so don't need to shop and cook for myself or be alone.

OLIVE
Retrospective: Monday 30 March 2020
At a personal level, I have decided to simply do what I am told. I am self-isolating, not seeing friends or family. I have had to cancel a number of things, or they have been cancelled for me. ... That's disappointing, but nothing compared with the catastrophic consequences for many people, so I feel I am lucky.

At the onset of the pandemic there were indeed many varieties of uncertainty. Daily lives had changed dramatically despite few tangible signs of the coronavirus. Symbolically, however, much was different. For example, there was an unusual tranquillity on the roads and in the skies, as well as new and life-changing legislation. These symbols were important in affording understanding of the situation (Berger and Luckmann, 1966; Blumer, 1969) but what exactly did they convey? There was a lack of information, especially in the early days, about how COVID-19 was transmitted, and how it might mutate. There was also uncertainty as to whether the virus would linger on food and parcels, whether it could be picked up from countryside stiles, and indeed whether face masks offered protection and, if they did, to whom. And, perhaps most importantly, there was uncertainty as to how and when an effective vaccine might be developed and distributed. The government issued guidance on these matters but was not always any better informed than the general public.

In addition, and despite the fact that COVID-19 had become dominant in their lives, most diarists were effectively isolated from the virus and all their information was vicarious and symbolic. Able to remain at home and protect themselves, only four were known to have contracted COVID-19 during the course of the diary project, two of these prior to the initial lockdown, one during the early days of restrictions and one after the lockdowns. They were, however, privy to a few high-profile cases of illness via the media, notably then prime minister Boris Johnson, who contracted COVID-19 early on in the course of the pandemic. Loseke (2016) discussed how personal narratives, particularly those of well-known figures, can be symbolically important in influencing public discourse, and this was a case in point. When the news of his illness first broke, Boris Johnson was working from home and still making video appearances, but after about a week he was admitted to hospital and, before long, placed on a ventilator. He was clearly seriously unwell. Witnessing daily reports on his decline, before his eventual recovery, was persuasive in bringing home the potential deadliness of the virus and the additional uncertainties if the country were to lose its leader.

ATHELSTANA

Monday 6 April 2020

For the first time I felt quite panicky, a real anxiety, when it was announced that Boris Johnson had gone into intensive care. For some reason, I suppose because he has become such a familiar face through Brexit and now this crisis, it made it more real and closer to home. Going into hospital rang alarm bells but to go to ICU was a shock even if half expected. Whether you like him or not, voted for him or not, he is another human being with family who will fear for his ability to overcome.

GATZOU

Tuesday 7 April 2020

I do a bit of ironing and cook a chicken 'stew'? Listen to Radio 4. Johnson is in intensive care, who is going to lead the country???? Do we know them? Are they intelligent? Being a good politician does not mean you are intelligent. ... We need brains now. Not ambitious public school boys.

TWEEGY
Monday 6 April 2020
Boris still in hospital. I have no great regard for him, but hope he's soon back at the helm, a change now would be difficult.

As time went on, and through their social interactions, more diarists came to learn of friends and family and colleagues – or friends and family and colleagues of other people they knew – who were exhibiting COVID-like symptoms or had received a positive test result. Increasingly they also heard about people who had become seriously ill or died. The cases were always shocking.

ANNA
Sunday 17 May 2020
My sister heard that a very close friend/colleague of hers had died of COVID-19. That is the closest I've got to a personal link to a casualty. A vibrant woman, in her 60s. She was only sick for four days – apparently it affected her digestive system and she may have had an aneurism. It is so shocking. And she lived alone.

APPLETREE
Tuesday 5 May 2020
Received a phone call to say the husband of a mutual friend has died of coronavirus. He had been in a care home for maybe five years with early onset dementia. Beginning to bring the reality close to home.

JESSIE
Wednesday 20 May 2020
Our window cleaner came today which was good as the windows definitely needed cleaning. He has sadly lost his father-in-law to the coronavirus and said that the funeral on Monday had been very strange with only ten people attending. His father-in-law was 91 and had been in good health until he had a fall which landed him in hospital where he contracted the virus. Sad.

JOJO
Saturday 9 May 2020
After all the lighthearted stuff, we heard from our daughter that one of her colleagues at the hospital had died from COVID-19. He was a highly respected doctor whom she had worked with for seven years. She was very calm about it but it had obviously affected the team greatly.

OTTOLIE
Wednesday 29 April 2020
Heard from a friend last night that her ex-husband had died of the virus. They had remained friends. It was sudden and shocking. The ambulance crew arrived in full protective clothing. They said to the sons, 'You have two minutes to say goodbye'. They didn't see him again. Six allowed at the funeral which will be short.

SQUEALS
Saturday 25 April 2020
We had street dancing for 15 mins last night – fun but I was shocked to learn that a near neighbour has been at home on her own quite ill with the dreaded C. She doesn't know how she contracted it. Don't know what I could have done to help but it was also yet another wake up call that the virus is all around us.

These cases, albeit fairly distant in the main, served as confirmation of the potency of the virus and underlined the need for caution and vigilance.

As well as adapting to the presence of the virus and the restrictions it brought in its wake, there was uncertainty about how long the pandemic would last. When Boris Johnson announced the first lockdown on 23 March 2020, he suggested it was for three weeks in the first instance. Just four days earlier he had suggested that the UK could 'turn the tide' of coronavirus in 12 weeks and on 30 April 2020, in his first Downing Street press conference since being admitted to hospital, he claimed that the country is now 'past the peak of this disease'. However, none of this was to be the case. The initial three weeks kept expanding, with a few reprieves, for almost two years. On 8 March 2021 England embarked on a four-step plan and a 'roadmap out of lockdown', but it was not until 21 February 2022 that the new 'living with Covid' strategy, removing all legal restrictions, was announced for England. Scotland and Wales were largely in step.

Human beings are used to organising their daily lives and planning ahead. Many people keep diaries of events to come, and make plans to see family and friends, take holidays, participate in leisure and cultural activities, and so on. Much of this planning involves others and depends on social interactions. The pandemic curtailed much of this level of organisation as there was uncertainty about the future. Cancellations remained cancellations.

FRANCES
Retrospective: Sunday 29 March 2020
Superficially the 'lockdown' has made very little difference to my daily life. ... But beneath this superficial sameness, I have found it difficult to

accept the new underlying reality. Existential questions intrude. Who in my family is really at risk? Are they taking the proper precautions? And more philosophically, when will it all end? And what will the world look like when it does? And will I live to see it?

GRACE
Tuesday 24 March 2020
Am thinking of Nella Last's Mass Observations (please don't let it be making three meals a day for a quite gruntled husband for the foreseeable future!).

JACCA
Sunday 26 April 2020
This lockdown feels not like a short inconvenient interlude but a complete and lasting life change. As a result, the emotional adjustments and life-style changes have felt enormous. In a world that is changing dramatically so our personal worlds must change. It requires focus and consideration if we are not to be swept along a tide of despair and fear and blind obedience. It has felt like a time to consider what is important to us as individuals and as a society, to develop strategies for survival and to find ways to question and influence where possible the actions taken by the government which affect every aspect of our lives.

JULES
Thursday 21 May 2020
Another aspect to this lockdown which is really galling me (and I think many others) is the lack of clarity from the government and media and the increasing forecasts of this going on for another year or more. It really does feel as if we are in some kind of limbo of uncertainty and it has never been more important for me personally to just take one day at a time; looking too far forward to an altogether unknown future is not doing me any good at all.

ROSA
Saturday 25 April 2020
How Long, oh Lord, How Long?

People are gradually absorbing the likelihood that this semi-imprisonment will be going on for much longer than originally envisaged. First it was for three weeks, then another three weeks. Now???? June? There is even talk in high places of Christmas. I prefer not to think about it, but sometimes things are forced in on you.

It was a long and bumpy road with many changes in rules and restrictions over the interim 23 months between the original lockdown and the transition to 'living with Covid'. Indeed Adam Wagner, a human rights barrister, calculated that lockdown rules had changed at least 64 times by January 2021, leading to confusion between laws and advice for the police, lawyers, ministers and the public alike (Syal, 2021). These rules were wide-ranging and included both national and local regulations. To add to the complexity there were, in addition, some differences in regulations between the constituent countries of the UK. Confusion and uncertainty were maintained by the constant changing of the rules.

News, news, news

A state of uncertainty and confusion was not relieved by messages broadcast by the media. If, as the symbolic interactionists such as Blumer (1969) suggested, personal perceptions of the situation were influenced by the exchange of meaning through language and symbols, there was much in the papers, television and other media with the potential for inducing anxiety. In an age of 24-hour news bulletins and extensive social media channels, few people can have escaped the graphic coverage of the pandemic in other countries, such as Italy, or the broadcast concern when the first cases emerged in Britain. The grave warnings from the government, and the onset of daily bulletins highlighting the escalation of hospitalisations and deaths, merely accentuated the message. This was serious and everybody was at risk.

COVID-19 was certainly hard to ignore. For many months the UK was submitted to non-stop news coverage of the pandemic, and indeed the *Press Gazette* of 9 April 2020 reported analysis by PR firm Resonance to show that five of every six BBC news articles was devoted to coronavirus (Mayhew, 2020). This was higher than any other news outlet. The trade press was also preoccupied with COVID-19, with travel (*Travel Week*), retail (*Retail Week*) and finance (*FN London*) having this focus in 99, 84 and 73 per cent, respectively, of their news output.

The diarists on the whole said they kept a close eye on the news, often because they found it compulsive even if gloomy and repetitive. Others, however, tried to ignore the coverage, or at least ration their exposure. Tuning into the daily television briefing, often with Boris Johnson flanked by his medical advisers, was for many either a regular fixture or something to avoid. This issued the latest figures on hospitalisations and deaths, much to the exclusion of information on other aspects of pandemic, such as the impact on business, the economy, and health conditions other than COVID-19.

BETTYMAC
Friday 8 May 2020
I have found the media reporting unhelpful on balance, apart from the *Today* programme. The daily briefing is repetitive and the format a turn off.

FISHERMAN
Saturday 4 April 2020
Listened to radio and decided to ration Radio 4 as suffering coronavirus overload. It appears that there is nothing else worth reporting in the world.

FRANCES
Thursday 9 April 2020
Reading the newspapers at the moment, and watching the news, is like a relationship that's gone sour; you can't do without them but you can't bear the sight of them. So I'm following others in my family to ration my intake.

FRANCIA
Sunday 29 March 2020
Watched *BBC News at 10* which has become a 'must'. This pandemic is still beyond my comprehension.

SARDOMIKE
Tuesday 12 May 2020
The 5 o'clock press briefing is our one fixed daily appointment.

With little else to go on, and whatever they thought of the presentation, the news and the daily bulletins became a prime source of information even if they did not convey much additional clarity.

JULES
Wednesday 8 April 2020
I'm getting very fed up with the media, BBC News especially (because that's the one I know best) telling us something and then getting their correspondent to say exactly the same thing they've just told us. For example, Boris Johnson: there's no further news than he's beginning to respond to treatment. Then to the political correspondent: what further news? We already know there isn't any! I think if I were in that position I would find it very hard not to be rude. It's such an annoying habit they have: the news seems to be 90 per cent conjecture and hypothesis and 10 per cent actual news if we're lucky. But I still watch it and get irritated by it.

The coverage was also commonly said to be alarmist and anxiety-provoking.

EDGAR
Friday 1 May 2020
When I watch the TV or listen to the radio, all I see and hear is doom and gloom. The daily bulletins are more positive which is why I watch them. I felt that the media and the opposition were grudging in their congratulations of

the target of 100,000 daily tests being reached by the deadline yesterday querying the method of counting. It's as if we can't be pleased about anything – there is always something to moan about, but I acknowledge the terrible difficulty of individual cases. I want to be reassured that all will be well. I find the doom-mongering of the media quite depressing. But then reading the above, I fear that I am just as bad. Maybe I don't want to face the reality which is what the press is doing.

EVE
Tuesday 21 April 2020

I wish the news could focus more on the recoveries from the virus rather than the deaths, as it is currently so depressing to only think about the negatives. I'm sure this focus must be contributing to the high state of anxiety everyone seems to be in.

HATTIE
Tuesday 19 April 2020

I'm still rationing what I read, and avoiding TV and radio news. Someone I spoke to recently was extremely anxious and depressed about things, but was continually reading everything possible about what is happening. I expect my approach is avoiding lots of issues but is also self-protection.

KATJA
Wednesday 20 May 2020

I feel I have to stop reading papers and listening to the news, it makes me more confused, upset and raises the blood pressure.

There was a feeling among many that the extensive coverage of the pandemic was disproportionate and that other newsworthy stories were being sidelined. It was also often felt that the predominant focus was on what some diarists called 'doom and gloom' and, accordingly, they reported pleasure when the focus shifted to more positive stories as well as coverage of international events. The media have indeed often been blamed for an increase in public fear due to the alarming language commonplace in news reports (Altheide, 2002, 2016). This is reinforced by Best (2021) who asserted that social interactionists frequently attribute public fear to media exposure. Whatever emotions it induced, the non-stop coverage certainly had the effect of keeping the pandemic at the forefront of everyone's mind.

Fear and anxiety

Fear may indeed be commonplace in modern societies (Bude, 2018) where a health and safety discourse has become prominent (Furedi, 1997, 2018).

This thesis maintains that a capacity for risk taking is becoming overtaken by a fear of danger. To the extent that this is the case, it may help to explain the high level of compliance with the new and uncompromising edicts of the government at the onset of the pandemic, and the bombardment of messages of uncertainty, illness and death that continued to herald from the media and designated experts on a regular basis.

Was the country in the grips of a moral panic, a sociological concept first introduced by Cohen (1973) as arising when a 'condition, episode, person or group of persons, emerges to be defined as a threat to societal values and interests'? According to Cohen, who introduced the concept to describe the public outcry accompanying tensions between Mods and Rockers in Brighton, moral panics may be responses to real events even if they can also be exaggerated. Interesting in this context is Gilman's (2010) observation that the term pandemic can in itself cause public panic. He noted how, in 2009, the then director-general of WHO had taken the impact of public health pronouncements into account in deciding whether to label an outbreak of influenza as a pandemic. A descriptor not only indicated the severity of an outbreak of illness but also had an impact on public perceptions.

Interactionists have long been concerned with the construction and portrayal of social problems. Blumer (1969) and others posited that perceptions of problems arise through a process of claimsmaking whereby influential persons make claims about the status of conditions of concern, and confer a social problem label. Others, whether governments, the media or the general public, may then join in as claimsmakers, on the basis of either observation or assertion. The outcome can be a competition for attention among all those wishing to put forward their view. In the instance of the pandemic, the seriousness of the situation was quickly augmented. Anxiety and fear were among the consequences.

Whether rational or irrational, there was certainly evidence of anxiety among the diarists. The novelty and uncertainty of the situation were probably important too. Carleton (2016) wrote about fear of the unknown, or FOTU, as a primitive fear that originated in very early times when dangers of all kinds were widely prevalent. The notion had currency well before the pandemic, but the idea was resurrected by some of the diarists. Psychologists, such as Gray (1987), have also suggested that the novelty of a situation, which is linked to uncertainty, has the potential to induce fear.

JENNIFER
Retrospective: Tuesday 28 April 2020

At the start of the pandemic I was in an anxious state generally, and this worsened considerably – with negative effects on my blood pressure. I would wake every morning with my heart racing and in a state of high alert throughout my whole body. I imagined I was ill and visualised being in hospital where there were not enough staff or equipment. I thought about death a lot and how to prepare myself and others for my death. I wrote a long letter to my daughters with all sorts of practical information. I also reminded them about my Living Will. I told them about the letter but placed it in the box of documents that contains my will, funeral plan, etc. I felt better for having done that.

OTTOLIE
Tuesday 5 May 2020

Cool and grey. Coughing a lot but don't think it's the dreaded. Stoical friend rang to say she cries when hymns play on the radio, or certain music. I am the same.

We decided that the hymns represent our childhood and in her case, her fear for her grandchildren. The hymns are mostly lost now, a metaphorical loss of beauty that we yearn for, even though neither of us was from church-going families. 'For the Beauty of The Earth'. 'Cherubim and Seraphim around the Glassy Sea'. 'Immortal Invisible' … all such, in their stained glass glory.

She said, 'I stand at the window and tears pour down my face'. It's unlike her. We are stoics, from naval families who moved constantly and had to cope.

Another friend, emailing about video clip: *It's surprising I am still sane. But am I?* Another: *The garden is immaculate but the house is a tip and I am sinking into lethargy.* These are all active, positive people. So, it's concerning.

Anxiety, as well as fear and uncertainty, figured in many diary entries and led to actions to keep the virus at bay (see Chapter 6). It also contributed to worries about personal health with many diarists wondering whether their own coughs or other symptoms were the precursor to COVID-19. In no reported instances did this turn out to be the case.

AUSTEN
Saturday 16 May 2020

I had a bit of a scare this week as had a bad cough and cold, and felt unwell enough to take to bed for a while. I think it was just a chill though with the change in the weather. Absolutely no fever and was better after 48 hours. Last week we were eating out in the garden and taking walks without coats, and this week turned so cold the central heating boiler turned itself on. Just shows though, worrying about a cold in normal times would never happen.

BONIVARD
Saturday 13 June 2020

I woke up one morning this week feeling distinctly under the weather. One's immediate reaction is – have I caught the C-virus? But I didn't have a sore throat or chest pains, I had my sense of taste and smell, and I didn't have a cough. I slept for most of the day and had little appetite. On the following day I realised that I had a recurrence of cellulitis.

LOUISE
Monday 6 April 2020
Yesterday had a bout of diarrhoea and got very frightened it might be a sign of Covid19. Today felt OK but legs a bit shaky. I have taken my temperature regularly and I don't have a temperature. Or a cough. This is just panic I think. Surgery rang me to go in for the blood tests at three. ... Had my blood tests done by a very cheerful nurse.

ROB
Sunday 24 May 2020
I feel like shit this morning. Maybe in my head?? Maybe not. ... In any event I have a temperature ... 38.6? ... very sweaty in the night? ... also achy and lethargic. ... Maybe nothing. ... Maybe a bit of a cold. ... Maybe the other 'thing'. ... 12 months ago I would have thought nothing of it.

TOPPER
Monday 30 March 2020
The vaguely alarming symptoms I had been having developed into a streaming head cold, rather than Covid.

Were some members of the government, as inferred from the *The Lockdown Files* (a series of articles in The Telegraph (2023) based on a large number of WhatsApp messages relating to the initial lockdown, sent to and from Matt Hancock, health secretary at the time), keen to encourage 'a climate of fear' – encompassing the fear of becoming ill, of contaminating others, and of dying – to ensure the maximum compliance with the new laws curtailing liberty? And was the opposition compliant? This is not an unknown political strategy, even in democracies, in attempts to take control of populations. As Harris (2023) documented, 'Project Fear' is nothing new and has been used by politicians over the past decades, recently in relation to the Brexit campaign as well as the COVID-19 pandemic. He wrote:

> When it came to Covid and the authoritarian measures deemed necessary to keep us safe, fear again won out. Even after the successful and ground-breaking rollout of the Covid vaccine programme, politicians raised the spectre of mass deaths unless we returned to lockdown – a controversial measure that will be examined, one day, by a public inquiry.

Dingwall (2023a), too, is of the view that 'Fear has, then, been a consistent, pervasive and amplified consort of the Covid-19 pandemic', citing the 'deliberate and calculated amplification of fear by state agents; the promotion of this fear particularly by broadcast media; and the infection of the scientific community itself, challenging its professed values of disinterest and objectivity'.

There has, certainly, been controversy about the messages sent from government to aid compliance. Nudges, which were widely used by the government's Behavioural Insights Team (commonly known as the Nudge Unit), at least in the early stages of the pandemic (Sibony, 2020), to urge people to follow the rules, have been seriously criticised for using frightening imagery to influence public behaviour. Indeed, an investigation into their use by the Parliament's Public Administration and Constitutional Affairs Committee was instigated in early 2022. It is of course not known how effective nudges actually were in their aims. Two experimental studies (Hume et al, 2021; Sanders et al, 2021) suggested that their impact, if indeed there was any at all, and especially in the unusual situation of the pandemic, may have been greater for intentions than for actual behaviour. Furthermore, there seemed little difference in the impact of nudges with loss or gain messages or, beyond the short-term, nudge messages that included further information on the beneficiaries of the desired behaviour or opportunities for self-reflection.

The role of the police

Social order is communicated symbolically (Schneider, 2021), and the police are, in Becker's (1963) terms, rule enforcers. Their role is to gain the cooperation of the public and maintain social order as determined by the government as rule creators. Accordingly they are expected to adapt in the wake of a moral panic (Hall et al, 2013), or as rules change, in order to encourage compliance with the new social mandate. All this materialised during the pandemic as lockdowns and the new legislation brought a changed role for the police. In addition, as suggested by *The Lockdown Files* (The Telegraph, 2023), this agency was brought further under the control of the government in the deployment of their role than previously.

Indeed, earlier normal behaviours became, almost overnight, the subject of police intervention. New police responsibilities came into being with Regulation 6 of The Coronavirus Act 2020 which stated that, in England, no person could leave their place of residence without a reasonable excuse. This legislation remained in force until 19 July 2021, after which all COVID-19 restrictions were lifted in England, with the exception of some rules concerning international travel. The police were charged with enforcement of this rule, representing a considerable change of emphasis as traditional forms of crimes showed a corresponding reduction. Analysis of crime reports from open police data, and comparing crime reports by type of crime for March to December 2019 and 2020, revealed a drop of nearly 12 per cent in the later relative to the earlier year (CrimeRate, 2022). Not surprisingly, with most people at home most of the time, personal theft from the person was down by 52 per cent, shoplifting down by 37 per cent, robbery and muggings down by 32 per cent, and burglary down by 30 per cent. Some other types of crime did, however, show increases. Drug offences were up 12 per cent, public order offences up 2.5 per cent, and antisocial behaviour up by nearly 40 per cent.

The new mandate was, however, no easy task, in part due to the ambiguity contained within the notion of a 'reasonable excuse'. The National Police Chiefs' Council and the College of Policing (2020) outlined a four-step escalation principle that underpinned the police strategy. These steps were engage, explain, encourage and enforce, with enforcement being only a last resort. It was accompanied by a non-exhaustive guide for officers who were given powers to report and prosecute breaches. Likely to be reasonable was shopping for food, including luxury items and alcohol, or a newspaper or other necessity, or buying tools and equipment to repair damage caused by bad weather (although buying paint and brushes to redecorate a kitchen was deemed unlikely to be reasonable). Going out for a walk or exercise, or travelling for a walk provided the walk takes longer than the drive, resting or eating lunch while on a long walk (although not a short walk followed by a long stop on a park bench), travelling to work if a key worker or otherwise unable to work from home, taking an animal for treatment, moving to a friend's house after arguments at home, or providing supplies or support to the vulnerable, were also seen as reasonable. Leaving home to seek medical treatment was also permitted.

The lack of clarity in this new role for the police inevitably meant varying interpretations and left much scope for the discretion that comes with the job (Reiner, 2010). How far what was commonly seen as an increased presence of the police influenced compliance with the restrictions is, however, unclear. Even if it did not engender fear among many diarists, it could cause annoyance and incredulity.

BARKLEY
Wednesday 22 April 2020
In the park we saw two female police officers enforcing social distancing rules – mainly telling people who were sitting on the grass in the sunshine to get up and walk or do some other exercise.

GRACE
Friday 3 April 2020
Walked to the local gardens today and mid-park I perched on a bench to get the stones out of my boots (boot removal needed as no Swiss army

knife with the correct attachment). Along came an immaculately made up police woman, who moved me on and told me the time outside was for exercising not sitting! I felt I had to explain about the stones as mitigation and wanted to show her my impressive steps for the day but felt the latter would certainly mean incarceration! She was very polite but I did notice further up the park many people were sitting in the sun! My guilt was easy pickings obviously!

The fact that English COVID-19 rules changed so many times during the course of the pandemic undoubtedly led to a considerable challenge for the police and, it can be argued, inevitable mistakes. There were differing views on police intervention among the diarists, some of whom pointed out that the law is always subject to interpretation. Many expressed sympathy for the task they were charged with, while others believed that excessive police intervention was counter-productive.

ELEANOR
Sunday 10 May 2020

We can now go out for exercise as much as we like and travel to get there. Does this now mean that seaside resorts will again be inundated with outsiders bringing in the risk of infection? I feel very sorry for the police who seem to have been left with an almost impossible task.

ELISABETH
Friday 17 April 2020

I just heard a man talking on the radio about the official attitude to lockdown, saying the government should be looking at facilitating things rather than penalising non-compliance and I so, so agree with that. He said most people are keen to comply with self-distancing etc. but threatening them increases depression and an inclination to rebel, push the margins etc. when the aim should be to say how can we help people get out and exercise with less risk – such as opening parks, golf courses, and other normally private places, would make life easier and thereby easier to comply without destroying our equilibrium. Thank goodness the local government minister was listening and has said this will happen!

MABEL
Thursday 26 March 2020

I do sympathise with the police who seem to have an almost impossible job on their hands. They will be criticised for what they do and for what they do not. And they are unlikely to be able to deal with many of the really stupid antisocial things some people are doing, such as stealing lanyards from medical staff so that they can get free or cheaper food and drinks, or coughing in people's faces and saying they have the virus. The other day some people let down the tyres of six ambulances, and on another occasion burnt out two food delivery vans. The news today, however, says that reported crime is markedly down. There may be fewer burglaries as everyone is at home, but petty crime hasn't gone away.

OLIVE
Monday 30 March 2020

Lord Sumption made a very strong statement on *BBC World at 1* regarding what he saw as excessive enforcement of lockdown by some police forces, particularly in Derbyshire, where drones were used to control movement and a lake was dyed black! He warned about the danger of turning Britain into a 'police state'. There is a demand, not least by police bodies themselves, to clarify how the crisis is to be policed. The strategy so far relies on the cooperation of the public, and excessive control tactics could undermine this.

Between March 2020 and May 2021, police issued over 120,000 fixed penalty notices for breaches of lockdown rules in England and Wales, with the greatest number of fines during the January 2021 lockdown when all of England was placed under Tier 4 restrictions. These were disproportionately given to males, younger people, those from ethnic minority backgrounds, and those living in deprived areas (McVie et al, 2023).

Not surprisingly, some so-called breaches of the law were deemed controversial. A much publicised case related to January 2021 when two young women drove five miles in Derbyshire to go for a quiet walk together by a reservoir. They were surrounded by police and issued with fines. One was carrying a cup of peppermint tea and told it was not allowed as it counted as a picnic. The police were subsequently quick to denounce their own action, stressing that they would not gain the confidence and support of the general public in their task of upholding the lockdown rules by proceeding in this manner. Although most diarists appeared not to have come into contact with the police during the period when breaches of the coronavirus restrictions were in force, they did report stories of police activity. Some regarded this as legitimate action.

CARACTACUS
Tuesday 7 April 2020

Have been doing a little gentle weeding in the strong sun (with sunblock). Had a chat over the fence to my next-door neighbour who works for the NHS as a printer. He is now on night shift, and very busy, printing all sorts of CV material. He drives to work and is occasionally stopped by the police, which must be annoying for him, but it's presumably good that the police are acting to deter non-essential journeys.

FISHERMAN
Tuesday 5 May 2020

Had drinks in our garden, and received a phone call from my son who advised me that his 10-year-old son had been told off by a policeman for skateboarding in an empty public square. I told him that he shouldn't be surprised, but, as the public park was closed, he would need to take some other form of exercise. Meal, phone calls, TV, bed.

HATTIE
Friday 24 April 2020

Living by the beach we are conscious of the number of people exercising on the prom and on the beach. Nearly everyone seems to be aware of the need to keep moving, though Friday was a lovely day and more people were on the beach with children. My daughter appeared with her daughter and we left buckets and spades at the front gate for them. She said would I go and sit with them, keeping well away, but I said I thought that wasn't in the spirit of things so didn't. The two of them spent about an hour in the sun, and then appeared at the front gate again to return things. They had been moved on by the police – shoes were being hastily put on when a policeman arrived by them but he just asked them if they were on their way now. My daughter had in fact noticed them clearing people away from the beach. I can see the sense of this as it would be very tempting for one family seeing others there to think they could be there as well.

In other cases, however, attitudes towards police activity, and inactivity, were more nuanced. Some suggested, in line with Blumer's (1969) principle that actions, such as police enforcement, are dependent on meanings associated with objects and contexts, that the focus might be on the easier targets. Others were concerned about enforcement for its own sake rather than to prevent the spread of the virus, and of freedoms being eroded without due reason.

JESSIE
Sunday 10 May 2020

We had a Zoom meeting with all the family which worked really well. Our youngest son also told us that he had gone to his local park and sat on a bench to read, but was moved on by police. The police then tried to move on a group of young lads each with a beer can in hand and kicking a football between them – their response to being moved on was they were exercising.

My son felt that there are real problems in parks about enforcing rules, as the police decided not to confront the lads and moved on.

JOJO
Wednesday 25 March 2020

Having dropped off shopping drove out to Dassett Hills assuming that would be fine as our one exercise of the day. When we arrived at top of hill there was a municipal van with three guys in it – one of them was gesticulating angrily at us and shaking his fists. We couldn't work out why until we parked up and read the sign that the Council has shut all parks to vehicles. You are supposed to stay local and walk or cycle round Dassett Hills – we counted about 30 cars (spread over the whole area) and everyone was keeping their distance apart from one group of about eight young people (foreign but couldn't recognise their language) who were taking no notice at all.

OLIVE
Tuesday 14 April 2020

I have become accustomed to seeing the police patrolling the prom where I have my daily walk. They have been moving people along from sitting on the wall, playing ball games on the sand, etc. These regulations are legitimately (?) in place for a particular context, but can slip into becoming normal/acceptable without democratic agreement if we are not careful.

TOPPER
Retrospective: Thursday 9 April 2020

Over the w/e we went for our usual day long walk round the Stourhead estate. We met two families and a dog walker throughout the day and social distance was maintained. It was a nasty shock to find a note from the police on the windscreen saying 'WHY ARE YOU HERE TODAY?' – and that the government restrictions did not permit us to use our vehicle to travel to this location to exercise. This has been a blow as we were looking forward to long walks away from people.

WARRENER
Wednesday 27 May 2020

L and C met at the weekend at Hampstead Heath, with C's wife also with them, and were chased off by a couple of policemen who threatened them with a fine. Seems it's OK for one person to meet with another (6ft away of course) but not for a couple to meet with one other person. All comes across as pretty arbitrary.

There could also be concern and anger at the threat of police action or rebuke.

BAREFOOT DOC
Thursday 9 April 2020
My older granddaughter's birthday is Midsummer's Day, and by her birthday the orchids are in full bloom on the downs. I know an ungrazed field under the shoulder of Wolstonbury where at least six kinds of wild orchid grow. The twayblades and butterfly orchids are often finished by the time we go there, we probably will see a bee or a fly orchid, the pyramids and spotteds will be plentiful, they flower all along the scarp slope, all summer. I wonder whether I will be 'allowed' to walk there when the time arrives; it's 25 minutes from my home. Whatever, I will. Maybe sneaking along back roads to avoid any patrol on the A23. It's absurd that I should even be thinking about such things.

Some diarists wrote how they were cross at the possibility of being stopped were they to carry out actions technically not allowed but which they had pragmatically judged to be safe. Did they need to have an excuse at the ready should the police intervene?

Under the watchful eye of offspring

Compliance with the mandated restrictions imposed by the government was influenced not only by formal policing or governance 'from above' but also informal policing or governance 'from below' (Stenson, 2005). The children of diarists, themselves adults, in a sense often took on the role of rule enforcers, instructing their parents on how they should take heed of the restrictions for their own well-being. Although diarists retained the capacity to make their own judgements as to what constituted an acceptable risk and what did not, it was nonetheless common for a degree of role reversal whereby parents were told by their offspring what they should and should not do. Most did appear to fall in line.

CARACTACUS
Sunday 3 May 2020
I have noticed that, in four or five families we know, the children are taking the lead in saying what should happen, and what their parents should do – or not do. In no case are the children still at home, but several people have said things like 'Our children won't let us go out … '. This seems to mark the transition from my generation being in charge, and calling (some of) the shots, providing cash, advising on things like house-buying, etc. to a dependent role, being regarded as hapless oldies who might become liabilities. Of course, such a transition has to happen at some point, but I feel that the process has been speeded up by the pandemic.

FRANCIA

Saturday 25 July 2020

Our daughter and son-in-law are visiting us this Sunday. The first time I have seen my daughter (apart from Zoom) since February and my son-in-law some time before that. Both daughter and son-in-law have been tested for the virus via some experimental procedure carried out by their local university. My daughter has stressed this testing to me on several occasions. I like to think my husband and I are fit and active but our daughter seems to think we should be wrapped in cotton wool. I think we are at the stage when the children take over the concern from the parents!!

HATTIE

Friday 10 April 2020

With family regularly checking up on us and giving strict instructions, we are being conscientious about these measures. Because my husband isn't yet 70 he does occasionally visit a shop and has been out to post parcels, but I don't do that.

MABEL

Saturday 21 March 2020

My sons are now insistent that I don't go to the shops anymore. One of them has even agreed to do my shopping for me as it has been impossible so far to get a supermarket delivery slot. I'll have to be very careful what I order so that I don't get any disapproving looks.

PETER

Friday 3 April 2020

Interesting how the 30 somethings are really hot on this stuff. I have several friends who are being policed by their kids. I guess they have so much more reason to get this thing sorted quickly. They have careers, small children and everything to look forward to. I'm not saying that I don't have a lot to look forward to, but I still feel that we've had such a great time to live through for so long, and they deserve that too.

While the majority of diarists concurred with their children's wishes and instructions, some were less willing to abandon their personal agency and decision-making.

HUMPHREY

Friday 29 May 2020

Of course it's our children who are already objecting to our easing off at all. They are so much stricter than us. There is an admirable TV series of short dramas, shot under lockdown, called 'Unprecedented' on BBC4.

There was a very funny but affecting one called 'Grounded' about a couple like us being lectured at by their worried daughter. It was very close to home.

SIMON
Friday 5 June 2020

Another down day. These are becoming more and more frequent. I'm going to have to get out of this place soon. To date I have only seen two sets of two people twice in ten weeks! My girls are worried that they or someone in their household might infect me if I go to stay with them. I understand that but have pointed out that I am coming up to 80 so really am more than capable of making decisions about my own life and that, if necessary, I shall take the train into London to meet O and go off to Whitstable for a few days staying in our friend's empty house. Much consternation on their part but I need to explain to them that staying alive for the sake of staying alive is really not on as far as I'm concerned and I am prepared to take calculated risks in exchange for a more social existence.

Evidently not all diarists were prepared to engage in role reversal with their children.

A question of morality

Inevitably new rules and restrictions gave birth to a new morality, with behaviours previously seen as taken for granted under question. Among the issues that gained attention from diarists were travelling to second or holiday homes, and gatherings on overcrowded beaches. Other dilemmas were whether lockdown rules could be broken to meet up with family or exercise the dog, and whether sitting down on a bench was permissible. A further issue discussed by diarists concerned payment for cancellations. A range of views were expressed on these matters, with decisions often reached pragmatically. While there was criticism of actions that constituted risk to others, there was more sympathy if they were risk-free. Most seemed to agree that payment for cancellations depended on the recipient.

ARAMINTA
Friday 24 April 2020

I do know two people who have elderly single parents who live on their own. In each case a daughter has decided to break the lockdown to keep their elderly parent company and the help they need. It's a moral decision and they have decided that this is the kinder way to treat their parent even though it does carry increased risk for them.

BETTYMAC
Thursday 23 April 2020

With regard to payment of membership fees. I had already paid for my tennis club membership which runs from April to April. I will not be asking for a refund. It could make the difference between life and death for the club. Of course, I am lucky enough to be able to make this gesture.

EVE
Friday 24 April 2020

In terms of 'new moralities' I am certainly doing several things that might now be regarded as 'wrong'. I am going for two walks most days and I am living between two homes, mine and that of my partner, which is not exactly the same as a second home but very close to it. My justification for these behaviours is that I am not doing anything that would harm others as I am very careful about social distancing on my walks and my partner and I make sure we keep our interactions in the area around each other's home to the minimum. Of course, it's always easy to justify the behaviours that make one's own life easy and I might be guilty of that and ignoring the 'mote in my own eye'. One thing I do try to do is not to condemn other people that have transgressed, although it is very tempting when they are public figures.

FRANCES
Thursday 23 April 2020

Indeed I can't see why people couldn't commute between their homes, as long as they didn't meet other people in either.

PANGOLIN
Thursday 7 May 2020

I don't feel critical of those sitting on benches for longer than they have been walking. They may have a heart attack if they don't rest.

Linked to the issue of morality is the notion of judgement, and several diarists drew attention to how the new rules and restrictions were leading to increased criticism of other people's behaviour.

ANNA
Wednesday 22 April 2020

My daughter today introduced me to the concept of lockdown-shaming – where people who are not into self-improvement or who can't account for their day are made to feel bad for not taking advantage of the circumstances. Delightfully, a cousin who in her professional life is probably one of the highest-achieving people I know (a 70-something now), rang up today objecting to the people she speaks to who are achieving – or meaning to – wonderful things, while she is just lying low in the country. What a relief (as I had assumed she would be of their party!).

OTTOLIE
Tuesday 21 April 2020

Two phone calls, one from a friend concerned that some evenings I sit on the bench in the sunshine with a glass of wine and some olives. I found myself furious. We, she said, only drink at weekends.

Well, how very dull. I sometimes don't drink, sometimes do, and not bothered either way. Right now, I think my birthday bottles are most enjoyable and so lovely to have a few decent ones. So far, haven't resorted to gin. But now, I just might. Pah. They've been to visit their second home, which I think is far, far worse than cradling a glass of wine in the sunshine and watching the robins. Lockdown overreaction on my part. I am fond of them. I don't care what people do normally, so I feel that this situation is changing me.

Some issues did, however, provoke a widespread reaction. A good example was the apparent rule-breaking by Dominic Cummings, chief adviser to the prime minister at the time. He had driven from London to Durham with his wife and young son, and later also made a 60-mile round trip with his family, apparently as he claimed, to check if his eyesight was good enough to make the return journey to London. Most diarists were highly critical of Cummings, particularly as he had been instrumental in helping to design the restrictions everyone was supposed to follow. Nonetheless, there were those who felt some sympathy for him, especially as he had not been the only one to flout the rules.

Another controversial and widely discussed question was whether or not neighbourhood watch should be swapped for neighbourhood shop. In September 2020, Priti Patel, the then home secretary, gave prominence to this issue by saying that she would inform the police should she witness her neighbours failing to observe the restrictions. Apparently the reporting line then set up by the police received numerous complaints about neighbours flouting the rule of six. Several diarists drew attention to how the new rules and restrictions had led to a change of mindset and increased judgement of others. There was a tendency for these judgements to be pragmatic and go beyond the requirements of the legislation.

LOUISE
Sunday 26 April 2020

I live in a very law-abiding area, especially now most of the students are gone, and by and large everyone is following the government's guidance.

However, in other parts of Bristol there have been more infractions. While this leads to a considerable amount of grousing on social media, I am more surprised by how many people are reporting these misdemeanours to officialdom. Avon and Somerset police have had 13,850 breaches brought to their attention. Out of these incidents they have only issued 211 fines, as thankfully their approach is to explain and engage with people initially rather than sanction.

ROSA
Saturday 25 April 2020

Various areas of discussion have arisen during lockdown about the behaviour of others. We had a WhatsApp group of immediate neighbours and very shortly after it started up one member made a report on another local resident, suggesting that there was someone staying overnight though not living at the address, against the gist of the rules we had been given recently by government, beamed in via TV each evening at 5 pm and some other times. I didn't like the idea of policing the behaviour of other members and texted that to the whole group. Various other members then backed me up and nothing like that has happened again yet.

In other ways, too, citizens were taking over. The National Rural Crime Network (Murphy, 2020) revealed reports of 'small-scale vigilantism' in April 2020. These examples of collective governance (Stenson, 2005) demonstrated how some residents, angry at people driving long distances to the countryside, including beauty spots, for walks or cycle rides, had taken matters into their own hands. In a worrying development, the organisation's chair said people had even been 'aggressively driving at cyclists'.

Summary

The first national lockdown during the COVID-19 pandemic brought unprecedented legislation in its wake. Never in the diarists' (and others') lifetimes had comparable legal restrictions been in force. Living in Britain, a liberal, democratic country, it was unknown to be ordered to stay at home and concur with a raft of measures that curtailed their freedom. There was, nonetheless, a high level of compliance with the new orders and restrictions, among the diarists as well as within the population at large. Whether this was expected or unexpected is debatable. It would seem that the uncertainty of the situation, the invisibility of the virus, the bombardment of messages from media, the daily reminders of hospitalisations and deaths, the continuous speculation about the progress of the pandemic, the surveillance by police and children, and the actions of other moral entrepreneurs, contributed to widespread anxiety and fear. These were almost certainly powerful motivators that encouraged a general culture of acceptance of the new emergency measures.

The pandemic and its attendant rules, however, did not impinge on everyone in the same way. The next chapter examines the sense in which everybody was in it together as well as the differences between individuals and social groups.

4

All in it together?

A common refrain throughout the pandemic was that 'we are all in it together'. While this mantra was widely used by politicians and others, perhaps to encourage national solidarity and compliance with rules and regulations, it was open to many different interpretations. There were senses in which it bore some truth, and others in which it did not.

Perhaps it was only completely true in that everybody could potentially succumb to the virus. COVID-19 in itself was not discriminatory. The actual risk of severe illness and death was, nonetheless, highly variable and dependent on such factors as age, personal vulnerability and exposure and, by extension, demography. All the same, everybody needed to be protected, not only for their personal well-being but also to prevent them passing the virus on to others. There was a strong collective interest in harnessing the virus.

The refrain also had some validity, although this is more debatable, at a national level on account of the enforcement model adopted by the British government. This putatively put the reduction of illness and death from the virus, and the protection of the NHS, at its heart, and sought to encourage all citizens, apart from the necessary exceptions, to behave in similar ways. Daily activities were prescribed and many behaviours were mandated. Social distancing was, for example, to be maintained at all times. Uniformity of beliefs and values relating to the pandemic was also encouraged.

Nonetheless, this model that prescribed the new social order and severely reduced personal agency, effectively meant – as a number of diarists pointed out – that the middle classes were staying at home while the working classes were bringing them things. Everybody was most certainly not 'in this' to the same extent or in the same way. This model, apart from reinforcing existing structural inequalities, also prioritised health above all else and gave relative disregard to, among other things, the needs of business, enterprise, the economy, and children and young people. There were myriad ways in which the pandemic impacted unequally on people across the nation. The diarists were the first to acknowledge that they were among the least deprived.

Although in many ways the pandemic did not strike equally, there were some ways in which a semblance of togetherness arose. Everybody was living through a period of uncertainty, with nobody really any wiser than anybody else about how the pandemic would progress and how long it would last.

Anxieties and restrictions thus affected everyone to some degree. Perhaps more importantly, however, there were many signs of significant mutualism within neighbourhoods and communities. As described elsewhere (see Chapter 6) there was a shared etiquette surrounding social distancing and other measures to keep the virus at bay, and much camaraderie. Friendships and humour were an antidote to the imposed isolation. Local communities also thrived and interacted as never before.

The over-70s – a special case?

The initial lockdown constituted a major upheaval to everyday life. As Berger and Luckmann (1966) would have described it, there was a severe impact on the symbolic universe governing the diarists. The old order had changed almost without warning and there was a new institutional structure. Values and behavioural expectations were in flux. Not only was there an erosion of liberty but, initially at least, there was a distinct possibility of additional discrimination against the over-70s. Prior to this point, there had been few restrictions according to older age. For example, anybody could carry on driving if they had good eyesight and no evidence of restrictive disability, continue to be employed in suitable work, go out shopping or join a tennis club, and take responsibility for personal financial affairs while remaining capable of doing so.

Nonetheless, at the outset of the pandemic, there was discussion of singling out the over-70s for special treatment. This was of particular concern to the diarists who fell within this age group and, indeed, had been included in the sample for this reason. It was suggested that they were especially vulnerable and thus should be isolated as far as possible. Indeed, by 29 May 2020 the official rate of deaths from coronavirus (the criteria for reporting has not gone unchallenged) among those aged 70 and over was twice that within the rest of the population (Webb, 2020). Moreover, while the death rate among 70- to 79-year-olds was two per 1,000, it was seven and 18 per thousand, respectively, for those in their 80s and 90s or above. There were more deaths among men than women in each age group.

The early plan was alleged to include a recommendation to keep the over-70s on lockdown for a year. This had been mooted on Sunday 15 March 2020, before the initial lockdown, and again in the middle of April in a leaked draft of a document by cabinet ministers that outlined how to get the country going. It did not materialise, but the damage had been done. The labelling had taken place and was exemplified by an image of a very elderly looking couple stooped and with sticks in *The Times* on 5 May 2020 with the title 'Coronavirus: Don't keep over-70s indoors, Tories warn' (Swinford and Courea, 2020).

PEN
Tuesday 5 May 2020
There was a very unfair photo in *The Times* accompanying a discussion about over-70s. A very overweight couple shambling along with sticks and propping each other up. These are not the over-70s that I recognise.

For this reason, and although almost all diarists were in their 70s and not their 80s or above, most did not feel that they were 'all in it' with everyone else. They had acquired a public image as elderly and at risk and confronted it with varying levels of acceptance and denial. They did not want to become ill, but at the same time did not necessarily feel that their vulnerability was determined by age. Some reported anger or shock at the label they had acquired.

APPLETREE
Retrospective: Monday 13 April 2020
I was furious about the over-70s being highlighted as vulnerable and like many was shocked to feel my age and the ghastly label elderly for the first time. Realised straightaway what the 'herd immunity' idea was – let the oldies and the sick die off and then we will have a young, fit herd left.

BAREFOOT DOC
Retrospective: Thursday 2 April 2020
'It's fine – for other old people, not for me.' I was angry when I got a text, telling me I should stay indoors. Mind your own business! You don't know my circumstances.

JULES
Retrospective: Monday 30 March 2020
During this time, and especially at the beginning, I became very shocked to realise that I was being grouped into an 'elderly', 'at risk' group which at first I found insulting. It has left me with the feeling that I have been forced to face up to the fact that I am not as young as I feel (or felt before this virus struck). Maybe that is no bad thing; it has certainly reminded me to take nothing for granted, especially my health and strength.

OTTOLIE
Thursday 7 May 2020
I was rather shocked to be labelled ELDERLY at the beginning of this. I don't mind OLDER. Elderly is a label of tottering helplessness.

All the same, there was acknowledgement that mortality rates increased with age and, although 70 was a somewhat arbitrary cut-off point, health risks were higher among older people than the young. Moreover, if the demand for medical services outstripped supply, there could be definite advantages to minimising risk. Diarists tended to be heavy consumers of the news, and the majority were also in contact with family, friends, colleagues and acquaintances online if not face-to-face. They were witness to the scare stories, the entreaties, and the statistics that were presented.

JACCA
Sunday 26 April 2020
Around the same time, I saw the document outlining decision-making strategy in the ICU and realised that just having hit 70 a bed or a ventilator might not be available should I need one. This was really depressing. Being 70 is bad enough but suddenly realising that being over 70 equated with being expendable was really hard to take. I don't feel old or worthless. I had a few days with a profound sense of helplessness and hopelessness. This is not normal for me.

There were those, accordingly, who saw some sense in offering extra protection to the older members of society, even if they were not too pleased personally.

ARAMINTA
Retrospective: Thursday 26 March 2020
Those over 70 are more likely to die if they get the virus so it's better to protect them more. Apart from saving lives it will decrease the pressure on the NHS.

CAMPBELL
Retrospective: Wednesday 25 March 2020
Of course, as an over 70, with an underlying respiratory condition, I'm glad about the emphasis on protecting people in my age group – I don't want to finish up overwhelming intensive care services any more than the government wants me to.

PERSIA
Retrospective: Thursday 26 March 2020
I agree about the government's emphasis on the vulnerable, i.e. those with underlying health issues and I consider the elderly to be from 80 plus – perhaps that's because I can't face up to being elderly at 71.

SWEETPEA
Retrospective: Saturday 28 March 2020
It makes me feel safer.

In the event, the over-70s were treated the same as everyone else. The most vulnerable were asked to 'shield' whatever their age. Diarists nonetheless did adapt pragmatically to the new restrictions, generally keeping themselves as free from risk as they could.

At unequal risk

Even if anybody could potentially contract the virus, there were enormous differences in the likelihood that they would. As Giddens (1984) and other sociologists have stressed, change at one level of society has repercussions at others. One implication of the pandemic, which almost all diarists pointed out, is that if older people, children and the vulnerable were staying at home, others were working to maintain the infrastructure of society and provide services for them. Thus many essential workers – including medical staff, transport operators, the emergency services, shop workers, delivery drivers, the police and justice system, and those working in public utilities – were not fully protected from exposure to COVID-19 and, accordingly, much more likely to succumb to the virus. Immediately everyone was not in it together. This reinforced a strong class division whereby the middle classes stayed at home while the working classes kept the country running and brought things to them.

The likelihood of illness and death varied even among essential workers. COVID-19 deaths were, for example, particularly high among women care workers and home care workers alongside the high rates of death among older people in care homes. The British Medical Association (BMA, 2023) reported how the need to free up extra beds to accommodate COVID-19 patients meant that many older people were sent home or transferred to care homes without being tested for the virus, 'a mistake that likely led to the deaths of many'.

HOLLY
Wednesday 13 May 2020

The state of things in care homes is so appalling and truly heart breaking. The residents and staff have been so neglected. While it was understandable that the focus, initially, should be on preparing the acute hospital sector, it is totally mind-boggling that so little attention was paid to care homes. There's a minister for care for God's sake. ... Word was getting out that there was pressure on care homes to take residents from hospital but as no tests were being carried out, there was no way of knowing if they were carrying the infection with them. We heard of some local commissioners putting a lot of pressure on both not-for-profit and private homes to take people from hospital. It was clear that not only was there no testing but that the care sector was completely lacking in supplies of PPE and the means and finance to secure it.

TERESA
Tuesday 14 April 2020
The news today is much more terrible than usual. This was the day when the extent of the deaths from the virus that have been taking place in care homes became public.

There were, furthermore, marked differences in rates of illness and death from COVID-19 according to demography. Bambra et al (2021) elaborated on how 'COVID-19 is a syndemic of infectious disease and inequalities. It has killed unequally, been experienced unequally and will impoverish unequally'. They described the pandemic as a perfect storm, explaining how risk factors become mutually reinforcing. Socioeconomic, geographic and ethnic inequalities co-existed and were linked with illness and the severity of illness. These authors analysed available statistics to illustrate how COVID-19 deaths were not evenly distributed but associated with disadvantage. This was demonstrated by Office for National Statistics figures throughout the pandemic. In May 2020, for instance, people living in the most deprived areas of the UK were twice as likely to die from the virus as those in the most affluent areas. Deaths were also much more common in urban conurbations than in rural locations.

Particular sections of the population, such as ethnic minorities, were at enhanced risk. Morales and Ali (2021) summarised studies to date and demonstrated how the pandemic highlighted the health disparities between ethnic and racial groups, with Black and Asian patients much more likely than the white population to receive advanced respiratory support or to die as a consequence of COVID-19. They concluded that the risks of illness and death among minority ethnic groups were attributable to factors such as a higher prevalence of co-morbidities linked to poorer outcomes, delayed access to health care, larger than average households, and greater social deprivation.

The pandemic also took a particular toll on those with pre-existing health issues. The British Medical Association report in 2023, mentioned earlier, documented how the NHS had already had a backlog of care at the onset of the pandemic, and how that just got worse as many treatments were cancelled in favour of treatment for COVID-19. Iacobucci (2021) presented statistics on the large numbers of people affected in terms of planned surgery, emergency care, the diagnosis of cancer, and heart operations such as coronary bypass and heart valve surgery. As pointed out, this could lead to moral and ethical issues in the provision of care.

OLIVE
Tuesday 7 April 2020
Judgements about who should have access to scarce medical resources is becoming a moral and political matter. Some groups regarded as 'very

vulnerable' or unlikely to benefit from scarce intensive care resources, have been encouraged to display 'Do not resuscitate' statements. Definitions of what constitutes a meaningful life and who decides was central to the disability movement from the 1990s on, and these insights should be drawn upon now. Instead, disabled people are bundled together as 'vulnerable'.

Not only physical health, but mental health too, was at issue during the pandemic. Two longitudinal surveys (Pierce et al, 2020; O'Connor et al, 2021) found that adults of all ages were adversely affected by the pandemic, with tolls on mental health and well-being. A study published by Age UK (2020), that included large numbers of participants over 70 years of age, served as corroboration, and reported how many older people were deeply afraid of COVID-19 and remained close to home. The findings from these studies suggested that many older people had seen their health deteriorate and their anxiety increase. In general, those with a long-term condition prior to the pandemic, particularly dementia, those who were isolated and did not use the internet, those from more disadvantaged groups without gardens, and those from BAME backgrounds, were especially affected.

As a number of authors have shown (Berg-Weger and Morley, 2020; Bambra et al, 2021), loneliness was a particular concern for older people living on their own. Indeed, this has been acknowledged by the English government that in June 2020, through the Department for Digital, Culture, Media and Sport, set up a £5 million fund to award grants to charities and local groups to tackle the problem.

Just under one in three diarists were living on their own at the time of the first lockdown. Diary entries suggested that a fluctuation of mood was common for everyone (see Chapter 7) and that it was not unusual to feel isolated even if not in a single-person household. Those on their own told how they had been alone in their house for weeks on end and some reflected on the importance of social contact.

ANNA
Wednesday 29 July 2020
I notice it seems to have been a pretty different experience for single people than for couples – mine being a single one. Also I guess if you or your partner were unwell (or had 'underlying health conditions') it would be very different. And if family members not with you got ill/went to hospital/died – well, thank goodness I've been spared that. And I keep my fingers crossed.

ELEANOR
Sunday 17 May 2020
Chatting to friends this week (week 9 of social distancing for me) and for those of us who live alone, we realise that it is nine weeks since we touched

another person. I am lucky that I have my cat for physical company and comfort but it brings home the reality of the extreme loneliness of those who live their lives completely alone.

JENNIFER
Sunday 14 June 2020

This week I have more often felt the aloneness of living alone during the pandemic. I quite often feel it in the mornings as I get up, or after I have done a Zoom session with people. In Wales we are allowed to go and sit in the garden of a friend or relative but the weather has not been good enough to do that for most of this week. However, yesterday a friend came and sat at a distance on my patio and we chatted for just over an hour. That was really nice – I have not seen her since before lockdown. And today, I may go down to my daughter's to sit in their garden. Hopefully this will ease the aloneness feeling.

ROB
Tuesday 16 June 2020

I am beginning to see that this period of lockdown has changed my view of myself quite a bit. … I am self-contained enough to deal with lockdown … (although … would I feel the same in a flat in an inner city high rise??). But it has highlighted quite how alone I am in many ways … despite friends and contacts who check on me from time to time … I have begun to miss human 'contact'. No chance of a hug anytime soon. … Cat is quite tolerant of my encircling him with both arms however … even not shaking hands at the end of a round of golf feels not quite right … and my semi regular Symphony Hall visits and the travel entailed … felt like being in society however slight.

ROSA
Friday 12 June 2020

My main fear for this period is social isolation, as being on my own for a day or two days has previously brought me to an edge. It only takes a time with a friend for a cup of coffee to guard against the great swoop down in my spirits. By pure chance the shape of my front garden and my neighbour's, forming an L shape on the grass in front of the two gardens, has meant that while we were in the sunny, early weeks of the pandemic, friends and neighbours were able to sit on spaced out garden chairs so that we could share a drink and talk. That was a lifeline to me. This reflects the need I always have. When I am living normally, I am used to living alone, but the rules were changed and I still have to work at arrangements to ensure I have social contacts with real people every day. The odd day with none is gloomy for me.

In various ways the pandemic impacted differently on individuals and population groups. Sometimes this was influenced by occupation and demography and sometimes it was linked to personal circumstances. There was unequal risk both in succumbing to the virus and in suffering collateral damage from the pandemic.

It's not just about health

The disproportionate adversity experienced by certain groups in society was not always about health and well-being. There were many other consequences of the pandemic apart from illness and death. Regarding finances, for instance, the Institute for Employment Studies (Wilson and Buzzeo, 2021) pointed to the often dire consequences for low paid and insecure workers, while a Comparethemarket survey suggested that more than half of households in the UK were, by January 2021, worried about having to spend all their savings (Osborne, 2021). The Office for National Statistics (2021e) highlighted the particular difficulties of families with children at home who, by December 2020, were finding it harder to keep up-to-date with their bills than at any other point over the past year. BritainThinks (2020) also concluded that the gap between families with young children and older affluent participants was striking. Diarists were in accord.

BONANZA BILL
Thursday 30 April 2020
As a pensioner, I am still receiving my full pension quota at the moment whilst younger people have lost their jobs or are on reduced incomes. This does make me feel guilty. I would like to be able to make a contribution to the welfare of others but am not sure how to go about it or who to support. I did give to Captain Tom's NHS Fund but that is a one off. I would most like to give to a fund that will help people who through no fault of their own are suffering real economic hardship.

There was concern not only for individuals but for the state of the economy as the country emerged from the pandemic. Enormous amounts of money had been spent, much business had been inoperative for long periods of time, companies were going under, and people were losing jobs. There was the possibility of recession and depression as well as the increased cost of goods and services. Worries of this kind were regularly expressed by diarists.

HOLGATE
Friday 12 June 2020
The other bad news this week is from the OECD that the British economy is likely to suffer the worst damage from COVID-19 crisis of any country in

the developed world. They have estimated that the UK's national income will fall by 11.5 per cent. However, this fall could increase to 14 per cent if the UK needs to impose a second COVID-19 [lockdown] later this year. In the meantime, the ONS has announced that the UK economy shrank by 20.4 per cent in April (the largest monthly contraction on record) as the country spent its first full month in 'lockdown'.

Most diarists had children and many had grandchildren. Concerns for young people – at school, at university or in early jobs and careers – were frequently forefront in their minds. There was, for instance, discussion of the merits and demerits of schools both closing and re-opening on children's well-being and longer-term educational attainment. It seemed from the early evidence that children from the most disadvantaged families were particularly affected (Pensiero et al, 2020). There were also worries about students studying online from home, and for young adults whose jobs were at risk.

There were many other sectors and groupings that also elicited concern from diarists, depending on their own interests and knowledge. Among those mentioned were the problems for courts that had postponed hearings and shifted to telephone and video hearings, the laying off of staff by airlines, the tourism sector in general, fashion retailers, charities, the hospitality industry, and the arts in general.

The conclusion to be drawn from what they wrote is that diarists generally considered themselves among the most fortunate. While they had their worries and concerns, they also iterated how they were comfortable and comfortably-off, less inconvenienced by the lockdown restrictions than many others in society, able to keep themselves to themselves but yet maintain internet and telephone contact with family and friends, and often supported by neighbours and communities. Some confessed to feeling a bit guilty and most suggested they had no real grounds for complaint.

CAMPBELL
Friday 27 March 2020
So since my last entry – and from before Max Hastings' now famous *Times* article saying the same thing in much stronger, over the top language – I do realise, as a self-isolating 70-plus with a good state pension, a flat of my own with no mortgage, a son who is all too keen to drop off provisions, how massively lucky I am compared with so many – maybe even the majority of – people. As a local doctor/writer I met on the Common pointed out to me the other day, for a couple living in a small flat with elderly, perhaps demented, parents and deeply restless and frustrated teenage children to worry about – let alone for those increasingly desperate about where the money is going to come from, this must be so much worse. Not to

mention those, including those with no more than an even chance of survival, actually suffering from the virus. And of course while I sit here at my laptop carping, all those NHS staff – not to mention all those long-suffering people on pretty low wages sitting behind the supermarket tills at the risk of their own health – have got so much more to worry them – not to mention the impressive army of volunteers who have now signed up to help. It was good to be out on the balcony clapping along with neighbours the NHS last night. But it's small recompense for what they are having to go through every hour of the working day.

JENNIFER
Friday 22 May 2020

I have been thinking about the phrase 'we are all in the same boat'. I don't think this is true. I have already written about the differential impact of the virus on BAME communities. But there is also a huge differential impact on younger people as against older people with secure pensions. And that differential will continue as we move back into a more active economy – which will be very inactive for many thousands if not millions of people chasing too few jobs. I cannot imagine what this situation must be like for those without a secure job or money. I don't think we hear so much about them. There are indications about how hard some situations are with the rise in calls to domestic abuse lines, and worries about children's welfare in locked down families.

We are in the same storm but not in the same boat.

Diarists did not agree that everyone was equally affected by the COVID-19 pandemic and strongly advanced the view that they were more advantaged than most. They (almost all) had no jobs to lose, were comfortably off, well-housed, and did not have to put themselves at risk of contracting the virus. They were not experiencing the hardships of children and young people in education or at the start of their working lives, the disruptions caused to most people of working age, or the potential dangers facing essential workers. They were also more fortunate than many others their own age or older, especially if in poorer health and with fewer material and social resources.

The commonalities

Despite the myriad ways in which the pandemic discriminated between individuals, communities and occupational sectors, there were still commonalities that brought the country closer together. Two positive news stories, for example, gained attention from diarists. These were the cases of Marcus Rashford and Captain Tom Moore.

ELEANOR
Sunday 19 April 2020

Positive thought of the week. The amazing achievement of 99-year-old Captain Tom Moore who has raised so many millions for the NHS by walking around his garden every day. A true example of stoicism and optimism to lift all our spirits.

HOLGATE
Thursday 18 June 2020

My, and I'm sure millions of others, hero of the week must be the 22-year-old (yes 22!) Manchester United and England footballer Marcus Rashford. His high-profile campaign helped raise £20 million for FareShare which has been able to hand out three million meals a week to vulnerable people across the country during 'lockdown'. Food poverty is a subject close to Rashford's heart. He remembers his mother, Melanie, working for the minimum wage and has said he would not have become an England player if he had not had free school meals. His brilliant campaign led to the government's U-turn on Tuesday and means it will now provide food vouchers for some of the UK's poorest families. ... I was struck by Rashford's short and perceptive tweet after the PM's humbling U-turn: 'Just look at what we can do when we come together, THIS is England 2020.' How right he is!

Furthermore, diarists expressed a shared sense, and often a heightened shared sense, of experience with those in their more immediate circle. In that regard they were all in it together. There were countless examples of reciprocity shown in permitted social encounters as well as the frequent rise in importance and support of the local community.

Social reciprocity was clearly demonstrated by the many behavioural adaptations they had made, such as the side-stepping and dance steps diarists had adopted for maintaining social distance when out on daily walks, the wearing of masks that may have been more for the protection of others than themselves, and the range of precautions they took to engage socially while still preserving their own and others' health. There was a strong sense of shared understandings with those they were in contact with. According to Mead (1934), they were taking the role of each other, and anticipating their reactions, in formulating their own thoughts and action. They were concerned for themselves but also for others. In this way, new shared normative behaviours and standards were absorbed and many diarists commented on how people generally seemed friendlier than usual. It seemed that there was a shared sense in which strangers often saw themselves 'all in it together'.

The wish for commonality and shared understandings also arose in more sustained settings as, perhaps, a substitute for direct contact with friends and families. Many diarists turned to close and further neighbours in a manner not experienced before, and the local community achieved a greater importance. With people confined to their homes and localities, and restricted in the possibilities for meeting friends and family, the immediate environment and neighbourliness took on a new meaning. More people were at home, exercise was to be taken locally, and all but essential journeys were disallowed. The communities within which they lived provided, for many people, the limit of their horizons as well as their main social contacts.

This reality was confirmed by the wider evidence. Nationally, for instance, city centres were being deserted in favour of suburbs and local neighbourhoods. Analysis of mobile phone data in early June 2020 by the Centre for Cities thinktank (Quinio and Ramuni, 2020) revealed that footfall in London, Liverpool and Manchester had fallen to one fifth of what it had been prior to the initial lockdown the previous March. People's daily lives had changed as they remained local. Data published by Ordnance Survey showed a drop in visits to National Parks and rural walks but an increase in urban walks, especially around the larger urban conurbations, between January 2020 and January 2021 (Horton, 2021).

A new sense of community

The diarists concurred with this new sense of community. Confined to barracks except for limited forays for supplies or exercise, it was not long before new forms of sociability began to emerge. Somewhat in parallel with what Putnam (2000) described had happened in the United States, neighbourhoods were reviving notions of social capital and engaging in lateral collective activity comprising self-help and mutualism. Many wrote about activities and forms of support that had emerged in their localities, quite independent of national and local government, as well as increased contact with their neighbours. This was a common pattern across the country. Bellotti et al (2021), for example, reported a survey of almost a thousand people across the UK that revealed how new relationships with neighbours had developed during lockdown. These new patterns of sociability also align with the interests and findings of the early interactionist tradition that was grounded in population movements and their impact on the social cohesion of individuals, groups and communities (Smith, 2021).

Jarvis et al (2020) referred to emerging patterns of community action as reflecting unleadership, meaning that ordinary people rather than the formal leaders, such as the government, were taking charge of the situation and organising activities such as distributing food to the housebound. Such behaviour could be seen as more than neighbourliness in that it was proactive and not for personal benefit apart from the satisfaction of being able to make a difference.

In many places this new sociability may have begun on the Thursday evening of the first week of lockdown, when people came out of their homes at 8 pm to clap and thank the NHS. This had been the idea of Annemarie Plas, a Dutch yoga teacher living in south London, and became a regular event for many, albeit with thanks soon extended to all essential workers. The initiative ran for ten weeks in the first instance. There was a later call for the event, renamed as a Clap for Heroes, to start again during the third lockdown in January 2021, but it never really took off. The reasons diarists gave were the weather, the lack of novelty value second time round, and the fact that the activity had had its day.

There was, however, a huge response around the country to the original initiative as, whatever the motive, there was an excuse to exit the front door and meet the neighbours. For many diarists, this new ritual got off to a good start. They referred to the regular event as 'heart-warming', 'very moving' or 'gently uplifting', and made comments such as 'it did feel good to be part of a community', or 'it is still a first for anyone on this posh road to get out and do something collective'. Often it was the social aspect that was pre-eminent.

CHARLES
Thursday 30 April 2020
Thursday evenings are becoming something of a social event! We go out at 8 pm to clap the NHS which we do for a couple of minutes. Then our neighbours, eight including my wife and I, get together for a chat. It is just so nice to talk informally about how things are going. Even one of our neighbours who is fairly antisocial and reclusive admitted that she looked forward to seeing us all!

SQUEALS
Friday 1 May 2020
Clapped last night as usual on a Thursday; it's strange to see everyone emerging from their houses when one is completely unaware of them the rest of the time.

A considerable number of diarists did nonetheless have reservations. They may have enjoyed seeing a few more people, but many questioned the motive of what for many weeks became something of a ritual. Indeed, the last 'official' gathering was on Thursday 28 May 2020 amid fears it was becoming too politicised and was losing its impact. In some places it had still gone strong until the end whereas in others it had all but fizzled out. There were mixed feelings about its demise. Some people missed the regular meetings, some were glad they had come to end, and others devised new reasons to meet up. Diarists reported congregating for drinks, street celebrations for birthdays, gatherings for new neighbours or those moving on, street concerts, and a Zoom theatre production. VE Day saw a host of community activities. For some this was another opportunity to get together with neighbours and others, whereas for others there was less enthusiasm, either because of misgivings about how it was being celebrated or as it might be an opportunity to spread the virus.

In many places clapping and street gatherings were accompanied by the setting up of WhatsApp groups or other neighbourhood sites that were open to all residents in the locality. These took on different characteristics in different places. Initially they were typically set up so that people could offer each other support, including getting groceries for those unable or unwilling to go out, and share information about local events. Over time, however, they took on different functions, depending on the locality and the residents. Many groups sent round a huge number of jokes and humorous videos, many going 'viral' as they were passed on to friends and family to be recirculated. There were, inevitably, mixed reactions to these groups.

JESSIE
Retrospective: Monday 13 April 2020
Our street has started a WhatsApp group – two neighbours leafleted the street suggesting that we get in touch to either offer help or ask for some – e.g. shopping. It has been very effective and created a wonderful sense of community with people we have never met before – so everyone was wishing each other happy Easter.

LYNNE
Thursday 23 April 2020
I keep up with the local mutual aid WhatsApp groups, but am finding as a format it doesn't make the retrieval of any useful information that I might pass on very accessible, and can get cluttered with entertaining stories of lost rabbits and general chit chat.

ROB
Wednesday 29 April 2020
More WhatsApp vids and funnies today from lots of contacts some duplicates ... many I am sad/ashamed to say ... featuring large ladies suffering from an overdose of lockdown eating.

Meeting on Thursday evenings, communicating on WhatsApp, and offering companionship and support to neighbours contributed in many places to a rise in community spirit. It was a pragmatic adaptation to unusual circumstances. Diarists reported the support they received from neighbours and volunteers, but also wrote about the ways in which they were able to help others. Collecting medicines for other people, delivering newspapers, carrying out grocery runs, making joint delivery orders, exchanging items, and much more helped to engender collective support in the locality.

CARACTACUS
Wednesday 1 July 2020

Reported to the Co-op to pick up food deliveries. This is the last week the Community support group are offering the service. Only three today, but that brings my total to 66 deliveries, of which five were prescriptions.

EDGAR
Thursday 9 April 2020

One thing to note which was quite different relates to Pesach and matzos (unleavened bread). Someone from my synagogue called to ask if I (we) needed any help etc. My synagogue had organised volunteers to call about half a dozen 'elderlies' including myself to ensure their well-being. I have nothing to do with the synagogue apart from being a member so I did not know this guy. ... I was still unwell when he rang and I asked him whether he might be able to procure six boxes of matzos. About a week later they appeared on our front doorstep. He had called me to say that he would be leaving them, and I asked him about payment. 'Don't worry about that,' he said, 'you can make a donation to the shul (synagogue) if you want to.' Note: something to do. I had not experienced this sense of community as I suppose I have always kept myself to myself and well away from the synagogue which I do not attend. I have not felt part of the Jewish community probably since the age of 13 and I have few Jewish friends – but that's another story.

HOLLY
Wednesday 6 May 2020

Food bank collection day has come round again. More people dropping stuff off and stopping a few minutes for a social distanced chat with us and with each other. The food bank weighed it in again – 195 kilos. The other food bank warehouse in the city was broken into overnight. Loads of things stolen – food, laptops, etc. – and the place trashed. What crap!

JANWIG
Sunday 28 June 2020

It continues to amaze me how long lockdown has been going on. I started the cake baking for the school on 26th April, WhatsApp tells me. Sixty-three days later the school has had a cake almost every day from about 20 different local amateur bakers. I'm so proud of this, even though all I did was put the message about that it was something people might like to do. One of those things that lockdown has fostered.

OTTOLIE
Sunday 12 April 2020
Leapt up at 5.30 and delivered a few eggs to all my neighbours, such fun racing around at dawn in my pjs, trying not to rustle. The path runs up and down in front of our only doors, narrow. Everyone asleep. I suppose I can call this exercise. I think my bunny hopping days are over though. Delivered myself one too so no one will know.

There was nonetheless the recognition on the part of diarists that, even within local neighbourhoods, everybody was not in it together. There were distinct social groupings and these often included those less fortunate than themselves. This might be because they were less well-off, because they were on their own, or because they were unwell. A considerable number of diarists expressed a general feeling of helplessness and wished they could make a greater contribution in some way or another. They wanted to do more for those less lucky than themselves. There were opportunities to donate to food banks, and give money to support community activities, and a few had managed to get involved in community schemes, but there was much expressed frustration at not being able help in more tangible ways. Several said they had offered their voluntary services, which had not been taken up, sometimes because they were apparently too old.

BETTYMAC
Thursday 16 April 2020
On the diary front I have still not had any call for my volunteering services although I have been advised it is taking time to set up procedures.

FRANCIA
Thursday 2 April 2020
Received email from village volunteer organiser saying that as we are 70+ we are not covered by the Parish Council's insurance for volunteering work. That halves the number allocated to our little patch. We will just provide telephone chat if needed. Still no calls for any assistance. Sure this will continue to be the case knowing the residents in our allocated area.

JULES
Tuesday 7 April 2020
I feel very spoilt and lazy. I'm thinking of volunteering once I get the antibody test done – although being 'elderly and vulnerable' may disqualify me for anything. It probably depends on how desperate they are by then. I'm thinking along the lines of being there to talk to the patients and offer them reassurance.

SARDOMIKE
Sunday 26 April 2020

I miss not being able to do something constructive, it feels wrong that I'm not volunteering, delivering food to the needy, something, anything. Hard to accept that I'm one of the vulnerable.

One diarist reported on her own initiative.

AMBER
Tuesday 16 February 2021

A few weeks ago, when daily news reports in the media showed ICU workers under unbelievable pressure and often distress, I heard a radio interview from one of them who said her team had been so touched by a delivery of fresh pizza from a group of women friends who had just decided on a whim to order the delivery to cheer them up on a shift.

I decided that this was finally something I could do something about, and I picked a hospital that had been featured as getting near to being overwhelmed – (where) with the help of the hospital's volunteer liaison officer, who told me that there were 200 staff in their three ICUs (far too many to do anything individually), I arranged for three huge 2.5 litre boxes of Celebration chocolates to be delivered to the units, each with an encapsulated note from me (anonymously) saying that each time they reached inside for a chocolate I hoped they would remember that thousands of people were aware of what they were doing and saw them as true heroes of our time. Apparently, it was really appreciated by the staff.

All these activities meant that new acquaintances and friendships developed in neighbourhoods and communities. Drinks over the garden fence, or shopping for a stranger, were not unusual. There was also a heightened sense of the plight of others and a wish to help. In line with Singer (1981), there was a widespread expansion in circles of altruism. Concern commonly extended beyond self and kin to the wider society and the nation state, for the duration of the pandemic at least.

Pets and other animals

Pets, too, had a considerable presence and importance during the pandemic. They were in it with everybody else. Their numbers in private households rose enormously, they provided company for millions, and they too could become affected and anxious.

With the working population and most other people spending the majority of time at home during the lockdowns, and with some people feeling lonely and isolated, getting a pet could seem a good idea. Indeed the Pet Food

Manufacturers' Association reported how over three million households in the UK had gained a pet during the year following the initial lockdown (BBC News, 2021a). The association said that meant there were around 17 million homes with pets at the later date. Cats and dogs were by far the most popular pets.

By no means all diarists had pets, but for a considerable number they featured heavily in diary entries. They provided company and dogs gave an extra reason to go out for a walk as well as a good excuse to start up conversations with other dog owners. Pets could be valuable companions, especially, but not only, for those in single-person households. They also provided a structure to the day, as well as new tasks as dog groomers were no more available than hairdressers. Not everybody, however, was sure that they wanted a pet.

BARKLEY
Wednesday 6 May 2020

Took the dog out at 8.30. Got to say it's been great having the dog over this lockdown period. It was great having him before, of course, but he's the reason I go for a walk at least twice a day. Not sure I'd be motivated to do so otherwise.

LOUISE
Sunday 7 June 2020

I haven't mentioned the cats much, but I should say that they are a big part of my life. Wherever I am in the house usually one of them is around, demanding food or cuddles or just wanting to sleep near me. They are in very good shape. It is very nice for them having us around so much. Pippin loves us both: but Merry is a one-human cat, fiercely and obsessively devoted to me. Bless them both!

OTTOLIE
Saturday 14 July 2020

Wonderful lunch with old friends then to their grandchildren my gorgeous god daughter who is so extraordinary with her outdoor camping and reading and general positive outlook. Or so it seems. Their dog is 'getting married' tomorrow and would I like a puppy? Maybe.

The emotional support from pets, and the interactions between humans and animals, have been much studied, especially in recent years. Research supports the benefits for mental health and general well-being, attests to the role of domestic animals in combating loneliness, and demonstrates how they can help in coping with stress (Palley et al, 2010). Aragunde-Kohl et al (2020) found from a study of almost 1,500 pet owners in Puerto Rico that some nine in ten talked to their pet or pets that provided them with company. Almost without exception pets were considered part of the family. These authors stress the therapeutic value of pet ownership and interaction.

Although social interactionist theories are essentially confined to humans, their perspective might predict that pets could also be affected by their interactions with their owners. Certainly, there seems to be some justification for this. Joyner (2020) reported on a Dogs Trust survey of 6,000 owners asking whether their dogs seemed affected by lockdown. Just over a quarter reported an increase in problem behaviours, such as biting, barking and whining. On the one hand, more dogs were seeking attention from their owners, while on the other hand a greater number were appearing more withdrawn than usual. It was suggested that a range of factors, such as less exercise and contact with other dogs – they had to remain on leads as they did not understand social distancing – and less peace at home, might be responsible.

A number of diarists concurred and indicated that their pet's behaviour had changed due to the pandemic.

BONIVARD
Wednesday 14 May 2020
I'm not particularly pet-centric and I'm not one to anthropomorphise animals but I've noticed a change in behaviour of our cat since the lockdown started. He is taking greater care of his appearance (washing more) and has become more affectionate, wanting to be with us through the day and at night. Does he think we need his support?

I've since discussed this with one of my cousins. His wife's 12-year-old Scottie has also become much friendlier and wants to be with him much more.

HATTIE
Saturday 24 May 2020
Just a brief comment on dog behaviour which I recognised after speaking to my daughter in Wales about her dog – our dog is becoming increasingly obsessed by food, hoovering the kitchen floor on the chance of finding a few crumbs and waiting hopefully when I'm cooking. She used not to pay any attention to us at our mealtimes, but now tends to hang about the table while we eat.

JOJO
Thursday 24 April 2020
Lily kept fussing round me when I was sitting outside – she is moulting so much that it makes me concerned that she is a bit stressed. I will have to keep an eye on her.

SKYE
Wednesday 21 May 2020

Interesting thoughts about animal behaviour during lockdown. Our dog thinks it's wonderful to have people around her all the time. It is going to be very difficult when she is left on her own again. Our chickens have become very tame. As soon as they see us in the summerhouse or on the patio they come waddling down looking for treats. They love apples and sit there staring at us whilst we munch away. It is now very silly as we have the dog and two chickens waiting for the apple core.

Of course there were always exceptions.

WILL
Thursday 22 May 2020

Our last cat, Alfred, was originally a stray who couldn't come with us when we moved into a flat temporarily until this house was finished (a whole new story!). So he went to stay with my partner's daughter and family and very rapidly took over the house from its two-legged occupants and the two cats already in residence, Petra and LaLa. ... Lockdown doesn't bother him as the rules don't apply to him, his people are available on tap at all times and there's always food available. What's not to like?

Not only domestic pets but other animals too were behaving differently during the pandemic. Diarists reported how they wandered further afield than usual and were found in strange places, such as wild deer in a family garden, a goose in a railway station, a fox on the porch, and, for one, a live grass snake in the middle of the living room floor. As one diarist put it, while humans are locked down, animals are roaming.

The role of humour

Goffman (1959) depicted social interaction using metaphors drawn from drama and the theatre and, for social interactionists generally, humour is an important aspect of the life-world. Best (2021) described how it provides an outlet for concerns and emotions that might otherwise remain unvoiced, as well as an opportunity to express attitudes that might be best not spoken in normal conversation. It is a form of communication that draws on shared understandings and commonly reflects on everyday matters and, particularly, a discontinuity in the social order. It is, in this sense, a form of reciprocity that employs escapism to reduce tension and encourage coping. From a physiological perspective, laughter reduces stress-related hormones such as cortisol, and increases endorphins. It is claimed it can strengthen the immune system.

Humour undoubtedly played an important role in maintaining a sense of connection with others as the pandemic unfolded. Obrdlík (1942) coined the expression 'gallows humor' to describe a form of humour that tends to arise in 'precarious or dangerous' situations. His own account related to his observations in Czechoslovakia following Hitler's invasion, where humour increased morale among the oppressed. There have been many subsequent reports of gallow humour, or black comedy as it is sometimes called, frequently relating to serious situations where illness or death is a distinct possibility. Although the pandemic cannot be equated to the wartime situation witnessed by Obrdlík, there were undoubtedly similarities in terms of uncertainty and risk.

A major difference, however, reflected the changing times and the new opportunities for interaction available during the pandemic. Most people were at home and many were spending long periods of time on their computers and phones. Using modern technology to design images and record videos, or simply to forward humorous items received from elsewhere, there was an endless circulation of jokes, cartoons, and videos.

HUMPHREY
Thursday 2 April 2020
There are so many video jokes swirling around to keep us all laughing. In a nerdy way I have to keep a spreadsheet of which ones I have passed on and to whom.

This, as Best (2021) has pointed out, is an important change. Goffman and others traditionally focused on face-to-face settings for the exchange of humorous interchanges, whereas contemporary possibilities rely heavily on electronic transfer. This enables mass sharing and is another example of togetherness during the pandemic. It allowed the airing of occurrences and concerns in common and legitimated their funny side. Initially at least, a well-featured theme was the shortage of toilet rolls.

BARKLEY
Wednesday 25 March 2020
Finally, a joke I heard yesterday that made me laugh – 'I can't get any supplies of toilet paper so I'm using lettuce leaves – it's the tip of an iceberg'.

Other frequent topics, among diarists at least, concerned the consumption of alcohol, disastrous haircuts, problems with masks, and much more. Very many of the diary entries were also imbued with humour whether overt, subtle or ironic. Writing the diaries was a performative act in that diarists knew they might be writing for an audience. Their diary entries were accordingly often an acknowledgement of the potentially threatening but intangible presence of the virus, but also a recognition of the strangeness of the situation. They were frequently humorous, with their authors no doubt revelling in the presentation of amusing observations and stories.

GRACE
Thursday 14 May 2020

Feel there must be a place for a *Famous Five go to Virus Island* book with Uncle Quentin, beige trench coat, pipe, trilby and dark glasses – a dead ringer for a lurker and with all these lerts around we need him!

I am going to make a fortune producing *Where's the Virus?*. It will have all the qualities of *Where's Wally?* but all the people will be dressed as a virus. I will partner that with the *Ladybird Book of Lockdown*. Peter and Jane go to the shops, Peter wears a mask. But Jane wears mascara, as she is only a girl!

Slowly but surely my tenuous hold on reality at the best of times is fast disappearing!

HOLLY
Monday 27 April 2020

We managed to have a laugh, though: she told me that her husband is officially in the 'shielded' category as he's in recovery from cancer. This means they get an unsolicited government grocery box and there's no way of cancelling it. She said that their last box had marrowfat peas and Spam in it! As they live in an impossibly trendy bit of Manchester, whoever put the box together must have had to go to extraordinary lengths to get the stuff that was in it.

OTTOLIE
Tuesday 21 July 2020

Walked up to H later, and on the way back took the long route over the hill. Blazing sun and the grass mowed for hay, the hay was baled. Seems so long since the buttercups blazed in glory during the worst of the pandemic. I lay on the slope looking at the view, amazing, then decided to just lie there, eyes closed. Lovely and peaceful. Suddenly, a voice called 'Helllllloooo'. I thought, Oh dear, someone needs help, sat bolt upright, only to find a woman racing towards me, who thought I had died.

We had a good laugh about how she nearly gave me the kiss of life (eeeeeugh, we both said together). Later had a gin and tonic. No olives.

There is little doubt that humour was an important coping mechanism during the pandemic. It provided a strong antidote to the uncertainty everywhere and brought people together. Laughing at both tragedy and the absurdity of the situation was a medicine of sorts.

Summary

Was everybody in it together? In the early days of the pandemic, diarists had been singled out for special protection on account of their age and supposed vulnerability. Many were unhappy about this, often because in their 70s they still felt fit and well, and as they were able to avoid contact with the virus. They were at much less risk of illness and death than essential workers, those with health conditions other than COVID-19, those in certain areas of business, and those in certain racial and ethnic groups and/or geographical locations. In this sense, not everybody was in it together. A sense of togetherness was not, however, altogether absent. For their own part, diarists wrote about their affinity with family, friends and acquaintances, the enhanced significance of local communities, and how they had forged stronger and more mutually supportive links with neighbours than ever before. Many also had their pets for company. Commonalities were further reinforced through shared humour.

Whatever their personal circumstances, everyone had to encounter and adapt to the 'new normal' heralded by the pandemic. The next chapter examines how diarists reorganised their time and activities as a consequence.

5

The 'new normal'

The new order introduced by the pandemic, and the rules and restrictions that came into place with little warning, called for a major change of mindset and a reconceptualisation of everyday life. Much that had been taken for granted was called into question. Schutz (1945), a phenomenologist, wrote about the taken-for-granted aspects of reality as part of what he termed 'life-world'. This referred to the social world shared by everybody and the 'fundamental and paramount reality', and underlined an understanding in common between oneself and others met in the pursuit of daily experience. For example, in the context of the diarists, the life-world included the ability to leave one's home, to meet and hug friends and loved ones, to travel near and far, and to exercise personal agency in going about one's daily business. Berger and Luckmann (1966) would have posited that their symbolic universes had changed. There was a new set of permissible actions and a new value system.

The sudden loss of previously taken-for-granted aspects of reality meant, for diarists, the need to restructure and reorganise their daily lives. They adapted, but adapted pragmatically. They wanted to make the most of the 'new normal' and take advantage of the opportunities offered by the pandemic, but they also wished to establish modes of behaviour that approximated, as nearly as possible, the behaviours they had been forced to abandon.

The reorganisation of time

This new construction of reality, and the restrictions to freedom of action, had a profound influence on the organisation of time. Fundamentally, at least initially, it affected the significance of social time, the position of the hands (or the digits) on the timepiece that allow the synchronisation of events and activities to take account of the perspective of the 'generalised other' (Mead, 1934). There were, to begin with, few events or activities that necessitated strict time keeping.

But beyond this, the new order affected perceptions of personal time which, sociologists and others would argue, are related to social phenomena. As the German philosopher Heidegger (1996) claimed, the human experience of time is not confined to what the clock might say, but also depends on our interactions within the world. No one time is ever the same as another. Flaherty (2021) proposed three elementary forms of experience that affect these perceptions. In brief, he suggested that time passes slowly when confronting 'extraordinary or problematic circumstances' as we draw more attention to ourselves and our situation. He termed this 'protracted duration' and contrasted it with 'temporal compression' when time appears to pass quickly, often when we are engaged in habitual activities. 'Synchronicity' relates to circumstances where the sense of time passed approximates to the time passed on the clock.

Diarists confirmed these changes in understanding. At the onset, and for some, time appeared to slow down or cease to hold any tangible meaning. Old familiar routines could give way to a kind of monotony in which the days had a certain sameness.

ANNA
Friday 3 April 2020
What did I do today? It's getting hard to account for time.

BARKLEY
Saturday 25 April 2020
There was an interesting piece in the editorial section by Jonathan Freedland on the lockdown and the 'warping' of time. He quoted a friend as saying, 'The weeks seem to pass surprisingly quickly, yet the days seem to last an eternity'. Freedland went on to make a comparison between the lockdown and prisoners facing long stretches of time without significant 'landmarks' to break up the monotony of every day being a repeat of the previous day. He quoted the former *Guardian* columnist and ex-con, Erwin James, who said, 'There are so many resonances with prison. ... The days drag and then you wake up and a month has passed and you think, "Where the hell has that gone?" '. Very true.

CLARA
Sunday 29 March 2020
What is striking is that time has been distorted and stretched. What seems like another era is only a few weeks ago. Today is March 29th 2020. February seems an age ago.

HOLGATE
Wednesday 13 May 2020
Is it really a week since I last wrote my diary entry? During this period time seems to have stood still. Which day is it? Is that the time?

HUMPHREY
Saturday 2 May 2020
As for the diary of events, or non-events more like, each day melds seamlessly with the next. Could this be what a prison stretch actually feels

like? We know that the best thing is to take it one day at a time, but this way years could slip by.

It has been argued that too much time on one's hands can prove problematic. Calkins (1970), for instance, discussed how a shortage of things to do could result in killing time with inactivity or displacement activity, and gave the examples of social institutions such as the army or old people's homes where such behaviours could arise. Many of the diarists appeared aware of the possibility of drifting within the 'new normal' and, for some, a first issue was getting up at a reasonable time if they were getting into the habit of sleeping later. Interestingly, but perhaps not surprisingly, John Lewis saw sales of alarm clocks fall by 38 per cent during 2020 compared with the previous year (John Lewis Partnership, 2020). They were beaten only by suitcases which fell by 69 per cent compared with the previous year and clearly reflected the fact that nobody was going anywhere much.

SIMON
Saturday 4 April 2020
In the words of the Beatles 'Woke up, fell out of bed, dragged a comb across my head' – though of course not enough hair for the latter – but it was a sunny morning so big effort to get out. But once again it was past midday before I managed it.

Many other diarists, but not all, wrote about establishing new routines, or at least ensuring that they put their time to good use, and did not waste it. Scheduling and creating timetables are, according to Glaser and Strauss (1971), important aspects of the social construction of reality. They provide a structure and they reduce uncertainty. Not everyone, however, felt this imperative.

HATTIE
Retrospective: Tuesday 7 April 2020
Our day-to-day life actually potters on very peacefully. We have no particular plan, apart from a vague intention to use the time to carry out some tedious domestic repairs, painting, etc., as well as clear out the attic and the woodshed. Achieving the last two tasks would be an enormous relief.

SKYE
Retrospective: Thursday 2 April 2020
I drifted for the first week and then decided that I needed a structured programme. It works as I now exercise regularly, do housework and

gardening as per schedule and still have time for me to knit and chat to friends.

SUSIEQ
Sunday 5 April 2020
Routine and a to-do list are my comfort blanket and my coping mechanism. They provide a defence against indolence and lethargy, help me feel productive, avoid the need for 'what am I going to do today' thoughts and assist me feel in control, especially when I am not. My standing joke was always that the first task on my to-do list was make list, so I could cross something off straightaway.

TARANAKI
Retrospective: Tuesday 24 March 2020
Not exactly a strategy but we hope to de-clutter, do gardening, read more, do jigsaws, take daily walks, maintain contact with family and friends.

With the loss of many habitual activities, there could also be a fear that time would run out, and that there would be nothing left to do once current tasks had been completed.

RAIN
Thursday 16 April 2020
I have been thinking about rationing, of activities and consumption.

I realised this was a connection, between remembering I think it was in the prison diaries of Albie Sachs, he had a comb, which he allowed himself to clean one spoke at a time one day at a time. I had been wondering what on earth I would do when all the weeding and clearing of ivy, and pruning had been done in the garden. But I have discovered so far that gardening is like teaching, it can take as much time and attention as you are willing and able to give it.

I fear housework is the same, but much less enticing.

In the event, diarists adapted rapidly to the 'new normal' with the vast majority appearing active and busy during the lockdowns. In part this seemed due to their own characteristics and experiences, and in part to the broader social environment and the activities that arose. On the one hand, they had grown up in the early post-war period and, as documented by Madge and Hoggart (2020) in *Sixty Somethings: The lives of women who remember the Sixties*, were accustomed to social change and the adaptations required. Additionally, almost all had already experienced retirement, or at least semi-retirement, and the challenge of structuring a new phase of their lives. On the other hand, however, new timetabled events quickly came into being. There were, for instance, the Thursday night neighbourhood clap for essential workers and the televised 5 pm daily briefing from the government that occupied diarists. But there was also the proliferation of Zoom meetings that diarists organised and took part in. And there were of course their diaries to write. There was soon little spare time.

LYNNE
Wednesday 29 April 2020

This is the first day I've actually felt 'what shall I do next?' I know there is de-cluttering still awaiting, but that is such a big job in terms of disposal and reorganising that it continues to be deferred.

PEN
Retrospective: Monday 30 March 2020

I had thought I was going to have lots of time for books and films. So far we have been so busy outside that we have fallen into bed at nine.

PETER
Tuesday 14 April 2020

I seem to be adapting to the whole thing! It has all become NORMAL. That's sort of comforting, but also very disturbing. It means that we could have anything thrown at us now, and we'd treat it as … normal.

What's more, I think I may be heading towards something like a routine. Which is weird, since I never really had one before coronavirus.

ROB
Sunday 19 April 2020

More jobs sorted today … and potential jobs listed … how did I ever have time to procrastinate??

This new engagement with time and its meaning was commonplace. It was, however, something that would evolve.

Wills and 'death stuff'

An early task for many diarists was to get their affairs in order. There was always the possibility, acknowledged indirectly if not directly, that they might not emerge from the pandemic unscathed and therefore never return to the old normal. They were pragmatic in minimising their risk of illness and death from the virus, but they could not be sure that they would not catch COVID-19 or otherwise become unwell. The rising deaths in the early months of the pandemic had concentrated the mind and encouraged many to deal with their wills and other 'death stuff'. They wanted to be prepared for any eventuality.

Indeed, they were not alone. Data collected by Farewill (2021), a will-writing fintech company, showed how surges in will-writing seemed to follow the course of the pandemic. Thus the number of people writing wills was almost three times higher in 2020 than in the previous year. Interestingly, however, the greatest rate increase was among younger people, probably because few had thought of doing so prior to the pandemic. Particularly large spikes occurred on the day Boris Johnson was admitted to intensive care, when the global death toll from the virus passed one million, and after the third lockdown in England was announced in early 2021. There was a notable trough on the day that the Pfizer vaccine for COVID-19 was approved in the UK. *Which?* also reported an increase in the use of its wills service during the early months of the pandemic: there was a two-fold increase in March 2020 over that for the same period in the previous year, and a seven-fold increase in April 2020 (Gifford, 2020). According to Hooson (2021), such surges reflected fears of the coronavirus.

BENCHMAN
Monday 6 April 2020
I suppose I ought really to review my will. ... Getting wills witnessed in current circumstances is somewhat challenging, as the two witnesses have to be present when the testator signs the will and when each of them does so as witness. A large room is needed for the purpose! I certainly can't complain that I don't have the time at present. I suppose it's a sort of cognitive bias; I feel perfectly well, am keeping my distance from people so consider that I am not at risk of infection, and hence there's no urgency.

Diarists were thinking not only about their wills but also about other tasks related to their own possible illness and demise. They were concerned with doing what they could to tidy up their affairs should they succumb to the virus. Sometimes it was a question of leaving instructions for their next of kin whereas at other times it was more about disposing of private information that was not for the eyes of their children.

ANNA
Tuesday 14 April 2020
Now, what should I do about my *diaries*? The boarding-school years could be historical documents for all I care, but it's the twenty-something years I worry about. ... I think they contain stuff that my daughters don't need

to know, stuff that would indelibly lurk around their memory/knowledge of me – and stuff I wouldn't be on hand to discuss with them. I suspect I need to deal with this quite urgently – not because I think I'll die soon, but because I think I know I don't want to leave it as part of my legacy. Some bits of one's life are private. ... So the job now must be to destroy them.

BEA
Monday 20 April 2020

I plan to do three things today. My son AKA the Lodger has acquired 3 kg of sugar which is enough to make three batches of Delia Smith's blackcurrant jam. Task number 1 is to make the first batch. Task number 2 is to write an 'In case of death' instruction. I am not ill and am not planning to die any time soon but if I should do so during the lockdown, I do not want people trying to travel to Cornwall in order to attend a non-existent funeral, therefore I plan to say that there should be nothing at all at the time of death apart from the simplest and cheapest cremation and that when/if this is all over the family may gather to hold a memorial or wake or both as they choose. Task number 3 is to wash the kitchen floor. The floor is made of traditional slate which looks great when clean but at the moment looks incredibly sordid.

JENNIFER
Wednesday 10 June 2020

What I have been doing in a more focused way is what might be called 'putting my house in order'. During the first panic I experienced at the outset of the pandemic, I thought a lot about illness and dying. I checked that my legal and other affairs were in order and wrote a long letter to my daughters about bank accounts, passwords, living will and other matters. I didn't send them the letter but told them where it was. When I calmed down a bit, this process led me to thinking about putting other things in order – relationships for example. So I have been doing that with the help of my counsellor – relationships with the living but also looking at my attitudes and feelings towards dead family and friends. It is a very interesting and revealing process.

LYNNE
Thursday 9 April 2020

I can report I finally made myself look at my legal file and ring a solicitor to check where my house deeds are (my old solicitor's firm had been taken over years ago!). A productive email exchange ensued. Something else to tick off the list.

Among other things, diarists wrote about living wills, powers of attorney, advance decisions, burial plans, and private documents. One wrote about her job which also suggested that the pandemic could prompt an urgency to trace family members.

DEMPSEY
Friday 12 September 2020

I would like to say something about my work. As a social worker who works with adopted adults who wish to understand their birth background and possibly reunite with birth relatives, I have been exceptionally busy since lockdown and post lockdown. Adopted adults are prompted to come to me to request their birth information by different triggers in their lives and so I work with adopted adults who may be 18 yrs old or 85 yrs old and in between. For some people the lockdown gave people more time to reflect on their lives and what is important to them. Also people have been dying in greater numbers so there has been more urgency to trace birth family members before they die. It has been very interesting for me to work in this field during these strange times. Unfortunately, it has also been very frustrating, because, due to lockdown and the restrictions accessing government and local government offices which are still continuing, it has been difficult to obtain the information that my clients need, so they are needing a lot of reassurance and support.

Times were strange and led to a heightened tendency for actions to sort out financial and personal matters.

Keeping occupied

On other fronts, there was plenty to do. With nobody outside the household allowed in the home for some time, except in the case of emergency, there was a need to be self-sufficient. First there were the daily chores, with additional cleaning duties for those who usually had the help of a cleaner.

CAMPBELL
Thursday 9 April 2020

And without the lovely Polish woman who in normal times comes to clean once a fortnight or three weeks – she didn't want to come at the moment any more than I wanted her to – I'm having to grapple with tidying and cleaning – not 'spring cleaning' though which would be much too thorough. So on a one room at a time basis – I've 'done' only the living room at the moment – I'll have to get on with it despite my hearty dislike of (1) hoovering and (2) changing bed linen. I guess at 73 it's about time I got used to it.

PEN
Retrospective: Monday 30 March 2020
The biggest impact has been that we decided two weeks ago to have no one else in the house so had to put off the woman who has helped for over 20 years. I'm ashamed to admit that I haven't done any regular housework for 40 years. We have designated Monday morning for cleaning and [my husband] and I reckon we can get through the essentials in two hours.

TARANAKI
Friday 27 March 2020
I spent the morning doing housework! Real fun – not something I usually do but of course my cleaning lady isn't coming now. I am sure she will miss the money. My husband helped which was good but he was soon bored!

Nonetheless, not everyone felt the same about these tasks. For example, while some diarists put extra efforts into cleaning, giving them a reason to leave their computer screens to do something useful, others saw little point in tidying up if they were not going to have visitors.

Diarists also commonly aspired to de-cluttering, whether or not they achieved their aims. Extra time did not necessarily provide sufficient incentive to be productive. Some diarists said that the good weather during the first lockdown lured them into their gardens or further afield, and the absence of social contact led to many long phone calls. Another disincentive to de-cluttering was the difficulty in disposing of unwanted items. Many household recycling centres closed at least temporarily due to social distancing and hygiene measures, particularly during the first lockdown, at the same time as 'non-essential' charity shops were often closed. Weekly surveys carried out by the Association of Directors of Environment, Economy, Planning and Transport (ADEPT) reported how dry recycling and residual waste collection services were also severely affected from the time of the first lockdown, with some disruption continuing for several months (Binns, 2020). Household waste and recycling centres, and other services such as the disposal of garden waste, were most affected. There was, however, a partial solution in at least one location.

CARACTACUS
Wednesday 27 May 2020
During the morning I heard the scrap man with his cry of 'Old iron' and his out-of-tune bugle, as he drove slowly round the local park. I expect that lots of people have been sorting out their old junk, but are unable to go either to a charity shop or to the municipal recycling centres, so are glad to get the scrap man to take things away. It's an ill wind … they say.

Being largely homebound was, according to many diarists, the impetus for dealing with other jobs around the home that had either just arisen or been on the 'to do' list for quite some time. Often these were tasks they would not normally do themselves, and occasionally additional help was called upon. Diarists described plumbing emergencies, blocked drains, difficulties in assembling new DIY purchases and, frequently, issues with laptops and technology more generally. A 'have a go' mentality was apparent.

AMBER
Friday 5 June 2020

I am probably sleeping well because there is really quite a lot to do – at the age of 72, in a new-build house with unfinished elements and no prospect of workmen to do them, we are slowly, with long rest breaks to ease our backs, laying 10,000 or so cement brick pavers on the floor of the large carport. We have been at it for three weeks, on and off, with about a third still to do.

ELEANOR
Sunday 17 May 2020

Biggest achievement this week – I managed to change the batteries in my car key fob thanks to YouTube.

FRANCES
Tuesday 31 March 2020

On the first day of the lockdown I had an electrical fault which outed all my kitchen sockets. My first instinct was to call on the nearest member of my family, and the second to get hold of an electrician. When I realised neither of these options was sensible, I had a few moments of panic and then tried to remember what the electrician had done last time this had happened. Eventually, this worked. I was hugely proud of myself, but at the same time ruefully aware of how unnecessarily dependent I had become.

FRANCIA
Wednesday 1 April 2020

Today we should have been starting a two-week holiday in Japan. Instead husband jet washed patio and front drive leaving the house looking like a mud hut so I have cleaned all external windows and doors.

JOJO
Thursday 19 March 2020

Finally the kitchen table collapsed at one end – good timing as my husband has all the time in the world now to fix it once and for all. It's been wonky for well over 25 years!!!!!

ROB
Sunday 3 May 2020
I note that the cooker needs a clean and set to it. … As I recall, the last time I cleaned a cooker … I got half a crown!!

TWEEGY
Tuesday 5 May 2020
Incidentally, on my long-term job list has been to clean behind the fridge, washing machine and dishwasher. We started with the washing machine. Huge struggle as so very heavy. All done. Then with the first load there was a leak of water!!

The good weather meant diarists spent more time outdoors. Quite apart from tending to gardens and allotments, they were encouraged to sort and clear sheds, paint garden furniture, clean gutters and outdoor cooking equipment, wash the car even if not going anywhere, as well as a wide range of other jobs. Tasks were made easier by the re-opening of many DIY and hardware shops by the end of April 2020 and garden centres from Wednesday 13 May 2020. These reopenings were certainly profitable for the businesses in question with, for example, the owner of B&Q and Screwfix reporting more than a six-fold surge in profits for the year to March 2021 compared to the previous year (Sweney and Butler, 2021).

BENCHMAN
Saturday 9 May 2020
Meanwhile, I am having to go to the allotment every evening to water the young plants. All my courgette plants have now germinated, but in view of the weather forecast I shall keep them at home in pots for a few days. More potatoes are now coming through, including some of the first earlies which seemed a few days ago not to have sprouted at all. Broad beans are in flower and more artichokes are forming. Some of the lettuce seeds are showing through among the weeds, but I am hard pressed to see any of the beetroot or spinach beet. The climbing beans are struggling but are still surviving; the dwarf beans are doing reasonably well.

LOUISE
Wednesday 1 April 2020
Did a bit more tidying in the garden. I am operating 30-minute stints as part of my evolving routine. To be honest the garden is now so well tended it is difficult to find anything to do! It has never been so tidy and weed free. I need new plants! But how to get them. As my garden is the local pleasure park for slugs and snails I cannot grow things from seed. I want some nice pots of bedding plants! Ah, deprivation.

PEN
Wednesday 8 April 2020

There is always a first time for everything. Began the day in safety glasses and a helmet with visor stacking up logs onto a saw bench, my husband wielding the chainsaw. We have a bit of woodland and every year there are thinnings which are stacked to start drying in lengths of about five feet. Then they need sawing into fireplace-sized logs, moved to a barn, split if necessary and stored under cover till they are properly dry. It's quite a palaver but satisfying when you finally get to light a fire. The ash is spread round the fruit trees and works miracles. Wood work has been a boy's job but with no help, it was needs must. I thought that heaving logs was harder than sawing them up but when I picked up the heavy saw I changed my mind.

WARRENER
Sunday 19 April 2020

After a couple of rainy days the sunshine is back, for a while according to the forecast, so back into the garden to trim the rampant rambling rose and dig up some of those outsize daisies to make room for the veg. We've bought seeds (cucumber, tomato, runner beans, courgettes) which we don't usually do and are making space for them. The urge to self-provide, even on a small scale, is definitely a result of the pandemic.

Some diarists embarked on major gardening projects. SusieQ and her partner Will are a good example. The progress on the garden in their new home was a major enterprise that was repeatedly mentioned in their diaries. Here are two of their entries.

SUSIEQ
Monday 13 April 2020

Big day today: it's not raining and work on the garden resumes after five months.

WILL
Friday 24 April 2020

Work on the garden finished today and we are delighted; it exceeds our expectations. The only issue is that the only plants we have been able to put in are those we brought with us or bought when we were expecting it to be finished last autumn before the floods. Garden centres are closed but some are offering deliveries. It takes some of the fun out of it when we can't browse and make our own specific choices. I suppose if we were allowed to visit we'd take the opportunity but is that breaking the rules? It's difficult to see how this would be worse than going for a walk if we maintain the physical distances. Or am I just rationalising it because I'd like to do it?

Going out for daily walks and exercise also helped to fill the days (see Chapter 7). In addition, diarists became involved in a wide range of projects, such as sorting old letters, photos and documents, writing of various kinds (memoirs, academic articles and books, fiction), or learning or playing a musical instrument. Others engaged in sewing, textile and other creative projects, or continued with existing commitments. A few diarists were still employed, for example as social workers, counsellors, university teachers, trainers, or working with the disabled, usually on a part-time basis, and others worked on charitable activities or had projects they were able to pursue during the pandemic via the internet. For some, however, prior commitments could not be met. Among these, two authors missed out on post-publication launches of their books, expert speakers had events cancelled, and others, such as a tour guide, had to take a period of abeyance.

The lockdowns also gave diarists more time and licence to spend on language-related activities. Completing crosswords and Sudoku puzzles, playing word games, doing jigsaws, playing patience, composing poems and, of course, writing diaries, were commonly mentioned. Indeed, for some they could become almost an obsession as well as a form of escapism and time out from endlessly watching the news. In one diary entry, attention was drawn to an anagram that, when circulated to the diarists, attracted much merriment.

BENCHMAN
Thursday 28 May 2020

Finally, in case this diary ever reaches a wider readership, here is a brilliant anagram (credit Tim King) whose topicality could not be more perfect: 'Stay alert, control the virus, save lives' is an anagram of 'Easily survives travel north to castle'.

Those who lived through the pandemic should understand its meaning.

Reading was another common pastime, although diarists were divided between those who spent more or less time on this than previously. Some had used their time to get through a large number of books, whereas others had not found reading as easy as they had anticipated.

SARDOMIKE
Monday 6 April 2020

Thank God for Kindle!!

SKYE
Thursday 21 May 2020

Interestingly I have found reading difficult too. If I have a good book then fine but not so good with one I have to get into. I'm glad I'm not the only one that has this issue.

There was also much more TV watching than usual, even sometimes during the daytime. Diarists reported an extensive list of films and other programmes they had been watching, often together with their personal reviews. This confirmed the national trend. According to an Ofcom report (2020a), people across the UK were spending an average of some six and a half hours a day watching TV or video content. This was almost a third more than in the previous year. Many older viewers were also using streaming services for the first time. This applied to one in three of those aged 55 to 64 and 15 per cent of those aged 65 or over. The respective rates before the pandemic had been 25 and 12 per cent.

Although there was much to do, there could be a feeling of sameness about the days. This led to reflection on the preciousness of weekends and how it was important to ensure they were in some way distinguished from the rest of the week. Maintaining this aspect of normality was important. This might mean getting up later, taking longer walks, doing different exercises, eating something different, special online family get-togethers, having a day of rest, or wearing different clothes. Whatever it was it seemed that the weekends could serve as a marker for the passing weeks. Bank Holidays were also seen as special.

And then there was Zoom

While the pioneering symbolic interactionists, such as Cooley (1902), Mead (1934), and Goffman (1959), wrote essentially about face-to-face interactions, Gottschalk (2018) introduced the notion of the 'terminal self'. This acknowledges how new digital technologies increasingly mean that interactions are virtual. He argued how these technologies mediate between parties that are not physically in the same place and, in so doing, moderate interactions and how participants 'self-reflect from their perspectives' (Gottschalk, 2021). Interactions may also be with several people at once, enhancing the performativity of the encounter. Users of digital technologies can, in addition, experience ephemerality as technological problems curtail interactions.

The terminal self was of key importance during the pandemic as the initial lockdown sparked a massive increase in internet use nationally. Ofcom (2020b) reported that by June 2020 the average adult was spending an unprecedented four hours a day on their computer or other devices, half an hour longer than in September 2019 and almost an hour longer than in September 2018. Twice as many people were having video calls to keep in touch with family and friends than had been the case prior to the pandemic. This was a worldwide phenomenon as restrictions forced large swathes of populations to stay at home. Shares in Zoom inevitably rocketed in value, with the company making as much money in three months as in the whole previous year (Washtell, 2020).

While nationally there has been some concern about the 'digital divide', whereby older people are less likely to have the skills to communicate in the virtual world (Martins Van Jaarsveld, 2020), diarists were all computer savvy as this was a requirement for participating in the diary project. They were all familiar with internet and computer use even if, inevitably, there was a sharper learning curve for some than for others. Suddenly cut off from direct contact with all but those in the same household, they missed their friends and families. Fortunately, however, there was Zoom. So, along with vast throngs of the population, they adapted swiftly and pragmatically to re-establish links with people and activities important to them. Although all diarists used computers, not all were acquainted with video conferencing at the onset of the first lockdown. It was not long, however, before almost all were using Zoom or an equivalent platform in some way or another. It could take up a considerable amount of time. The proliferation of Zoom events called for serious diary management as it was easy to become double booked.

HUMPHREY
Sunday 14 June 2020
Have I mentioned Zoom before? Only every epistle.

OTTOLIE
Monday 11 May 2020
What is social media now but a virtual dinner table?

WARRENER
Friday 17 April 2020
A Zoomless day. A blessing.

The ways in which these platforms were used were endless. Diarists mentioned coffee mornings, virtual drinks and supper parties, birthday parties, Gareth Malone's home choruses, quizzes, book and film and investment clubs, book launches, webinars on various topics including craniosacral therapy, committee meetings, consultations with colleagues and students, political party meetings, exercise (Joe Wicks was very popular) as well as pilates, yoga and tap dancing classes, online bridge, language lessons, a BSL class, church services and prayer groups, art tutorials, meditation, live streamed concerts, and so on. The possibilities were enormous. Many activities were imaginative.

PANGOLIN
Friday 5 June 2020
I'd been looking forward to a real online treat on Sunday – a Zoom party to replace an annual event in our street of a party with [a theatre group]. We

are doing the Bronte Saga ... I must sort out my costume and set for Nellie Dean. Now we probably need an understudy for Heathcliff and Catherine Earnshaw (my daughter's partner and my daughter).

STRATHSPEY
Friday 17 April 2020

I am a member of a large dancing organisation and have done voluntary work for them for the last 20 years, it all involves working on my laptop so it has been relatively easy to continue it during lockdown.

I have been very impressed by the efforts made by others in the group to provide dance-related activities that can be done during lockdown, a variety of related quizzes, lessons on Zoom, virtual dances (tunes and videos so that we can imagine an evening's dancing). There are even dance classes, which although we can't get together, they lead us through step practice. One brilliant group performed a 'Toilet Roll dance', a couple of couples and singles all dancing in their own homes, the videos superimposed to give the illusion of a complete dance with six people and passing the toilet roll to one another.

Keeping in touch with family was, nonetheless, often paramount. The proficiency with Zoom that most diarists had achieved came into its own and led to many activities with families and friends, such as celebrations of birthdays and other events, quizzes, and general chats and meetings, sometimes with those spread across the globe, and much more.

HOLLY
Retrospective: Friday 27 March 2020

We have a daily 'cuppa' via FaceTime with my mother-in-law who is 86 – actually having a cup in your hands and sitting facing each other really works better than a phone call. She's being amazing. She hates being alone but is of the firm view that you just have to get on with it.

HUMPHREY
Thursday 2 April 2020

Our dance card is filling up with social invitations. A Zoom drinks here, a Zoom family quiz there, our daily Zoom pilates class, and lots of FaceTime calls. What is the right protocol for keeping up with friends? How often should one talk? Should one phone or email? Does one chase up the ones who have not replied? It's a facer.

JESSIE
Sunday 12 April 2020

Easter Day – very strange not to be with family on this day – however we did have a family Easter egg decorating competition on Zoom – which was fun.

SUSIEQ
Friday 10 April 2020

My 70th birthday present from my sisters is a Spa day and one sister suggests we might have a go at a virtual one in the interim. I am very concerned that she's about to suggest we do this from our respective baths with lots of bubbles, but fortunately all she has in mind is each having a face pack.

TERESA
Wednesday 22 April 2020

This evening got ready for a Zoom Cocktail 75th birthday party. Dressed up in best clothes, although best only on top half, set up tablet with cheerful lighting, carefully chosen pictures in background. ... It was good to see friends, especially some with whom we hadn't been properly in touch. Son had produced a quiz about M's life, vetted by her beforehand: where had she grown up? Names of brothers and sisters? Where did she lose her virginity? Did she eat the cannabis cake offered to her in 1968? Where had she taught? Etc. This was fun but I felt mildly alarmed at the challenge of celebrating my own birthday in a couple of weeks' time.

Diarists with grandchildren frequently singled them out as those they missed most. They were losing out on watching them grow and develop and were often forgoing regular childcare duties. Many devised creative (usually online) strategies to keep in touch and appraised of how they were doing. Needless to say, some were more successful than others.

BEA
Friday 1 May 2020

In 1964 I achieved (if that is the right word, at least it wasn't a fail) an E grade for Advanced Level French. 1964 is a long time ago so I have probably forgotten most of what I learnt, however I got a request yesterday to write in French to my grandson so that he could do a translation. I sat for a long time with a notebook and a dictionary and managed to write a few lines in long hand to 'Mon cher petit-fils'. I then transcribed it onto the computer so I could email it to him. Unfortunately I have no idea how to get the laptop to write e acute or e grave. So the first thing that has got to be done at his end is for him or someone on his behalf to put in the accents. I did tell him where they should go, i.e. J'espere (there should be a grave accent on the middle e!). I am not sure that they will ask me to repeat the process.

CHARLES
Thursday 16 April 2020

We joined the grandchildren in a Zoom children's book group this morning discussing the 12 labours of Hercules. They seemed to enjoy it and had drawn some good pictures. Good ideas came out about some of the peripheral animals. I loved a little story from one child of a fish being swept through the Augean stables and suddenly realising it was swimming in poo. They always love a story involving poo!

GATZOU
Retrospective: Tuesday 7 April 2020

I Skype now. I have started just over a week ago, just in time to teach my grandchildren French one hour a day. It's working well. Surprisingly. They live nearby, I don't miss them because I speak to them every day. They talk to me more than when I was trying to get their attention in 'real' life … they are 7½ and 5 (in a couple of weeks).

HATTIE
Sunday 26 April 2020

Make rainbow jigsaw for grandsons and send it off. This was a pleasant activity. I painted a rainbow onto thick card, with bits and bobs in the background and the colours written out – reading practice for 4-year-old – and my husband cut it out beautifully into quite complicated shapes. My daughter sent a text today to say they had spent a very happy half hour doing the puzzle. I had warned her that she might need to be on hand to hold it together from time to time in case the pieces drifted apart from each other.

JESSIE
Friday 24 April 2020

I realise that I have not recorded a 'game' I am playing with my granddaughter (7) and grandson (4) who live in Devon. While doing some tidying up I found some postcards of places I had visited in the past. So devised a game with my granddaughter that I was going to go on a pretend holiday and send her postcards. I asked her where I should go and she suggested Madeira – where her other grandmother has a holiday home – but she then said I should also go by way of our holiday home in Spain. I started this game on 6.4.20 with a card from St Pancras station and I have been sending cards at three- or four-day intervals of my travels so far by train through France, Spain and now in Portugal. I always label the card Pretend Holiday but give her a bit of detail of what I might have been doing. My granddaughter has really entered into the spirit of this and will ask me when we speak if I am on a train or on a beach, etc. I too am enjoying this game and enjoy planning on how to proceed with it.

JOJO
Retrospective: Monday 30 March 2020

I am reading my granddaughter her bedtime story on WhatsApp video every evening so that's a plus!!

LYNNE
Tuesday 26 May 2020
I had quite a long WhatsApp video chat with my daughter and granddaughter this morning, who is standing and taking her first steps. I was treated to a lengthy demonstration of how to take things out of drawers in her bedroom. We can play 'boo' and wave.

TARANAKI
Saturday 18 April 2020
Yesterday I spent quite a lot of time talking on FaceTime with my two oldest grandchildren. I have been setting them 'schoolwork' style activities to do. They seem to have really enjoyed this latest one which was to imagine themselves as farmworkers and to describe a typical spring day's tasks. It was real fun and got them thinking and talking at length. A good mix of preparation and delivery in a question-and-answer exchange in which they had to validate the jobs they had chosen. I am pleased to see how well they are working together.

Inevitably Zoom gave rise to much of the ephemerality discussed by Gottschalk (2021) and it was not always a positive experience. There were many problems with sight and sound and much frustration, especially in the early days of the pandemic. Diarists reported not managing to join a meeting, failing to position the camera correctly or achieve a split screen, or viewing people upside down. One diarist wrote how a virtual church service left her feeling sad and grieving for earlier times of social interaction and activity.

The significance of food

Food assumed a pre-eminence during the pandemic for almost everybody. The nature of its significance was, however, variable. Shortages of certain items (not all edible), notably loo rolls and pasta, during the first lockdown were universal, as was the impact of shop closures and restrictions. Beyond that there was divergence, with major differences in taken-for-granted aspects of reality between the more advantaged members of society and those existing on low incomes and reliant on food banks. In other words, there was a difference between those who needed food to survive and those who also saw it as a major source of pleasure. This reflects Bourdieu's (1984) distinction between a 'taste of necessity' and a 'taste of luxury'. Food preferences and practices are linked to social class and the availability of time and money. The French sociologist Poulain (2017) concurred in his book *The Sociology of Food: Eating and the place of food in society*, originally published in 2002. His view was that eating is not simply a biological requirement but also a social act. Food and patterns of social interaction are intimately intertwined.

In accordance with these perspectives, many diarists – who fell within the relatively advantaged category – devoted considerable space in their entries to documenting the planning, sourcing, preparation and eating of food, often suggesting that these activities had assumed a new importance in their daily lives. They also wrote about growing things and eating from the garden, and paying more attention to healthy eating. As ever, of course, this did not apply to everyone. For some, provisioning became an endless and unwanted chore.

Having grown up in the early post-war period, diarists were used to notions of rationing and 'waste not want not' (Madge and Hoggart, 2020). Many wrote about not throwing things away and making do. Not surprisingly, therefore, an early task was to use up anything edible.

APPLETREE
Retrospective: Monday 13 April 2020
I checked store cupboards for tins of tomatoes/beans/tuna, tea and coffee, etc. using my mother's groceries mantra from the fifties (adapted). Butter, lard (oil), marge, bacon, cheese, sugar, tea, cereal, soap. ... Plenty of toilet rolls thanks to J's visit. Her inordinate use meant I always had plenty even after her roll-a-day visit!!!!

BENCHMAN
Monday 6 April 2020
I cooked us an odd meal yesterday, using mainly store cupboard ingredients. It was a mixture of chopped onions and brown lentils, cooked separately at first until both were soft, and then combined with some cooked pine nuts I had in the fridge and a few anchovies and spices. I served it with some grilled halloumi. It proved surprisingly tasty, although the lentil mix was a little dry. I should have added some vegetable stock.

TERESA
Saturday 28 March 2020
Ate up food from the freezer and immediately regretted choice. Stale couscous, dry chicken and elderly peas.

Others relied, perhaps more than in the past, on being self-sufficient by growing their own fruit and vegetables, or making staples like bread. During the pandemic there were copious internet sites providing recipes for lockdown loaves and, anecdotally at least, it seems that sourdough competitions were commonplace within certain sections of the locked down population. There was certainly discussion of sourdough among the diarists as well as a few photos of loaves that had been baked. Rahman (2020) suggested in a blog for *The Conversation* that baking became a lockdown coping strategy. It enabled a tangible accomplishment with a 'delightfully carby end-product'.

Pursuing an interactionist line of thought, she discussed how posting photos of newly baked loaves was (among other things) a form of self-presentation. They provided a narrative of our lives in lockdown that could be shared with similarly minded others. They conveyed a message that all was okay.

One way or another, most (but not all) diarists said they spent much more time thinking about and preparing food than they had previously. It had become a new priority, whether this was viewed positively or not. Meals and their preparation took on a greater significance when many other customary activities were prohibited. Indeed, Public Health England (2020) reported on how the sale of food and drink from March to June 2020 was more than ten per cent up on the same period the previous year. And, even more remarkably, sales during the week immediately prior to Boris Johnson's announcement of lockdown on 23 March were over 40 per cent higher than the equivalent week in the previous year. As these figures take account of purchases by both households and outlets such as cafes, pubs and restaurants, the impact of the COVID-19 pandemic on everyday grocery shopping may have been even greater than suggested. Households were taking stock and stocking up.

EDGAR
Monday 27 April 2020

I am not sure if it is these strange times or my age but meals have become a big feature in the day (they may always have been – I cannot remember) and I look forward to the next one even before I have finished the last.

PERSIA
Thursday 2 April 2020

I am amazed at where the time goes each day and when I look back in the evening feel I have achieved little. An enormous amount of time seems to be spent on food. Compiling the next shopping list for the neighbour, preparing it, cooking it, eating it (the smallest amount of time!) and clearing up. I certainly never spent this amount of time when I was on my own thinking around eating!

TARANAKI
Sunday 28 June 2020

We have never been at home for such an extended period! I worked out the other day that I had cooked 90+ dinners on the trot. It was a depressing thought.

WARRENER
Wednesday 27 May 2020

We constructed a menu for the next few days, listing meals in one column and main ingredients in the other. Ingredients column includes stuff in the fridge, stuff in the freezer and stuff to buy, thereby feeding into (ha ha) the shopping list. Then I did the order. Never before have we taken food planning and organisation to such levels. More evidence that eating and drinking have moved centre stage in our lockdown lives.

Stocking up with food did, nonetheless, present challenges, with many diarists reliant on others to send or bring food. Relatives, friends, neighbours, students and other volunteers, local businesses and others commonly came to the rescue. Sometimes neighbours took it in turns to do shopping for each other. Some in remote areas faced particular difficulties.

PETER
Friday 3 April 2020
We ran out of gin today. Which of our small army of shoppers should I ask? Would any of them think it an excessive luxury?

TWEEGY
Retrospective: Tuesday 31 March 2020
In our village the parish council and the church have together organised efforts to help. Volunteers are shopping and delivering, etc. A food bank has been established at the church. Friends shopped for fresh stuff for us on our arrival, and I have two chest freezers of veg and fruit from the garden and soup, stews, etc that I have made. A man selling fresh fish calls weekly, and I already have a 'milk and more' account.

Some diarists were nonetheless happy to venture out to do their own shopping. Many national supermarkets were quick off the mark in introducing special early morning shopping slots for the over-70s, as well as instigating one-way systems, protective perspex screens and other measures to encourage social distancing. Those who had given these slots a try had mixed views. For some they worked well whereas for others they were crowded, with long queues at every checkout.

A report from the Office for National Statistics in September 2020 (Dalgleish, 2020) suggested that the pandemic accelerated the shift to online shopping although, interestingly, food and drink were not the most affected. At the date of their report, online groceries accounted for around ten per cent of the total. Online food sales in August 2020 were about twice what they had been in February 2020, but still only around 10 per cent of the total. The trend continued. The *Retail Gazette* in December 2021 reported how the spend on online groceries almost doubled in that year compared to 2020 (Parr, 2021).

In line with the general pattern, diarists sought food deliveries, or sometimes 'click and collect', in the first weeks of the pandemic. At the beginning, however, they did not always meet with success. At this point demand far exceeded supply. Even the 'elderly' and 'vulnerable', often given priority, could find it difficult to access the service. In these early stages of the lockdown, numerous diarists wrote about the time spent trying to find home delivery or 'click and collect' slots.

BARKLEY
Wednesday 25 March 2020

I've been trying, so far without success, to log on to Sainsbury's online delivery service – I read that they were prioritising the over-70s by providing this service. However, every time I try to log on I get a message saying, 'Due to the huge increase in online orders, we're pausing new registrations for the time being'. There's also a phone number for over-70s and other vulnerable people to call to register for online deliveries – and guess what? – it's permanently engaged.

TARANAKI
Sunday 29 March 2020

My husband and I spent an age placing an order with Morrisons for click and collect at a branch some 15 miles away (the closest possible). When we first got online, there were in excess of 50,000 people in the queue. The wait for connection was about 45 minutes. We are not used to shopping this way so the actual selection and payment processes were slow and frustrating.

Success could be seen as a major achievement and cause for celebration.

PERSIA
Friday 15 May 2020

Second cause of celebration was our first online delivery slot – from Sainsburys. Having tried Waitrose, Ocado and Tesco, Sainsbury finally came up trumps. Great excitement to get a slot however a complete novice at doing online ordering such that I realised after the first go that we had ordered one mushroom and one banana – however we soon caught on and all arrived in good time. I would certainly never have believed six months ago I could get so excited from a grocery delivery.

PETER
Thursday 2 April 2020

Deliveries to the house are a treat, like receiving Christmas presents.

Sales of alcohol boomed during the lockdowns and the pandemic, with the consumption of wine, beer and spirits all showing an enormous increase.

As Janet Street-Porter (2021) suggested, perhaps many people got through house arrest in 2020 and 2021 by drowning their sorrows and drinking more. Many, but by no means all, diarists confirmed this trend for themselves, often also mentioning a resolve to cut down, but not just yet. It seemed that an increased emphasis on food, and a cutback on other activities, could be linked to a greater consumption of alcohol.

BONIVARD

Saturday 2 May 2020

My son who manages some wine shops confirms that demand is up by about a third. There was an initial rush but this has been maintained. Home deliveries are popular and some customers are ordering more than one case a week.

JOJO

Saturday 4 April 2020

My first evening without any alcohol since the lockdown – YAY!

New patterns had been established.

Keeping up appearances

Personal appearance also assumed a new significance during the pandemic and lockdowns. Diarists were not unlike other groups of the population spending most of their time at home, but encountering others when they went out for walks or took part in video meetings. According to Goffman's (1959) dramaturgical analysis, the social world is a stage and people actors who present themselves according to the situation and audience. They are more conscious of their self-presentation in formal settings imbued with perceived expectations than when on their own or just with significant others. Did this accord with the diarists' attention to appearance during the lockdowns, especially as hairdressers and other personal services were not operating?

So far as dress was concerned, diarists gave the impression of wearing casual or 'gardening' clothes much of the time. According to the Office for National Statistics (2021d), sales of clothing fell by just over a fifth during 2020 compared with 2019, and remained below pre-pandemic levels into the following year. Marks & Spencer also reported a fall in clothing sales of nearly a quarter in the final three months of 2020, even though they sold 20 per cent more pyjamas than usual during this time, attributing this in part to the increase in time people spent at home (BBC News, 2021b). Despite all the jokes circulating at the time, diarists did not indicate that they had increased their consumption of sleepwear.

FRANCIA
Saturday 4 April 2020
Have worn nothing but jeans and old jumpers for two weeks.

JOJO
Monday 6 April 2020
I have to confess however that on our daily walk yesterday I didn't change out of my gardening clothes – Sod's Law we bumped into (at a distance – 2 metres at least) two people we knew!!

MABEL
Wednesday 1 April 2020
Today I scrubbed up. I washed and coloured my hair, painted my nails, put on makeup, and even some perfume. I also looked in my wardrobe for something different to wear and found some patterned black denim jeans that I'd bought in a sale about three years ago but had never worn. I tried them on first to check that they fit and, deciding that they were quite nice really, found a black jumper to go with them. My partner said he had a new girlfriend when I emerged!

OTTOLIE
Saturday 28 March 2020
An old friend sent me 'Coronavirus Rhapsody' which cheered. I danced about in my pyjamas, then read Terry Waite's article about trying to keep disciplined and not wearing pyjamas all day. So got dressed.

An interesting point, first mentioned by one female diarist but then taken up by others, concerned wearing a bra. There had been a number of articles in the press suggesting that many women had ditched this garment during lockdown, and it emerged that this was also the case for some diarists. Others, however, felt that it might not be an altogether sensible idea.

ELEANOR
Sunday 19 July 2020
As for the relaxation of supportive undergarments – I certainly haven't abandoned them! If anything, I have tried to shorten the bra straps to try and uphold my frontage and prevent any further descent!

JANWIG
Friday 17 July 2020
I have sort of abandoned a bra, but put it on for going out to the pub and shops. Like a mask maybe! Keep it by the front door. Not that I always wore one anyway. So that has not changed much.

TOPPER
Saturday 18 April 2020
I've dispensed with my bra since social distancing as everything is so baggy no one will notice.

Hair was another significant aspect of appearance for many diarists, especially as hairdressers and barbers were closed for almost three and a half months, from the beginning of the first lockdown on 23 March 2020 until 4 July, and then again later that year. Some discussed hair colour as well as cut, and how the solution might be to wear an Alice band or a scarf. Others decided to let their hair grow long and/or revert to their natural colour. A few took matters into their own hands – or perhaps the hands of their partner. Similar issues arose with regard to the closure of other types of personal service.

BARKLEY
Monday 13 April 2020
Just before going to bed I decided to have a go at cutting some rogue hairs that were sticking out over my right ear. Not a good idea at that time of night, especially after two and a half cans of lager and two gin and tonics. Result? I took a small chunk of flesh out of the top of my ear that just would not stop bleeding. Eventually, I went to bed with a towel covering my pillow.

BETTYMAC
Tuesday 21 April 2020
Very early on I stocked up with hair dye, however I have not used it yet for two reasons. Firstly I have decided to give my body a break from chemicals and secondly who knows how long this might last, I might need it later!

HOLLY
Wednesday 29 April 2020
Husband announced that he had a dental hygienist appointment in his diary for 4 o'clock and that he intended to keep it. I began saying that he couldn't possibly go and anyway they weren't open etc., etc. He explained with exaggerated patience that he hadn't meant that he was *actually* going to the dentist – he intended to go to the bathroom at 4.00 and spend the half hour that the hygienist usually takes, doing it himself. OK, then.

PERSIA
Sunday 21 June 2020
One of the great positives was finding a box of 'hair colour for roots' at the back of the cupboard with an end date of 2014. My guess bought whilst [partner] was ill but must have got to the hairdressers so never used. However – with two inches of grey things were now desperate. But how to

do it when the worst part was at the back – enlist the help of brother who I have to say was much better than my attempts at the front and took over the operation with a most successful outcome and perhaps a new sideline in the offing! The next day I felt really good with no grey hairs! How vain can you get?

SUSIEQ
Tuesday 7 April 2020
This morning it was our weekly treat and torture session. Not half as interesting or racy as it might sound – my partner washing my hair for me backwards over the bath. Lovely to have clean hair but a serious pain for both of us.

There were clear ways in which the diarists conformed to Goffman's notion of front and back stage performative behaviour, with many demonstrating a clear distinction between the presentation of self in public and non-public contexts. Previous attention to dress, hair and other aspects of appearance was, to a considerable extent, abandoned during the early period of lockdown when most time was spent at home and there was little contact with anyone outside the household. As time went on, however, there seemed to be some reversion to norm. The hours spent on Zoom, and the loosening of restrictions enabling greater sociability, no doubt contributed to some restoration of front stage behaviour, as did perhaps a measure of dissatisfaction with a more dishevelled appearance and a wish not to 'let oneself go'. Diarists began to pay greater attention to how they looked, even if aspects of their prior identity kit, such as smart clothes or makeup, were not restored.

Not only how they looked, but also how they felt, was important and there was much resolve among the diarists to be healthy during lockdown. They were largely in line with their age group more generally in this respect. In one study, researchers used activity-tracking devices to monitor the physical activity of different age groups before, during and after the initial lockdown in March 2020 (Bu et al, 2021). Interestingly, they found not only that over-65s were exercising more than others during the lockdown but also that they even increased their levels of exercise after lockdown was eased. A separate study linked loneliness and a lack of exercise during lockdown with a rise in depression and anxiety symptoms (King's College London News Centre, 2021).

Diarists wrote much about ways in which they were exercising. Going for regular walks was a key aspect of this, but step counters, exercise bikes, Joe Wicks video sessions, online dancing and daily fitness routines were all important too. Several wrote how they had got their bicycles out and dusted them down, while others ventured back to tennis, golf and swimming as soon as they could. Weight was a related concern for many. The increased emphasis on food during lockdowns was not always helpful. Portion creep and chocolate biscuits could be unwelcome temptations.

Spending and spending less

A YouGov survey in May 2020 charted increases and decreases in spending on specified items since the beginning of the pandemic (Nolsoe, 2020). Looking at the 873 participants in the 55 years and over group, 51 per cent said they were spending less while 20 per cent said they were spending more. The rest said there had been no change. Overall, they had spent somewhat more on groceries, alcohol for drinking at home, and books, and a bit more on supplies for hobbies. There had been less spent on other entertainment, services such as cleaning and haircuts, take-away food, clothes and beauty products, active wear and sports equipment, and significantly less on transport, holidays and travel. A further report from the New Policy Institute (Inman, 2020) suggested that the richest 20 per cent of Britons, which would include people from a similar age group to the diarists, would have spent around £23 billion less over the first three months of the pandemic than they would have had there been no lockdown.

The patterns of spending indicated by the YouGov study resonated with the reports of the diarists. Certainly, their patterns of shopping and spending had changed markedly since the onset of the pandemic. In addition to buying items, diarists mentioned donations to charity and food banks, and gifts to children. Many said they were spending more on food and alcohol, not always because they were eating more, but in order to keep well stocked up to avoid frequent shopping trips. Among other things, they were spending less on meals out, petrol, holidays and leisure activities, clothes, and cleaners (although they might be offering retainers).

EVE
Thursday 9 April 2020

I am in the very privileged position of keeping all my income because I am working from home but I have reduced my expenditure a lot during the lockdown. Normally I eat out at least once a week, each month I have my hair cut, a massage, see a play, watch a film, hear a concert and go to an exhibition and I'm no longer able to do any of these activities. As well as these regular commitments we have had to cancel our walking holiday in Italy and cannot go to the Edinburgh Festivals as they have also been cancelled. By the end of August I think I will have saved at least £3,000 most of which I will pass on to charities that support community arts.

HOLLY
Wednesday 22 April 2020

Then, I sat down at my laptop and did a back of the envelope job on my finances. Spending has certainly gone right down. We do one food and household shop each week and that lasts the whole week – the only time we've done more than that is when we've run out of milk a couple of times. Other than that, there've not been any other big spends. Oh – apart from the Easter choc parcels I ordered for my kids and their kids which cost an arm and a leg and have yet to arrive! Fuel bills will probably be a bit higher but not hugely so as we work from home anyway. So I guess one positive spin-off of the terrible COVID 19 crisis is that I'm saving money towards the eye-watering cost of the orthodontic treatment that is in store for me once I'm let out of the door.

Most diarists had at least a state pension coming in even if, as some mentioned, their investments and pension pots had taken a hit as the stock market took a sharp tumble in the early stages of the pandemic. For a few, however, other sources of income had suffered.

BARKLEY
Thursday 9 April 2020

At this time of year I would normally be starting to get some guiding work, so I'll lose income in this respect. Last year was my most lucrative yet in the six years I've been guiding. This was mainly due to the eight days I spent over the 75th anniversary of the D-Day landings, acting as both guide and tour manager for a group of Americans in both the UK and in France.

JACCA
Sunday 26 April 2020

My financial situation crumbled very early. Fortunately, being of pension age there is always something coming in but generally I rely on income from letting out a small property and a couple of rooms. I closed in early February not wanting to be exposed to risk myself but also aware of the risks to the community here. Suddenly not only had I lost the income but was in a position of trying to repay all the deposits that had come in last year and paying the winter bills and refurbishment costs.

The pandemic undoubtedly led to changes in consumer behaviour, reflected in the Office for National Statistics basket of goods used to calculate inflation. The items newly added in 2021 (Office for National Statistics, 2021a) included loungewear, dumbbells and hand sanitiser as people spent more time at home, devoted more time to keeping fit and healthy, and became more aware of hygiene. While the diarists did not necessarily choose these items, they did still find things to buy. These might be practical aids to ease their everyday life, purchases to support their current activities such as gardening, their online life, or extra luxuries including food and drink. Specific purchases mentioned were new laptops, either for themselves or their children, webcams to use with Zoom, other computers and accessories, trainers, a shopping trolley, kettles, food mixers and other kitchen aids. Plants were near the top of the list and clothes near the bottom.

BONANZA BILL
Monday 18 May 2020
I find that I am starting to spend money online – on things that are useful like a new bed – but I suspect this is part of trying to keep busy and involved.

ROB
Wednesday 6 May 2020
One of my tasks will be to flatten for a collection, tomorrow (green bin recycling day) … the mountain of cardboard and packaging I have accumulated with a flurry of lockdown online buying.

Occasionally there were reports of purchases that would not have been made in pre-pandemic times.

FRANCIA
Saturday 30 May 2020
The unbelievable happened. My husband bought a car without seeing it and the garage took his in part exchange without setting eyes on it. … Surely, under normal circumstances we would not have parted with such a large amount of money without first being satisfied that the car we were buying was to our liking. We may never have considered a new car anyway had things been normal. We would have treated ourselves to a holiday abroad instead.

GATZOU
Thursday 4 June 2020
Guilty. I have spent money whilst in lockdown on rubbish clothes that sending back would have taken a year of my life to manage. I also have bought a brand new iMac which I am not using now because I need to sort a problem with my Outlook on the old one to make sure I don't lose emails before transferring. I thought my 'old Mac' was too old but I realise now that all I needed would have been to give up Outlook for something else.

One consequence of the pandemic appeared to be a sharp decline in the use of cash. This was inevitable as people were very limited in their ability to go to shops, they were not using services where they might previously have paid with notes and coins, and bank transfers were necessary when purchasing online. Diarists were not going to cash machines and, nationally, Link (2021), the largest cash machine network in the UK, reported a 37 per cent decline in ATM transactions in 2020. More than one diarist said they had forgotten their pin number as a result.

Summary

The 'new normal' prohibited many of the taken-for-granted aspects of daily life, but diarists quickly adapted to their changed circumstances. Time took on a new meaning and, especially in the early stages of the pandemic, there were likely to be few commitments to give structure to the day. As the weeks went by, however, many diarists developed routines or otherwise found things to occupy their time. Homes, gardens, puzzles, TV and reading were among the occupations that diarists turned to. Projects of various kinds, and sorting and de-cluttering, were also commonly mentioned. Zoom, however, was perhaps the new activity that became pre-eminently important. The internet enabled not only communication with family and friends, but a wide range of other activities to keep diarists busy during lockdowns. Food became another preoccupation for many. Planning meals, and sourcing, preparing and eating ingredients, took on, for many, a heightened significance. Attention to appearance, and spending patterns, were also affected by the pandemic.

The pandemic brought uncertainties to contend with and the COVID-19 virus to keep at bay. Behaviours and strategies to avoid becoming ill are considered in the next chapter.

6

Keeping the virus at bay

The ostensible purpose of rules and restrictions during the pandemic was to keep the virus at bay. There was also a call to protect the NHS by staying safe and not requiring hospital attention. Individual precautionary behaviours had the same aim. All these actions were, nonetheless, framed by uncertainty. It was easy to understand that close proximity to somebody exhibiting the symptoms of COVID-19 put oneself at risk of illness, but other measures were commonly based on conjecture rather than known fact. Little, at least in the early stages of the pandemic, was understood about the nature and operation of the invisible and intangible virus. Interactions with others, and in particular the media, generated anxiety and fear rather than more specific information on COVID-19, even if the public was bombarded with statistics and graphs to provide a semblance of greater scientific certainty.

The symbolic universe (Berger and Luckmann, 1966) that the nation inhabited had changed. There was a new institutionalised structure and a new set of values. The issue in this case was that the new set of beliefs accompanying the new symbolic universe was not well established. There was no clear explanation for the new order other than the continual reports of illness and death.

So, as Blumer (1969) might have asked, how did diarists and others make sense of their lives in relation to prescribed rules and personal precautions? Ultimately they were agents of their own behaviour and needed to construct their own actions and cognitions to deal with the situations they faced (Hannem, 2021). Only four diarists reported having contracted the virus over the period of the study, and few had come into direct contact with it during the early stages, so they acted in line with their own understandings and interpretations of the situation, and in negotiation with others with whom they might be interacting. Nobody knew much but life went on.

Diarists, as a group, were comfortably off and living in spacious homes and usually with gardens. They were mostly retired even if involved in many outside activities in pre-pandemic times. Many lived in rural or semi-rural areas where it was not difficult to go for walks without close encounters. For these reasons, they tended to be ideally placed to avoid the risk of contracting the virus. Nonetheless most did not want to stay at home all the time, and many needed to venture out even if for a hospital appointment or to service their car. Just about everyone had occasion to practise social distancing, wear a mask, and apply their own pragmatic agency in taking additional precautions.

Social encounters

The pandemic fundamentally changed the rules of social interaction. With the initial lockdown announced by Boris Johnson on 23 March 2020 came an instruction to stay at home (unless essential workers) other than for a few allowed excursions and, when out, to 'socially distance' from others. This meant keeping at least two metres from anybody not in the same household. While the two-metre rule remained in force, restrictions were relaxed from 1 June 2020 to allow groups of six to meet up, but only outside. The two-metre rule was later changed to one metre on 4 July 2020 as other restrictions were also eased. September 2020 had further seen the introduction of the 'rule of six' in England (with a similar rule in Scotland, albeit with a slightly different definition of what was permissible) whereby up to six people could meet in either indoor or outdoor settings under socially distanced conditions. Indeed, it was not until Monday 19 July 2021 (and Monday 9 August 2021 in Scotland) that the requirement to socially distance was finally lifted.

Diary entries suggested that diarists generally observed the two-metre rule as it was something they felt kept them safe. This accords with responses to the Opinions and Lifestyle Survey conducted towards the end of July that year (Office for National Statistics, 2021b), with 74 per cent of those aged 70 or over reporting always or often maintaining social distance. Nonetheless, diarists might recognise that the rulings were somewhat arbitrary and not necessarily 'following the science'.

> **CARACTACUS**
> *Tuesday 23 June 2020*
> New regulations have been announced for July, which will relax the restrictions on socialising, and allowing certain categories of business to re-open to the public. One of the dubious rules is that the two-metre separation must be observed – except where it can't be, in which case one metre will do. That seems to be a product more of optimism than of science.

Going out for daily exercise, and encountering acquaintances or strangers, was a key setting for social distancing. 'Normal' social interaction had been suspended, with the old social order replaced by new shared meanings and collective acts. Strauss (1978) discussed what he termed negotiated orders (more recently termed generic social processes: Prus, 1996), that are continually reconstituted as structural conditions change, and that involve joint agreements. In this context, they had come to mean an agreed physical proximity, the management of boundaries, and movements to facilitate the pathways of all parties. Those complying were exercising what Mead (1934) would describe as the human capacity for perspective taking and taking the role of the other. Understanding one's own behaviour and hence understanding others' needs and behaviour too. Goffman's (1959) work followed this tradition with a focus on face work, or face-to-face interactions. He was interested in how people present themselves and believed that life and theatre are very similar.

The validity of these various theoretical concepts was demonstrated by the cooperation and drama reported in social interactions during the pandemic. Avoiding one another in a friendly manner, or jumping aside to let somebody else go past, were good examples of what was happening within the new temporary social order. The reciprocity of action was endorsement of these new patterns of behaviour. Changes to the old micro-social rituals of everyday life (Goffman, 1967) were under way.

BEA
Tuesday 12 May 2020

Walking around town this morning, a man coming towards me said, 'We are all becoming very good dancers', as we moved apart the requisite two metres.

GRACE
Thursday 9 April 2020

As I go on my much loved daily walks, the social distancing dance struck me as a game of chess no one quite knew the rules of. Some just take rook steps sideways, others diagonally walk across the road, the bishop's move, some make knights move forward, across. When I see it as draughts jumping over pieces I will know that it has all become a game of leap frog!

MABEL
Wednesday 1 April 2020

We went out for our daily constitutional, taking yet another route. In the last ten days we have managed to do a different walk each time. Today we did around 13,000 steps. Most people keep as distant as possible, which can involve sinking into a prickly hedge on some of the narrow paths, but some continue to walk two abreast and pass much closer than they need. Two women stood out in the efforts to observe social distancing. One appeared hiding in a gateway and almost made me jump as I hadn't seen her. And the other made a great show of moving off the path onto a green bank. She commented on how adaptable human beings are and how, although our daily life has changed dramatically, we are all just getting on with it.

While reciprocity and mutualism were much in evidence, this was not always the case. Goffman contrasted focused interactions, where the people involved take notice of each other and make concessions accordingly, and unfocused interactions where there is a lack of mutual awareness. Diarists reported reciprocity and mutualism in the main, often saying how people were generally more friendly than usual, but there were certainly exceptions. Some commented on individual behaviours during encounters, sometimes critically and sometimes with incredulity. Cyclists and joggers were particularly likely to be regarded as deviant. In the language of Cohen (1973), they could be seen as the folk devils flouting the rules of the new temporary social order.

BONANZA BILL
Friday 15 May 2020

Social distancing has obviously paid dividends but the etiquette of implementing it can be quite diverse. Some people stand respectfully aside, often with a smile, which I find quite acceptable. Others make a big play of putting lots of distance between you and them which I do not. In fact, I find it rather offensive. Some people, of course, don't even seem to be aware of the need for social distancing which can be a bit awkward if you don't want to get too close. I suspect the ways of doing 'social distancing' could be a good basis for a comedy sketch.

BONANZA BILL
Tuesday 19 May 2020

One friend who is taking 'social distancing' to the extreme has asked when we can chat. She refuses to talk in person even from a distance of six to 12 metres as if that could spread coronavirus. I feel unsympathetic to this blind adherence to 'the rules' without any real reason so I feel somewhat reluctant to arrange to chat on social media.

FRANCIA
Friday 31 July 2020

Something that I did catch on TV a few days ago. Two footballers obviously pleased with some triumph in their game, touched elbows (permissible I think) then they hugged each other. Since March I have been left speechless on more than one occasion.

SWEETPEA
Sunday 26 April 2020

In my daily walk in the park, I've found most people are really good with social distancing. However, it really annoys me when walkers or particularly joggers keep to the path and force me off into the grass. I've also nearly been mown down twice by cyclists. I tend to look upon this type of behaviour as just selfishness and lack of awareness of other people, which some people are exhibiting in stark contrast to others who are politely self-distancing.

Social distancing as prescribed conferred some level of security in the prevailing uncertainty as to the whereabouts and transmission of the virus, and there could be considerable consternation when people failed to remain at a 'safe' distance.

FISHERMAN
Thursday 4 June 2020

I was outside the house when my neighbour and his wife, who were going for a walk, mentioned that they had found difficulties with some local paths. I explained the reasons, but there was one that I could not identify and envisage. Amazingly he came right next to me to show the location on the map on his phone. I could actually smell his breath! This was the man who had been identified with coronavirus on his return from Thailand, and had suffered scarring of the lungs.

JACCA
Sunday 26 April 2020

For four weeks we had no other face-to-face contact, with the exception of an Open Reach engineer. When I met him at the gate I was at a complete loss as to know what to do and wondered if I should hold up a clove of garlic or something.

JENNIFER
Friday 1 May 2020

Got ready and went for a walk down to the beach – a longer walk than usual. The sun was shining and the tide was out so there was quite a lot of room on the beach. I then walked back through two lovely parks and some streets. Normally this walk takes me an hour but today it took me nearly an hour and a half because of having to avoid people who are not helping to maintain two metres distance. … I got home feeling very stressed. This happens most days when I go out for a walk.

STRATHSPEY
Friday 17 April 2020

I arranged to accidentally meet a friend at the gates of a nearby park and planned to just walk and chat while observing social distancing. It was a lovely day and before the schools closed. It became immediately obvious that large numbers of people were just out to enjoy the lovely weather with no intention of observing social distancing, in fact were picnicking.

> This just wasn't going to work and in fact I am now paranoid about strictly maintaining the rules.

The official view for the first few months of the pandemic was that social distancing was most important of all and that wearing a mask would make little difference. The argument was advanced, and debated, that a mask would protect others from the wearer but would not protect the wearer from others. Indeed, it was not until 15 June 2020 in England, 22 June in Scotland and 27 July in Wales that the first legal requirements to wear face coverings came into force. Initially they were mandatory only on public transport, and it was not until 24 July 2020 that masks were made compulsory in shops and supermarkets in England. Similar policies came into force on 10 July in Scotland, and 14 September in Wales. Failure to comply without a good reason risked a £100 fine in England despite the acknowledgement that the policy was difficult to police. The announcement in England had come some ten days before the new law came into force and, in the interim, Michael Gove, then Minister for the Cabinet Office, had been spotted coming out of a sandwich bar without a face covering. He had previously been at some odds with Boris Johnson and took the view that wearing masks should be advisory rather than obligatory, and based on common sense and good manners. One upshot was a subsequent government statement outlining how masks would not be obligatory in take-away outlets. As one diarist wrote, the virus does not know whether or not a shop is a take-away.

A poll by Opinium published on Sunday 19 July 2020 in the *Observer* (Savage, 2020b), just before masks were made mandatory, suggested that 71 per cent of adults in England supported the new order, with just 13 per cent in opposition. The majority support was confirmed by a YouGov snap poll (Nguyen, 2020) around the same time, albeit with 60 per cent in favour of mandatory masks and 34 per cent believing they should be optional. In addition, the Opinions and Lifestyle Survey (Office for National Statistics, 2021b) revealed that nearly everybody polled said they had worn face masks outside their home once they were obligatory. Several diarists felt that masks should have been introduced earlier.

JESSIE
Friday 31 July 2020

> Masks – wearing masks in shops started and I have found it difficult to wear a mask but have done so. However, when going to our market I noticed that most people were not wearing them in the open although wearing them in shops. It feels a bit late to have started this rule and it would have been better to start it much earlier so that we were in the habit of wearing one and it had become part of the norm. My sister who lives in France has

been wearing a mask when out of the house right since the beginning of lockdown so thought it odd that we did not have to wear it.

LYNNE
Sunday 28 June 2020

An anecdote from my social Zoom of relevance to this project – there was a perception from one that the over-70s wearing masks can be quite a nuisance in shops. They are not considerate about where they walk and who they bump into, possibly they assume the mask absolves them of all responsibility. I haven't seen this myself as I still only rarely go into shops, but 'just sayin'' (as it would be put on social media).

PERSIA
Friday 15 May 2020

I cannot understand why face masks aren't obligatory. The government are now coming round to saying they *should* be worn on the tube and buses but I would like this to be they *must* be worn at all times outside. Some Asians have always worn them to stop them passing on germs when ill which seems to apply in the current situation. I was recently out gardening in the front when a runner came by at a fast rate panting heavily and I was most alarmed he wasn't wearing a mask and felt it quite intrusive that he didn't even bother to run a few feet away in the road (it is a cul de sac).

Others were less convinced.

BETTYMAC
Tuesday 21 April 2020

I have not been out of the house for the three weeks other than a very early walk when there are only a very few people around. I do not have a mask. I am unsure what I think about them and do not need one really.

ROB
Tuesday 31 March 2020

I note a number of people wearing face masks??? My understanding is that in general circumstances out and about they are of little use in preventing infection unless you have IT ... when it will minimise a little the risk of your passing it on via coughs and sneezes?? So did the seven or eight people I saw have it?? In which case why are they out? Just a comfort blanket I guess???

STANLEY
Thursday 4 September 2020

I shop once a week at the local Morrison's which is less than pre and early lockdown mainly because I strongly disagree with wearing a face mask. I'm with the original group of scientists who said, 'Don't wear a mask 'cos you could catch it as it likes damp bits of cloth'.

Many of the arguments advanced in relation to social distancing apply similarly to mask wearing. The notion of reciprocity, and protecting others as well as oneself, are much the same. There is, however, an additional factor in that masks obscure facial expressions and gestures, both with known persons and strangers, and thereby affect the nature of face-to-face interactions (Smith, 2021).

So far as it was possible to deduce, most diarists were compliant with mandatory mask wearing. They said it was not too much of a problem, although many found masks uncomfortable and impractical if they were wearing glasses that became steamed up. Diarists also lamented the old ones left to litter the streets, and there was criticism of the fact that many were imported from China.

Pragmatically determined precautions

Aside from social distancing and wearing masks when around others, there was considerable scope for taking personal precautions, at home or elsewhere, to prevent transmission of COVID-19. These precautions were, however, taken in a context of uncertainty about the nature of the invisible virus. Accordingly, diarists and others constructed their own notions of vulnerability based on their interactions with the media, friends, families and others, and the messages they received (Moore and Khan, 2021).

One of the clear messages from the outset was that preventing transmission of the COVID-19 virus depended on regular hand washing and the use of sanitiser. Boris Johnson, on 3 March 2020, had publicly said that he would continue to shake hands with everyone, but that hand washing was key. It is not known how he contracted the virus, but on 27 March 2020 it was announced that he had tested positive. This occurrence was perhaps a symbol of the danger of the virus. Even if it could not be seen, it could still be touched.

For many diarists, pragmatic adaptations to the novel situation included the development of new everyday rituals to minimise the risk from anything entering the house from outside. If you could become ill from shaking hands, then perhaps you were also at risk from touching something somebody else had touched. So far as groceries and other material items were concerned, the government's Food Standards Agency (2020) recommended thoroughly cleaning food surfaces and regular hand washing. It also stated that as COVID-19 was a respiratory illness, it was not known to be transmitted by exposure to food or food packaging. There was no official guidance to quarantine food and other goods. Diarists faced uncertainty but used personal agency to make their own decisions.

CLARA
Tuesday 31 March 2020
I had two food deliveries. Good, but stressful. I have to assume everything has the virus on it, so have a system at the front door, of emptying fruit and veg from packaging into a bowl, and taking packaging and cardboard straight downstairs to recycling. Wearing gloves, wash all fruit and veg. Oranges that had been in netting I even put into bleach and then rinse. It is all scary.

ELEANOR
Sunday 24 May 2020
A definite feeling of battle weariness at the beginning of this week. Must I really continue to sanitise everything that arrives at the front door? I did order a set of colourful collapsible sieves for washing fruit and veg which cheered things up, once I'd wiped down the packaging they arrived in before opening them up! I never want to wash another banana or wipe down another cardboard box!

FRANCES
Friday 3 April 2020
The contamination problem: how far do you need to go in wiping down every item that comes to the door? If it's through the letter box I put it unopened on the floor and wash my hands, then write on it with a marker pen the day of the week (Mon, Tues, etc.) and leave it for three days before opening. If it's groceries, I put the perishables in the fridge or freezer – on a separate shelf if possible, and leave the rest in the bag or box for three days. Then I wash my hands and wipe down fridge and freezer handles. The whole ritual is ridiculous, but I can't convince myself that it is either necessary or unnecessary.

SKYE
Saturday 18 July 2020
Coffee and chat with a friend. I managed to cut a slice of cake and butter it without touching said cake. I also found a pair of tongs to place cake on plate. Sense of achievement afterwards. This friend has had a kidney transplant so I was being exceptionally careful with food prep, etc.

Similar issues arose for other objects coming into the house, or activities close to home. Occasionally matters did not go fully according to plan.

ANNA
Sunday 29 March 2020
Short walk in (long) evening to post birthday card. But inadvertently I TOUCHED THE MOUTH OF THE POST BOX! Felt contaminated. The rest of

the walk I had to hold my phone (Hilary Mantel continues to absorb me) in my left hand which got frozen, so I turned round sooner than I'd have liked.

CARACTACUS
Wednesday 25 March 2020

With our new 'post box' at the front door, we need to know how long the virus might survive on the packaging. Current advice is that it can last up to four hours on copper, up to 24 hours on cardboard, and up to two to three days on plastic and stainless steel. This is influencing how we deal with items put into our box. Interestingly, despite the message we put on the front door asking deliverers to ring the bell after a delivery, the last two haven't done so. Maybe they have been instructed not to touch bells, etc.

GATZOU
Wednesday 8 April 2020

I have not opened either parcel yet as I was told I'd better wait a few days so all traces of virus would have gone – I picked it up at the corner without gloves and I just realised, I forgot to wash my hands!!!!!! So, I may have it now.

RAIN
Thursday 2 April 2020

Today I phoned my sister happy birthday early, and with my morning coffee made a few housework and creative gestures (dusted a window sill, used felt tip pens to draw a rainbow, hung the washing out in the sunshine, wrote a birthday card ready to post to our granddaughter), and read the newspaper. The paper had a hot iron first, and my hands were thoroughly washed.

There was little formal guidance on the precautions to be taken, and those that were issued could be viewed with amusement.

WILL
Friday 15 May 2020

There are some inadvertently amusing (if I can curb my anger for a while) aspects of the revised 'guidance', my favourite being the one about tennis. Apparently, I'm not allowed to touch my opponent's balls and should initial my own so that my opponent doesn't inadvertently touch mine. I'm not sure how this would go down in LTA circles but it bears little relationship to any tennis I've ever played. Still, in for a penny …

As people were ultimately deciding for themselves how best to avoid risk, or the risks they were prepared to take, there were inevitably disagreements in social interactions. Mutuality and reciprocity were not always in evidence.

CLARA
Thursday 23 April 2020

[Another resident in the building] came upstairs for some wine for his cooking. I am finding the disjoint between his and my disinfectant practices stressful. I bleach plastic bottles and packaging when I unpack a delivery. Does he? I woke up in the night, remembering he had handled the bottle of wine. Had he touched something which could have had the virus? Had I washed my hands or touched my face after pouring a glass of wine? These are sudden anxieties which hit in the middle of the night.

ELISABETH
Friday 17 April 2020

Yesterday I went to collect a package for a friend in the next village, took it to her and sat in the garden with her and her partner for a half-hour chat. I came home feeling a little aggrieved because they didn't offer tea because, I suppose, handling things together would break the rules. My friend threw the drill I was borrowing from her on the grass rather than putting it in my hand because that would have meant getting too close. Now this I regard as unnecessary caution when they and I have been nowhere for the last week and had contact with no one. Common sense has been chased away by an unjustified ramping up of the fear factor, in my view. Of the 800+ deaths yesterday, only nine were in Wiltshire – one of the largest counties with a population of only half a million.

Creativity and ingenuity were commonplace in the fight to keep the pesky virus at bay. Many and varied precautions were reported, including playing tennis in gloves.

Life is 'done differently'

Despite the pandemic, life went on. Many activities were curtailed, as witnessed by the cancellations, the quiet streets, and the other symbols of a national shutdown reported by diarists. But many events and services persisted throughout lockdowns and despite restrictions, or started up again after a brief interlude. These events and services were, however, changed in their nature.

Medical services are an important example. Hospitalisations were increasing rapidly in the early months of the pandemic, and doctors were either dealing with coronavirus patients, off sick or compelled to self-isolate. Face-to-face appointments accordingly became few and far between, the people allowed into hospitals were severely restricted and, one way and another, there was a major interruption to normal provision. Diarists that managed to have contact with services reported on the changed practices.

CHARLES
Monday 4 May 2020

Yesterday was rather exciting. We had a trip out in the car! Had we been stopped by the police we could have justified our journey as necessary. Overnight one of my normally thin and bony feet had swollen, for no particular reason we could see. So we were heading to A & E at our nearest hospital, my wife fearing possible cellulitis.

Sent to 'Minor Injuries' I walked into a large completely empty waiting room. There was no one at the desk. I said 'hello' a couple of times but nothing happened. Two minutes later a staff member popped her head in and reassured me that someone would see me shortly. Sure enough a 40 something consultant in a specialism I didn't catch asked me into a small cubicle. He was all kitted up in maximum PPE, and I hoped he was comforted by my mask.

The examination was thorough. Not cellulitis but just as well to make sure because of my lowered immune system. No diagnosis but a 'not to worry about it' message, which was all I wanted. I asked how things were going. He told me his main worry was that hundreds more people were likely to die unnecessarily, because they were too afraid to come into hospital. He put a lot of the blame onto the scary media coverage.

The return journey was uneventful and the parking slot outside our house was free, unheard-of previously on a Sunday afternoon in May. Almost as unheard-of as getting in and out of the A & E Department of a major Midland hospital in ten minutes!

LOUISE
Tuesday 7 April 2020

I thought I would write about my visit to Southmead Hospital yesterday as it is something others may not have done. My appointment was at 8.40. Not allowed to eat, which was no hardship as I find it difficult to eat anything in the early morning, and had to drink a litre of water, which is quite a lot.

The drive to the hospital was the longest trip I have taken since lockdown started. I noted that those who were up and about were mainly athletic types: joggers, cyclists, Nordic pole walkers, a couple of people doing yoga stretches. Not very many cars. The car park at the hospital which was full the last time I visited there was basically empty.

Southmead was recently modernised and is a strange place. One extremely long main building for most treatments: it is like an airport, with locations labelled 'Gates' and a lot of coffee shops and other facilities among the gates. Usually there is a little trolley-train which takes the infirm to stations at the far end, but it wasn't operating yesterday. In fact there was none of the hustle and bustle which typifies any hospital I have spent time in. It was strangely empty, with a handful of maintenance staff and a smattering of patients. But the bizarre thing was how different it was from my visits to the surgery. There was no attempt to keep anybody out, nobody in the concourse wore a mask or other protective clothing except one elderly patient. Anybody could have walked in! Whereas the surgery was plastered with KEEP OUT notices.

I had to go to Gate 19 for radiology. It was accessed by a lift and when I reached the desk there was a notice two metres away telling us to stand behind it. I did, but some of the other patients ignored it and went up to the desk. The reception nurse did wear a mask, as did the others, but there was no attempt to make us patients wear a mask or use hand sanitiser.

The radiologist did wear mask, gloves and coverall when I got into the scanner unit. I have had one before and it is a painless operation apart from the injection of dye which makes you feel you have wet yourself – a weird sensation. After the litre of water I did need a wee by the time the exercise was over. The cannula was removed and then it was back home. I passed Waitrose and there was a long but very orderly queue well spaced out and looped back along the street.

SARDOMIKE
Sunday 26 April 2020

Our big moment was my visit to the Marsden Cancer Hospital in London. My sister, who drove, and I were like little children out for a treat! She was not allowed in the hospital, but parking in London has never been easier, lots of spaces and no traffic wardens, so were able to park in a side road almost opposite the hospital.

Surprisingly, few members of staff were wearing masks, and no social distancing. Where I came into contact with a receptionist there were markings on the floor, and the Dr. who dealt with me sat 2mt. away wearing a mask. I'm now on tablets to reduce my PSA and others to counteract the bad effects etc. I have to return on 7th May to check I'm ok on this new regime.

Funerals were another example. Unlike weddings, they were permitted to continue throughout lockdowns and the pandemic. They were, however, carried out with a difference, albeit with restrictions. The Royal London (2020) National Funeral Cost Index Report highlighted a survey showing how, due to restrictions on travel and the number of people allowed to be present at gatherings, three in five mourners arranging funerals after March 2020 said they had had to cut back on plans. This proportion rose to some 70 per cent among those aged over 55 years. Several diarists had attended funerals over the period of the project, usually online but occasionally in person. Such events are important status passages (Glaser and Strauss, 1971) that mark key points in the life course. It appeared that the essential elements of these rituals had been largely retained.

ELEANOR
Monday 22 June 2020

My daughters and I decided to watch E's funeral [online] separately as we weren't sure how each of us would feel about it. It was all beautifully done and despite the distanced involvement, it was moving and I did feel involved, following the prayers and joining in with the hymn, 'Morning Has Broken'.

There was no black and yellow tape and the 25 allowed congregation were able to sit comfortably and socially distanced in the sun-filled chapel. One daughter said afterwards that it was easier to imagine ourselves there as we had all attended E's wife's funeral less than two years ago. My son-in-law said that the hardest thing was being unable to hug and comfort each other.

I hope now that we can all breathe a little and take some time to look to ourselves and our families, knowing that E is at peace. In a strange way, I think that the lockdown restrictions may help us all to do that as social mobility is still limited and we can still shelter ourselves from the wider world. Will we experience delayed reactions once lockdown is over? At the moment, for me, grief becomes an almost impersonal part of our current surreal existence.

JENNIFER
Friday 10 July 2020

This week has been difficult and I have felt very exhausted after our trip to Leamington Spa on Monday for my friend's funeral. We had boxes of masks and gloves in the car, wipes and hand sanitiser plus flasks of tea and sandwiches. We wore masks in the car and I sat in the back. We wore a new mask in the ceremony (we were the only people wearing masks) and a new mask for the journey back. I also wore gloves. We set off really early as I was worried there would be huge amounts of new traffic on the road. My daughter is a great driver and we didn't hit any jams (although there was a very long one on the M5 going the other way). We got there an hour early so that was fine. The crematorium was located in some beautiful woods so we had a lovely walk before eating a sandwich. Fortunately there was a loo available! but no waiting inside. The cortege got stuck in a traffic jam coming from Coventry so the ceremony was late starting. So many stunning flowers arrived for her – absolutely gorgeous. My friend was Swedish so several people including her daughters wore blue and yellow.

In the chapel, the chairs were set out at a distance – there were no more than 18 of us there in all. There was a celebrant who told the story of her life. Friends, including me, read out tributes that we had written to her. Lovely music – she loved jazz. Her ex-husband arrived late! And her daughters spoke beautifully about her. The whole ceremony was on Zoom so people in Sweden could watch and my other daughter was able to see it too. I am really glad we went.

In many other ways too, things were being done differently. The shopping experience was much commented upon, with supermarkets and other outlets in public spaces frequently restricting numbers and marking out safe distances between customers. This could be interpreted as a semblance of rational decision-making in the face of uncertainty. Nonetheless, dangers and anomalies remained, as remarked upon by Fisherman.

FISHERMAN
Friday 15 May 2020

After lunch drove to the pharmacy to collect my prescribed medication and, on return, called into the local Co-op for some items. Long delay on the outside queue, shopped, then attended the checkout. Cashier behind perspex screen and wearing mask and gloves. When passing the basket with groceries through to her she returned the plastic bag to me, saying that it could be infected? I queried this because I had handled that in the same way as all the goods I was purchasing and, as she was wearing gloves, she should be OK and I was the person taking the risk? Anyway, rested on the bed on my return, meal, TV, bed.

FISHERMAN
Monday 8 June 2020

I went shopping in Tesco for groceries, which was fine until I reached the checkout. My purchases were on the conveyor, being recorded by the cashier when he sneezed. He belatedly buried his nose in his sleeve but I was not impressed and waited for some time before going to his end of the conveyor to pay. I mentioned the incident to my partner when I got home and she donned some gloves and wiped containers with disinfectant, and fresh items with soapy water, whilst I put the empty bags etc. in the shed. Then I washed my hands thoroughly. It's very easy to become paranoid at the moment.

Many other examples of change to everyday activities were also reported. Sometimes these were rules and restrictions imposed by agencies and organisations, sometimes they were the outcome of personal agency on the part of diarists, and sometimes they were a combination of the two. In some instances the external changes were for behaviours enacted at home. The following varied examples are illustrative. Daily life was affected from top to bottom.

APPLETREE
Tuesday 28 July 2020

Dropped into Oxfam bookshop on the way having phoned beforehand. They'll only accept up to 12 books at the moment as they have to be quarantined. Overheard the volunteer asking if they have to go and wipe a book or quarantine it if a browser has picked it up. Mercifully, no.

ATHELSTANA
Wednesday 9 July 2020

The long-awaited hair appointment arrived today and quite a relaxed experience despite the Covid secure measures in place. Mine is only a small hairdressing salon with two stylists, a family concern. Visors were worn and for only the second time did I find myself wearing a face mask. The only real differences were in procedures like waiting to be allowed entry, hanging your own coat and following the floor markings whilst every time a new seat was used it was immediately wiped down afterwards and towels and gowns washed after each use. … There was only the annual rise in the cost of treatments which was limited to £1 which I thought was rather fair considering the outlay involved for extra gowns and towels, not to mention the purchase of a washing machine on the premises and the general loss of income over the lockdown.

BAREFOOT DOC
Wednesday 6 May 2020

It was a grey day and chilly, and the same-as-every-other shopping mall was empty save for a small queue outside M&S. It was WH Smith, in an empty roofed avenue, that gave me a jolt. I was peckish and decided to have a bar of something to snack on as I drove back to Brighton thro the spring woodlands and verges. Chocolate bars were near the front of the store, I chose what I wanted, looked to pay. There were no staff to hand, and a self-serve till next the exit. I scanned my chocolate, waved my contactless card over the machine, re-entered the empty avenue. It felt like a scene in some 80s post-holocaust sci fi movie, where all the humans have been wiped out and only robots continue dutifully to serve until they rust into stasis. I was shocked to find myself inhabiting, in the live flow of my perception, what had been merely a dystopian future of earlier imagination. It took some minutes to shed the feeling of a bad dream, and see ordinary Sunday-emptied grey streets again, in a town of commuter offices and homes that once, before my time, beat with a marketplace- and courthouse-centred pulse.

BARKLEY
Saturday 28 March 2020

Around 8.15 am I took the dog out for his morning walk. Being a Saturday, I thought the park might be busier than during the week, but it wasn't – it was quite a lot quieter. … There were a couple of people in the park I know, and one of them pointed out that there was a notice next to the park entrance saying that dogs should now be kept on a lead while in the park. Feeling suitably chastened, I grabbed the dog and hastily put him on the lead. Three laps and back home.

BEA
Sunday 5 April 2020

I watched virtual mass from the cathedral. I had an edict from the Parish to say that if we attended virtual mass we should not do it lolling on the sofa in our pyjamas ... As if! Standards ... standards.

BONANZA BILL
Sunday 5 April 2020

Now here's a funny one that has come up as a result of the coronavirus lockdown. I need to take a Speed Awareness Test for a speeding offence. Under normal circumstances, you attend a training session at a venue in the local area. Because of Covid-19, these courses are now being run as virtual sessions. I booked to go on the course and it was only when I received the confirmation email that I realised I do not have all the equipment required to take part in a virtual session. You need a mic and a camera as well as downloading the Microsoft Teams app. I tried to get through today (Sunday) to chat to the team as advertised only to discover the Drivetech offices are closed. I am not particularly techno-savvy, cannot ask anyone to come in and help me because of social distancing, yet have to complete the course before 15th August. What happens if I cannot attend a physical course by that date or cannot get the help I need to do the course online??

CHARLES
Friday 12 June 2020

Yesterday we had the car serviced. A week or so before lockdown the garage had said the car needed a recall to do with the seat belts. We were going to take it in but as the day came nearer we got scared of going out and cancelled. A routine service and the MOT had fallen due a month ago so we agreed to do that, the recall and the MOT in one go.

The garage was quite well organised. Arrows on the floor, 2-metre markings, but staff walking around without face masks and the receptionist also maskless. Although I had a mask with me I decided not to wear it. Peer pressure I suppose! They have far fewer staff than before as the receptionist also went and fetched the car and emerged from it, now with a mask on, having removed a plastic sleeve from the steering wheel to avoid virus transfer.

MABEL
Tuesday 7 April 2020

A notice has emerged on a gate on our local walk saying 'Do not touch gate with your hands'. We have been being very careful with this for a while now, taking kitchen towel to touch any fastenings that we can't avoid, but otherwise using our feet where possible, or another part of the covered body, to push gates open and shut. We have watched other people's actions. Some seem to take no precautions but open and close gates much as they have ever done. But others are consciously using their clothed wrists, feet or protection on their hands.

WARRENER
Tuesday 21 April 2020
And also after boxing up five bottles of Heineken for the bin men. We've taken to putting some bottles of beer on top of the bins to show our appreciation. It's so true that this crisis has demonstrated who and what are the *really* essential services. It's as though all the flab and soft stuff has been stripped away and what we now see is the skeleton, the structure that holds us all together, off which everything else hangs.

Pragmatic adaptation abounded. Diarists had quickly adjusted to the new situation, both cognitively and behaviourally, and used their personal agency to determine their own reactions. Humour and stoicism were also in abundance.

The rules – what they say and what they mean

Rules are rules, or are they? There has been much public debate about compliance with COVID-19 regulations and how much it really matters. Are there extenuating circumstances which render the rules breakable? Witness the case of Dominic Cummings and his trip to Durham with his family and the uproar it caused (see Chapter 3). But perhaps some transgressions are worse than others. Certainly an Ipsos Mori poll during May 2020 found differing levels of acceptability (Buck, 2020). For instance, while roughly equal numbers in the survey thought that going out for more than two hours to exercise, or going out in the car to relax, was or was not acceptable, there was much greater condemnation of other forms of rule-breaking. Thus 73 per cent of those asked regarded letting a cleaner into the house as not acceptable and 68 and 57 per cent, respectively, thought similarly about friends or family over 70 looking after children, and socialising with friends and family in the garden. In other words, a still considerable minority considered some restrictions to be negotiable.

Other studies have enlarged on these findings. Data from the Office for National Statistics, for example, suggested that age may affect the likelihood to break lockdown rules (Swerling, 2020). In particular, it was found that, by November 2020, physical contact indoors with at least one other person not in the same household was most commonly reported as acceptable by those aged 50 to 69 years (25 per cent) and least commonly by the 70s and over (17 per cent). There was a suggestion that the pull of families was, for many, a stronger pressure than the requirement to comply with rules. This thesis gained some support from a later smaller survey carried out for *The Observer* in March 2021 which found that a quarter of parents in England were planning to break lockdown rules to take their children to visit their grandmothers for Mother's Day (Ferguson, 2021).

As the entries so far suggest, diarists had their own opinions about how they should react to the coronavirus pandemic, and what was and was not acceptable behaviour. For their own part, and in the main, they based their views on whether or not they thought their actions would put them at risk from COVID-19. However, they commonly reported how this was an area in which there was considerable individual variation. Pragmatic decision-making extended beyond deciding what precautions to apply to deciding which rules and restrictions not to follow.

STANLEY
Saturday 27 June 2020

So lockdown is coming to an end. Looking at the news I think for many people it's already over. The country seems to be divided into three groups, those who think it's over and life is back to normal, those who will go with the flow, and those who are still very worried, not to say terrified, and will not leave their safe environment any time soon. There is a lot of the latter down here in Cornwall. If they had enough barbed wire they'd have a barrier along the natural barrier of the Tamar River. My beloved and I belong in the middle group, we'll do a bit more of what we enjoy doing but won't be dashing off to any beaches any time soon. Interestingly we were going to do some retail therapy in Plymouth but decided not to as there were no cafés etc. open and we realised that half the pleasure in going shopping was sitting at a table outside a café watching the world go by. The result of many foreign holidays on the continent got us into the *Café und Kuchen* culture. I don't think we'll be taking any foreign holidays soon. I think life will just carry on.

Most diarists cited something or another that they had done over the period of the pandemic that was not strictly in line with the rules and restrictions. They mentioned social distancing that was forgotten, having seven people for lunch when only six were permitted, going for more than one walk a day, engineering an apparently chance meeting with a friend, going inside somebody else's house, taking someone to hospital, having family bring food and medicines, failing to wear a mask, and much more. In many instances these were their own pragmatic assessments and adaptations. They were usually, however, adhering to the purpose of the rule and were fully able to justify their own decisions. This calls to mind Wittgenstein (1953) who posited that the meaning of rules is dependent on how they are applied. Grasping a rule does not necessarily mean attributing a single interpretation to that rule. Although his account was essentially tied into language and the understanding of individual words and phrases, there is a clear parallel with his position and the way some diarists adhered to the reasoning behind a rule rather than to its precise wording. It could be seen as perfectly legitimate to exceed an hour's walk or to fail to wear a mask in certain circumstances, as well as to 'break' rules where there seemed good reason.

BONANZA BILL
Thursday 4 June 2020

I have taken a fairly relaxed approach towards the lockdown. I do not want to contract the disease, it is true, but I guess I switched off slightly at the beginning when everyone over 70 was told that they were vulnerable and should isolate. I could not see why just because of my age, I should be any more vulnerable than someone a lot younger than myself who suffered from specific health conditions such as obesity, diabetes or heart disease. I have seen people in person, attempting to keep a social distance, and have travelled a little within my area. I have even taken my first trip on public transport. I accept that I may therefore be at an increased risk of getting the virus but the balance of risk seems to weigh in favour of trying to lead as normal a life as possible whilst taking basic precautions. For example, I have been to the supermarket every morning to get *The Times* which has been a godsend and picked up any shopping needed at the same time. This has given a focus to the morning and helped me to feel connected. Who knows, it may prove my undoing but I am willing to take the risk. Am I a serial rebel?

EVE
Friday 1 May 2020

In addition to the discussion of the book, people were sharing some of their transgressions of the lockdown for example by visiting elderly parents in their homes or taking care of their grandchildren. We were justifying these 'interpretations' of the rules on the basis that it was reasonably safe and prioritised the well-being of the people we were relating to which I think is a reasonable justification.

PEN
Sunday 21 June 2020

Question: does a conservatory or garden room with open doors and windows count as outside? Probably, though I wouldn't want to justify it.

ROSA
Monday 1 June 2020

It is a peculiar situation for all of us, going in to watch the Coronavirus News at 5 pm. One of the Cabinet addresses us each evening and gives us their latest decisions on the rules of our lives with the virus. How far can we walk from our houses? Can we drive our cars? Will the shops open (other than food shops)? What can shielded people do? Are we to be allowed out of our houses? Will the voluntary groups continue to shop for those of us who are not to go into shops? The government essentially dictates the latest rules at these 5 o'clock moments.

Then people interpret what we have been told.

In any case, as the diarists amply illustrated throughout the project, there was much confusion about the rules. They had changed so often that it was hard to keep up. The introduction of bubbles and tiers only served to increase the difficulty of remaining current. There were also many anomalies besetting the restrictions. It was easy to get lost in the detail.

SUSIEQ
Monday 11 May 2020

Did we obey or break the law and if so, which law, which country?

First we went to a garden nursery in Shropshire that has only pretended to close and filled up with petunias and fuchsias (which will all have to be hardened off). Driving in Shropshire is okay, but we should have been doing so to exercise. The garden nursery should have been closed and our journey was hardly essential. From there we went to a garden centre just over the border in Wales. Fine if we were travelling from within Wales but possibly not because we were travelling from England. But at least the garden centre was legally open. Bought many of the items on my planting list for delivery later this week, not known when.

Negotiations are commonplace in all areas of life (Strauss, 1978) and were clearly evident amid the lockdowns and restrictions of the pandemic. Diarists were negotiating with the rules, with themselves as they used their personal agency to make sense of the situation they found themselves in, and through their social interactions. Their adaptations were pragmatic and individual.

Summary

The new order brought expectations of acceptable behaviour. In some cases this was mandated by law, such as social distancing, wearing masks, and restrictions on encounters in homes and gardens. Most diarists were generally compliant with the formal restrictions, even though almost everybody admitted to some counter behaviour at some time. In other respects, diarists and others were required to make their own assessments of risk and decide on their own precautions. Uncertainty about the presence and transmission of the virus prevailed and diarists responded variously, either largely discounting risk from everyday objects or adopting stringent measures to ensure they were virus free. Institutional change took place as well. Hospital and medical services, for instance, were still functioning for conditions other than COVID-19, but were doing so differently. Funerals could still go ahead, but these had moved online for the majority of mourners. And shopping had become a different experience, as had almost everything else. These changed circumstances called for widespread and pragmatic adaptation.

Dealing with the pesky virus could be onerous but it was one of the necessities of the pandemic. Diarists could, nonetheless, point to many positive aspects of their new life-world. The clouds and silver linings are considered in the next chapter.

7
Clouds and silver linings

The coronavirus pandemic was a time of contradictions and mixed emotions for the diarists. There was an uneasy juxtaposition between their own daily and often peaceful lives, that involved generally positive communications with those known to them, and the illness, anguish and suffering further afield. In a sense they experienced what Festinger (1957) termed cognitive dissonance. As outlined earlier (see Chapter 4), they recognised that everyone was not 'in it together'. They might be alright themselves but things were not okay everywhere else.

Clouds and silver linings could, moreover, be inextricably linked. The restrictions on freedom, for instance, gave licence to staying at home to relax, while the inability to meet family and friends gave rise to enjoyable activities on Zoom and increased camaraderie within the local community. The closure of hospitality venues led many to a new or renewed interest in experimenting with foods and recipes, while the banning of all but essential car journeys encouraged walking and an appreciation of the local environment. In many ways the adaptations made by diarists went a long way to compensating for their previous taken-for-granted activities. Not all, but many, clouds had silver linings.

This chapter considers the ups and downs engendered by the rules and restrictions in relation to remaining in households, keeping in touch with non-present family and friends, the absence of many taken-for-granted aspects of daily life, the obligation to stay close to home, and cancelled celebrations.

Households together

At the onset of the pandemic, there had been a small window when everyone could decide where they would live during lockdown and with whom. The implication was that they would then be confined to close face-to-face contact only with other members of their chosen household. There were 21 diarists who lived on their own during this period, with the rest living with a husband, wife or live-in partner or, occasionally, an adult child or another person living in the same building.

How did relationships fare when partners were locked down together? One study carried out from UCL (Zilanawala et al, 2020) suggested that almost one in five people across the age span said their relationship with a partner had suffered over the first four months of the initial lockdown. Nonetheless, breakdowns in relationships were most common among younger groups and rarer among those aged 60 years or more. Another study (Bellotti et al, 2021) carried out a survey of almost 1,000 people in the UK and reached similar conclusions. Again, almost one in five respondents living with a partner reported a deterioration in their relationship during the initial lockdown. However, on the other hand, about half said that relationships within their household had got better over the same period. No breakdowns by age were given by the researchers.

Most diarists reported little impact of the pandemic on their relationship, and a considerable number specifically said it had improved or consolidated how they were getting on with partners. Some negotiations had been required (Melville and Wilkinson, 2020) but these seemed generally minor. Marriages or partnerships had usually stood the test of time, and couples had often become used to spending more time together if they were both already retired. Diarists also had the advantage of spacious living conditions, often with private gardens, which meant they could be together or apart, as they chose.

FRANCIA
Saturday 27 June 2020

So has there been any change in the relationship between my husband and myself? After nearly 51 years, we are still the best of friends despite the lockdown. I am extremely fortunate in being married to a trustworthy, caring and considerate person. We have differing interests but we have the same principles. Our different interests have been mostly curtailed for the moment but the lockdown has meant we have spent far more time together but this has been a joy. We have walked together, gardened together and most importantly of all, laughed together. I would say, however, that my husband is now playing golf again and it is nice to have the house to myself occasionally!

GATZOU
Wednesday 29 April 2020

Personally, I am enjoying this lockdown ... and we get on better with H. He is much more relaxed. I now cook for both of us all of the time, something which had gone down drastically in the last few years. Mostly because our times did not coincide. He seems to be enjoying my cooking. It has to be hot though where I am more of a salad person but anyway, I made some compromises and he has too. He has also put some hooks where I wanted them ... (they had been waiting in my drawer for years). He does not know but I have bought some more.

HOLLY
Thursday 4 June 2020

In more normal times, my husband and I do quite a lot together but also quite a lot apart. ... Being in lockdown for the past almost three months, has brought us together in the space of the house and garden more. ... Some things have stayed the same (e.g. time apart in our work rooms) but we've been thrown together on each other's and our joint resources more somehow. One result of this, I think, is that there's been more of a focusing down on each other – we've been showing more interest in each other and we've been making more of an effort to get the very best out of each other. We're pretty interested in each other anyway but it's a bit more distilled right now. I spoke to one of my women friends about this and she said that something similar has happened to her and her partner.

HUMPHREY
Sunday 28 June 2020

As for the answer to the personal question, part of the reason why I feel so smug is that I not only enjoy so many benefits (health, wealth and happiness) but most of all I have a wife whom I love, who is my best friend and who despite being nearly my age, I still think of as attractive and sexy. So, no problems there. Indeed, it has been a rather cosy time.

There were, however, some admissions of how lockdowns could spark occasional arguments between partners.

BARKLEY
Sunday 21 June 2020

Just before we went to bed we had a row – the first one we've had since lockdown began. As usual, it was over something trivial, but the underlying issues weren't. One of these issues was to do with the fact that during this lockdown period I have become more distant and inward looking. I'm sure this is to do with the repetitive nature of daily life under lockdown. Our routine is quite rigid, and I feel I have become more robotic and ritualistic. If I wasn't aware of it before, I am now.

Nonetheless, it was only in a small number of cases that diarists acknowledged more serious strains in their relationship exacerbated by the lockdowns. These seemed to stem from disagreements over the government's handling of the pandemic, clashes over the television programmes to watch, and other matters relating to everyday life. There was some suggestion that discord might be more likely in relationships with pre-existing tensions.

The pandemic could also have an impact on relationships with non-live-in partners. The following diary entries are illustrative.

BAREFOOT DOC
Thursday 2 April 2020

I'm tired. Time to stop. Frustrated not to have moved my work forward as I really needed to. Pleased to have sat in comfort in the park with a sense of the long span of the place I first came to live in 50 years ago. Pissed off that my lover seems unable to get into a video hook-up with me, when she's spent hours in Zoom and WhatsApp, dancing and gossiping.

HOLGATE
Friday 26 June 2020

I have seen my partner twice since mid-March and I think that has been OK. We have been meeting at National Trust gardens! Both of us are relatively self-sufficient independent people and I think we best operate not living together. The 'lockdown' has been a bit of a test, but we seem to have come through it reasonably well.

OTTOLIE
Friday 15 May 2020

Walked to see partner through buttercup meadows, as usual with shopping and to sit three metres away and see if he is well. We have not even held hands for ten weeks.

For diarists with live-in partners, the pandemic seemed much more likely to consolidate than disrupt relationships, even if there could be minor disagreements.

Staying in touch

Almost all diarists had children and grandchildren outside their households and these were commonly missed the most during the early stages of the pandemic. This confirmed the findings of a Statista survey (Stewart, 2020) carried out during May 2020 in the United Kingdom which found that around two thirds of the respondents said that they missed seeing family and friends more than anything else. Diarists wrote about wanting to be able to do things together, help and support each other, and maintain and cement relationships. Several had never been able to hold their new grandchildren and, for many, the pandemic interrupted regular taken-for-granted grandparenting duties.

JACCA
Sunday 26 April 2020

Although we have not always got on, my sister, she is the person I would most like to see. She is my closest family member and this crisis has really brought that into focus. There are probably very good psychological as well as social reasons that families get together for weddings and funerals. I feel I need the continuity and blood ties of family now more than ever. I am relieved though that I don't have parents or children to worry about. If my mother was alive at this time, I would have had to break all rules to get to her to look after her. I simply would not be able to bear her vulnerability.

PEN
Sunday 12 April 2020

So really the only downside of our life at the moment is not being able to mix with the rest of the family. We used to have the grandchildren for Secret Breakfast at the weekend (excessive carbs, normally forbidden). It was a time to catch up with what they were up to … films, books, friends etc. Now feeling rather cut off, but they are obviously having a wonderful time.

PETER
Tuesday 7 April 2020

Woke to find my wife in tears this morning, watching the latest video of our grandson. She rarely expresses emotion through tears. I think the pressure of tears had grown to the extent that a burst was inevitable. I'm glad it happened, though not glad about the circumstances that caused it.

Keeping in touch to share experiences and views was also important for maintaining a perspective not completely dominated by news and government updates. Indeed, as described earlier (see Chapter 5), practically everyone had adapted to become 'terminal selves' (Gottschalk, 2021) and, in the main, kept in touch via Zoom or other means. They initiated enjoyable and creative activities and some reported being in more regular contact than in pre-pandemic times. The availability of modern technology provided the means to see and communicate with family and friends. It was the best they could do in the circumstances and diarists tended to accept the new restrictions with a good measure of stoicism.

HATTIE
Sunday 26 April 2020

As my Edinburgh daughter said today, better to miss seeing relatives for several weeks than never to see them again.

Nonetheless, virtual meetings were not the same as physical contact, and many diarists told how they longed for hugs. Indeed a survey carried out by Demos in May 2021 found that a quarter of their sample said they had not been hugged for over a year (Swerling, 2021). According to Bloom &

Wild (Nazir, 2021), an online florist whose sales doubled over the pandemic, bouquets of flowers had come to be viewed as 'substitute hugs'.

ARAMINTA
Friday 17 April 2020
I mentioned in an email to my niece that although I was fine I could sure do with a hug. Next thing I know is she's put on FB that I could do with a hug, and lots of my family and friends have sent me hugs. It did actually warm my heart although I was embarrassed that she did this.

CHARLES
Thursday 16 April 2020
What I miss most is the possibility of a hug with friends and family. Of all the forms of social interaction I like a good hug the most. I would happily break the rules to have a good hug with someone I care about and who cares about me. But I know I can't and I won't, because a hug is spontaneous and I would have to ask permission, which would probably be denied, and that would only makes things worse!

FRANCES
Monday 27 April 2020
The new more recent innovation of kissing on both cheeks with all and sundry – even on first acquaintance with people you've never met before – is one I will be very happy to ban. But I hope that with close friends and family a bear hug with faces averted will become acceptable again – someday!

ROB
Friday 22 May 2020
I have begun … even in my limited way … to miss human touch … I really would like a hug from someone … Anyone … The cats help … But it's not the same is it??? I can't begin to imagine how grandparents of young kids must be feeling.

Friendships were also important to almost all diarists during the pandemic, many of whom reported increased contact to check up on how they were doing. Often they felt helpless and concerned they could not offer the support they would like to for those who, for example, were ill, had cancelled operations, were isolated, or were unable to go online. Many kept in touch through Zoom (and other forms of social media) and telephone calls.

APRIL
Retrospective: Thursday 16 April 2020
Most worrying are friends my age who live alone, are not very healthy, and have no family near. Who will look after them? The first few days of this

house arrest the phone was constantly ringing with worried friends about what was going to happen and how they would cope. This has slowed down to occasional calls just checking up on each other.

JENNIFER
Tuesday 16 June 2020

At the beginning of lockdown, I contacted most of my friends to see how they were doing including some friends abroad. In some cases, I have maintained more contact than usual, in others it has lapsed somewhat. I can't say I have made more or new social contacts. I have certainly maintained contact with existing friends on a regular basis.

With extra time to spare, and in addition to maintaining current friendships during the pandemic, there was much restoring and strengthening of older relationships, with messages sent and received 'out-of-the-blue'. Several mentioned how it was particularly comforting to talk to long-standing friends.

ELISABETH
Thursday 7 May 2020

I have just telephoned the person I have known longest in my life. A friend I met when I was 18 who remained a friend until around 20 years ago when he moved further out of London and I moved west. We haven't spoken for about four years but it was as if we still met up every week. ... This sort of thing makes you think about the friends you have lost touch with and should make an effort to re-contact. It was perhaps easier to be mutually supportive.

JACCA
Sunday 26 April 2020

I have a monthly Zoom with another circle of friends from early school life. We have seen each other possibly four or five times in 40 years and are now communicating monthly with emails in between. It doesn't seem too strange. We are essentially the same people we were as teenagers but with a whole different life experience. I feel seen and cared about and connected in a way that I would probably find uncomfortable in the flesh. ... It's particularly tough for people going through traumas alone and in a way the fact that the lockdown has in a way made us all isolated makes it easier to have these supportive sometimes very emotional online exchanges.

The clouds of isolation from family and friends were thus tempered by the silver linings afforded by Zoom and other means of communication that allowed interactions to continue, albeit in new ways. There were many instances where interpersonal contact appeared even more intensive and extensive than in previous times. There was also some compensation gained from the increased neighbourliness and community togetherness (see Chapter 4). Diarists were among those to adapt creatively to the new life-world.

Losses and gains

Quite apart from face-to-face interactions with family and friends, many other things previously taken for granted became out of bounds during the lockdowns and restrictions. While generally accepting and stoic, diarists reflected on what they particularly missed. Beyond human company and touch, they commonly mentioned haircuts, open-air and televised sport, dentistry, travel, singing, and cultural activities. There was also a wish to be spontaneous, and to be stimulated by the company and conversation of others. And to have things to plan for and look forward to. The little things were important too.

ANNA
Saturday 11 July 2020

What am I most missing? It is making plans. Planning excursions, holidays, visiting. I love having plans of that sort to look forward to. Even jaunts in the car with someone I can trust to be 'safe'.

BEA
Thursday 16 April 2020

Yesterday I found homes for another 23 plants. While I was out in the yard I realised how much I was missing the chiming of the town hall clock. It chimes the hours and marks the quarters, with one chime for quarter past the hour, two for half past and three for quarter to the hour. It stopped at 9.05 on 29th March. ... It is the little things that you miss.

HUMPHREY
Saturday 2 May 2020

I call friends, particularly those on their own, but all of us are running out of conversation or rather interesting conversation. Already I am conscious of repeating myself even in this diary. ... It's the lack of meeting others that encourages me to this idleness. I have always thought by talking. How does one think when there is only one person to talk to, stimulating though she is? I need someone who disagrees heartily with whatever I come up with.

JULES
Friday 10 July 2020

What do I miss most about the lockdown? Very little. I think the chief thing, on reflection, is the lack of freedom to do anything spontaneous. To be able to say at 6 pm – 'let's go to the pub for a meal tonight; it's a lovely evening' without being 'stopped and searched' for personal details and then herded to some distanced table with perspex down the middle and generally made to feel like a leper. I know it's necessary but normal it isn't.

Of course, not everything that diarists had previously taken for granted was enjoyable or even as important to them as they might have expected. An important human characteristic is the ability to adapt and embrace change. There were certainly things that diarists did not miss, even if it surprised them. For some, not having to commute, or having a good excuse not to attend events and gatherings, could be another silver lining.

BARKLEY
Thursday 4 June 2020

And I'd say one of the main things I've learnt is that I'd never have believed I could go for so long without going out in the evening and not missing it that much. Mind you, as soon as we feel it's safe to do so, we'll be down the pub again like a shot.

BENCHMAN
Thursday 18 June 2020

I have done nothing myself about playing bridge online. I suppose that if pressed to do so, I might accept an invitation but I wouldn't want to do it during daylight hours (the dog would not tolerate my being occupied for three hours at a stretch) and during the evenings I am generally too tired. Strange how two of what used to be my chief leisure activities – bridge and singing – now have no place at all in my life.

JANWIG
Friday 22 May 2020

So yes, I'm sustained by work, by gardening, cycling, dog walking, neighbourliness, nature, birds, growing veg, and I am happy with shrunken horizons in a way I would never have thought possible.

RAIN
Wednesday 8 July 2020

What has been amplified in me is the tendency to think a lot and stay around the house. I have not missed going shopping or finding new things. Although I had thought that, in different times, I might have replaced my hairdryer which packed up (after 40 years). But I can manage without. Or I might have taken my sewing machine in for service/repair, but I can manage without. And it would be nice to have more fabric patches to range and stitch into greetings cards, but I can manage without by using the bought card store for greetings. If times had been different I might have walked into town to buy food, and bumped into someone while I was out, and had a chat. But everything is being delivered. I might have arranged an outing to visit somewhere with friends, but going in separate cars doesn't make sense. I am as reticent as ever about initiating everyday meetings up although I am positive when others suggest it. ... So I do feel trapped by inertia, which has been amplified.

The removal of many social obligations meant that individuals could restructure their time. Diarists found many ways to occupy themselves, whether it was doing jobs they considered useful, being creative, engaging in hobbies, interacting with others in whatever way possible, or something else entirely (see Chapter 5). There were many compensations.

GRACE
Saturday 12 July 2020
However there has been much I have enjoyed – the feeling of a 1950s' world and appreciation of quiet, clean air, wildlife enjoying freedom, families walking and playing together.

LYNNE
Sunday 19 July 2020
The main silver lining to lockdown for many, myself included, was possibly about just having more time, whether or not we did anything especially productive or novel with it, but again that was associated with the concept that lockdown itself was time-limited.

OLIVE
Monday 8 June 2020
One positive thing which has emerged from the current context is a recognition of the preciousness of simple human encounters. My experience is that people now make more of an effort to connect in circumstances where distance is imposed.

Other matters that might be seen as relatively minor in the greater scheme of things warranted mention in diaries. Quite normal occurrences could become exciting after a prolonged period of restrictions and staying at home. The arrival of a window cleaner merited an entry in several diaries as did the return of the cleaner after a period of enforced self-help. Gaining refunds from cancelled holidays and travel, the return of live sport, and greater freedoms to go out and resume previous sporting and other activities, were also noteworthy. Issues with cars were commonplace. Disuse for many weeks led to flat batteries, but services and MOTs continued nonetheless. And, of course, there were numerous problems with computers and telephones.

Further noteworthy events were more personal and individual. These included a letter published in *The Guardian*, finding an old letter card from an ex, winning a small amount on the Premium Bonds, watching a cat catch a rat, a first flowering in ten years, putting the duvet cover on inside out, intimidating behaviour from a 'particularly nasty dog owner who recently served a 12-month court order banning him from the park', a dead body in the local river, helping neighbours heave an enormous outdoor bed over their fence as it was too big to go through their house, a local cannabis factory back in action, theft from doorsteps, problems with submitting tax returns, unidentified bleeping at night which turned out to be an absent neighbour's alarm system, outside doors that would not lock, and viewing the supermoon.

In some instances, diarists attributed the impact of incidents directly to lockdown. Often these were seen as a relief from the daily monotony of their restricted lives. Small matters could acquire disproportionate importance.

BONANZA BILL
Sunday 3 May 2020

Yesterday my partner lost his specs, presumably after falling while taking a photo on the edge of the Thames. We could not be bothered to go back and check yesterday but decided to take a long shot and see if we could find them. We got to the spot where we thought they might have dropped and there they were! Such are the little joys of the lockdown.

CHARLES
Saturday 16 May 2020

Last night my wife dropped a pair of scissors down the side of our sofa. The sofa converts into a bed for when all the children come to stay so there are considerable workings underneath. We could not find the scissors last night. We tried again this morning and still no sign. A few minutes ago we had another look and finally found they had dropped into a box-like void which cannot be reached from the top and is stitched at the bottom. Impasse! Unpicking the sofa underneath is the only way, but it is so heavy that we are not sure we can tip it over so that unpicking is possible!!

These are the kind of events that give some kind of strange relief from the monotony of lockdown. Here was first of all a puzzle to be solved, then a technical challenge to overcome. Before lockdown we would probably have said, not to worry, let's just buy another pair of scissors. Now we were determined to overcome all difficulties to solve the puzzle and succeed in the challenge!

OLIVE
Thursday 21 May 2020

Today we forgot to put out the recycling bin! They're only collected every two weeks, and it's full to overflowing. We remembered yesterday, but had forgotten again. It's not that unusual – forgetting to put out the bin. We're usually a bit frustrated, but have a laugh and that's it. This time felt different. We were both slightly on the verge of hysteria as we ran down the garden path to find the bins had already been emptied. We very nearly blamed each other, but held back just in time. Nonetheless an atmosphere prevailed as we began our morning walk. It eventually dissipated as we reached the estuary, and perspective returned with the familiar view. It did strike me, though, that for those who don't have such an outlet, small irritations can become magnified when people are in each other's company so constantly.

While the pandemic led to losses, there were compensations too. There was more time to spend on old or new interests, and there was a valid excuse to abandon certain earlier obligations. Many everyday occurrences also took on a new significance, often becoming linked to the pandemic in one way or another. These were unusual times.

'Environmental citizens'

The instruction to most people to stay at home apart from daily forays for exercise or other essential activities was, initially at least, a pandemic cloud. It led to innumerable cancellations of activities and plans, and forbade diarists from meeting non-household family members, partners and friends. But an important silver lining was commonly mentioned in diary entries, and this was the good weather. According to the Met Office at the beginning of June 2020, May had been the sunniest calendar month on record (Madge, 2020). Following the wettest February on record for England and Wales overall, it had also been the driest May since 1884 with very little rainfall and much parched ground.

The wonderful warm sunny days during the first lockdown attracted frequent comments on how it made lockdown more bearable and affected mood and energy levels. When it was cold or windy, or wet, this was remarked on as well and often seemed to be a cue to go indoors and catch up on emails.

CARACTACUS
Wednesday 20 May 2020

The weather continues so warm and dry that I have a fancy that we might come to talk, in future years, of a 'Covid Summer', meaning a long spell of clement weather.

SKYE
Thursday 2 April 2020
Woke up to sunshine and an online food delivery this afternoon. It's amazing what becomes important in your life!

The good weather lured diarists outside. Quite apart from tending to gardens and allotments, and doing outdoor jobs, they went for walks around their neighbourhoods, often mentioning how they had got to know their local area better than ever before. Most also took advantage of the daily hour's exercise beyond the confines of their own homes and gardens permitted by the original COVID-19 regulations. As the restrictions changed, and driving to take a walk was allowed, and as visitor attractions opened, these outings were extended. Additionally, a number of diarists wrote how they had got their bicycles out for the first time in years. This is in line with the findings of another study which reported how over-65s were more physically active than other age groups during lockdown, and how they continued to exercise more when the lockdown restrictions were eased (University College London News, 2020a).

GRACE
Monday 20 July 2020
Walks have been the way through Covid, locked down but able to break free, and the sight of families and couples and lone walkers nodding and greeting from the two metres away is the enduring image I shall retain. When in doubt go out for a walk – gets you away from those jobs you mean to do and anyway there is always tomorrow – the diary was always empty!

HOLLY
Monday 25 May 2020
My trusty Fitbit tells me that we've walked or run around 350 miles since we went into lockdown.

JIMMY
Thursday 2 April 2020
My life is circumscribed to two walks per day (each of about two miles). I don't bother so much about corona as most people because I am old and not so afraid of dying. I am negligent about social distancing.

PERSIA
Thursday 2 April 2020
The garden is my escape and how glad I am to have it. It is both therapeutic to tend as well as enabling me to have a 30-minute brisk walk around it each day. The latter is slightly monotonous as the garden is quite small

but hopefully this means I am walking at least 1½ miles each day so feel I am having some exercise.

For the diarists, exercise was often combined with an increased focus on the local environment. This accords with an Office for National Statistics (2021c) report that showed how interest in nature increased during lockdowns. More people were spending time outside and there was much increased traffic on the RSPB website. In addition, almost everyone participating in the People and Nature Survey for England between April and June 2020 (Natural England, updated 2021) believed that the natural environment was beneficial for mental health and well-being.

Puddephatt (2021) argued that 'there are both intellectual and political pressures for symbolic interactionism to retool and find a more prominent place for the natural environment in its theoretical scope'. Some theorists have called for the inclusion of the natural environment as a nonhuman actor within the construction of reality. Brewster and Bell (2010) built on Goffman's theory to describe how it is possible to have a dialogue with nature, whereby natural elements such as trees, flowers and streams become the centre of focus while the artificiality of barriers such as fences become relatively ignored. There is evidence, from the diary entries, that diarists increasingly saw themselves as 'environmental citizens' during the lockdowns, as Puddephatt suggested. They wrote about engaging with nature to a heightened degree, and having more time to potter and observe.

ELEANOR
Sunday 24 May 2020
The garden continues to provide pleasures and treasures. ... The potatoes are determined to burst through however much earthing up I do so am just letting them get on with it now. Having time to potter and look closely is great soul food and it is amazing the changes that can occur in 24 hours.

HOLGATE
Tuesday 14 April 2020
I'm enjoying the slower pace of life and the space it has given me. I'm enjoying the birdsong in my garden and the opportunity to stop and stare at the flowering trees, shrubs and plants as well as those in the beautiful area I live in.

RAIN
Monday 25 May 2020
Never before I have looked so closely so long over so many weeks at what is growing, and the state of the soil. Indeed I have been out so often that

the robin comes as soon as I step out of the door, and follows closely and sings out for me to dig.

SIMON
Monday 18 April 2020
Finally got out at 10.00 and walked around and through the park and across to the bandstand where, for the first time in my life, I sat on a bench for one hour in the sun doing absolutely nothing. Clearly have now joined the ranks of the ancient.

The peacefulness of the outdoors led to an increased awareness of birdsong – until interrupted by noisy motorbikes – and turned many people into birdwatchers. The British Trust for Ornithology (2021) reported how the number of participants in their Garden BirdWatch scheme (which was free during lockdown) more than doubled during 2020 as homeowners appeared to be taking a heightened interest in their gardens and wildlife.

AMBER
Saturday 4 September 2020
There have to be some positive things in all of this. Lots of people have reconnected with nature, birds, the pleasure of time to oneself, values may have shifted, skills learned or honed, appreciation of things once taken for granted – whether this will endure, who knows.

APPLETREE
Sunday 3 May 2020
Amazed myself by getting out of bed at five this morning to go out for a walk and listen to the dawn chorus. Really pleased to see two swallows (my first) and hear several chiff-chaffs and a black cap.

CHARLES
Sunday 26 April 2020
We walked around eight miles in total, with a delightful picnic halfway beside a small stream. In the warm sunshine we saw blue tits, sedge and hover flies, bees and even an early leatherjacket come and go from the stream. The quiet and peace was wonderful. No aeroplanes, very few cars, lorries or other noise to drown the birdsong as is usually the case. Lockdown does have its advantages, at least for us!

EVE
Thursday 9 April 2020
After lunch I went on my usual walk and heard a woodpecker. This must be the first one I've heard in Scotland in about 40 years. They have probably

been drumming away but the sound has been drowned out by the noise of traffic and other people.

Sightings of many types of insects and animals were also recorded. These included hedgehogs, sheep, bees, butterflies, rare breeds of cattle, black hens, a fox, and much more. It seemed that the diarists were not alone, as the UK Centre for Ecology and Hydrology (Natural History Museum, 2020) reported that users of the website iRecord saw many more insects, squirrels, rodents, deer, bats, hedgehogs, moles and shrews during lockdown in 2020 compared to the previous year.

JANWIG
Thursday 14 May 2020

Nature such a consolation. But even it has its minor tragedies. One of the joys of this period has been our first garden hedgehog in 20 years. Maybe because we have time to notice it? Anyway, have heard it snuffling away for many evenings, including last night.

And then, sadly, this morning, found it disembowelled, just the prickles left. It seems likely to be a badger. EXCEPT we have never had a badger in the garden and it did no other damage. But what else could it have been? Apparently their cubs have been born, and the ground is so hard worms are hard to come by. So they are on the lookout for other prey. So sad.

Copious observations of flora, sometimes aided by a plant identifier, were also made.

BAREFOOT DOC
Thursday 9 April 2020

And an hour's walk, along the lip of Devil's Dyke. It's the yellow flowers' season right now. Gorse. Celandine. Dandelion. And ravishing shy cowslip, startling lemon petal, sage sheath, bright apple leaf. The blues are bubbling under – bluebells in the wings, violets small and intense. Periwinkle the first, speedwell close second. Borage already tall. And at head height, white white white sloe blossom. I sat on a felled tree. Bark had come off, and beneath were wonderfully wrinkled mazes of borer beetles' tunnels. I snapped them with my phone's camera. If they come out (I doubt they will, close-ups generally don't) they might make good calendar images at the end of the year. At the end of the year. It doesn't bear thinking about.

Engagement with nature, the countryside and open spaces had become widespread among the diarists, many of whom lived in rural or semi-rural locations. Place had gained a new significance and meaning. This was a clear silver lining of the pandemic cloud.

Celebrations and rituals

Apart from many inevitable cancellations and changed arrangements for weddings and funerals (see Chapter 5), diarists commonly wrote about their low expectations for birthday celebrations. Although not as significant as the status passages (Durkheim, 1912; Glaser and Strauss, 1971), such as births, deaths and marriages, that were postponed or took a different form during the pandemic, these events were important rituals in their everyday lives (Goffman, 1967). Nonetheless, many went on to write later about how enjoyable they had turned out to be. Whereas they had not been looking forward to the occasions, and would not be able to spend them with family and friends, they outlined a long list of phone calls, deliveries of cards and presents, Zoom parties, children turning up out-of-doors, take-away meals, and socially distanced meetings in the garden wrapped up in rugs, that had made them a success. The looming clouds had turned out to have silver linings.

JANWIG
Tuesday 14 April 2020

[D]espite the lockdown [I] had an amazing day. Helped by weather, but also messages from far and wide, from almost every segment of my life too. My daughter-in-law baked and posted a cake. My daughter and son-in-law composed two songs in my honour, one a pastiche of my favourite folk song, 'Stewball'. And there was a quiz about me too. I suspect it was actually better than what was originally planned, a week with all the family in Lincolnshire Wolds.

OLIVE
Friday 15 May 2020

I turned 70 two days ago. BC (before Covid) I had been planning a party with 40 or so people: friends and family. We would have had curry and wine; music and poetry and fun. Of course it had to be cancelled. As it turned out, though, I had a ball, courtesy of friends, family and technology. … The extent of kind deeds and words was unexpected and, frankly, overwhelming. There may be something about current restrictions on social contact that stimulates a need to communicate in a more expressive and unambiguous way; an added impetus to ensure that feelings are fully expressed. I feel blessed to have such a loving, lively, funny, creative and kind hinterland.

Several diarists mentioned wedding anniversaries in their diary entries. Although these had not materialised as planned, they also turned out to be positive occasions. The following two accounts are illustrative.

APPLETREE
Saturday 18 July 2020

Golden Wedding. Afternoon tea delivered plus enormous cake. And a bottle of Bolly. We set up in the garden but it was too dreich so came inside. L and kids had made two cakes: a five and a nought and decorated them, as requested … *BLOODY HELL WE MADE IT*. M set up her laptop to Google Teams (I think) so that K and her family in France could join in. … Later friends came round in ones and twos and we sat outside with them for tea and cake. … Not the Golden Wedding we had planned in France with all the family. But good nevertheless. … Went for a twilight walk together round the field, Jupiter low and bright in the southern sky.

JESSIE
Monday 13 July 2020

To celebrate our anniversary – we decided to go to the beach – after looking through my book on hidden beaches we decided to go to Kent, taking a picnic. It was a lovely day, the beach is not as hidden as the book suggested but we still found plenty of space. We had a swim before our picnic, lay on the blanket reading when the lifeguard came and told us that in half an hour the tide would be in and the bit of the beach we were on would be cut off from the main bit of the beach so we then packed up and moved. I got another swim before deciding to go home. The car was parked next to a pub with views of the sea so we made a last minute decision to eat there before we left, a great way to end a really lovely day. We realised it was the first time we had eaten out in four months.

Christmas 2020 was another instance where celebrations did not usually go as planned, following a U-turn on the initial announcement on 24 November that up to three households or bubbles would be able to meet up during a period from 23 to 27 December. Although this was still the plan in England on 16 December (although not in Scotland and Wales), it had been dropped by 19 December. By this date more than a quarter of the country was in Tier 4 and consequently not allowed to mix with anyone outside their household or bubble on and around Christmas Day. Those in other tiers could come together in their three households on Christmas Day but were not permitted to stay away from home for the night.

An Opinium poll for *The Observer* (Savage, 2020a) pointed to the implication of these restrictions for those in older age groups. They meant that as many as 1.7 million people aged 65 or more could be expecting to spend Christmas Day on their own, around twice the number in a 'normal' year. This did not apply to the majority of diarists who were living with partners, but the ruling did nonetheless affect plans for family gatherings. Most, however, took the directive in their stride and regarded it as inevitable.

Indeed, and reflecting at the time of the second follow-up, some voiced incredulity at the original plans as well as relief that they had been scrapped.

AMBER
Tuesday 16 February 2021

Christmas came and went like just another day – we haven't made a support bubble and did feel, as many did and have since proved correct, that allowing families a Christmas meet-up was too risky. One of my daughter's friends spent Christmas as a family with her parents – her, very fit, father is now dead from Covid – they all have to live with that.

HUMPHREY
Tuesday 9 February 2021

We were very much hoping to have our close family with us. We are lucky enough to have a barn and we thought with the high ceilings, the heating on and the windows open it would be safe for the 12 of us to meet even if we needed to be a little spaced out. We went to town decorating it with coloured lights and a large Christmas tree. Our three children all took Covid tests and once school had finished started to self-isolate with their kids. They were all scared of giving us the plague. When the PM changed his mind and limited Christmas to two days, we thought we should be the ones to cancel it. Although it was a big disappointment, we feel it was the right decision and I think our kids felt the same and probably felt relieved as well.

Most of these diarists were still determined to keep Christmas special. They planned a nice meal, perhaps put up a tree, and made the day different. They were also in touch with family, either face-to-face at a distance or via video calling, and generally made the most of the situation. The majority accepted the new restrictions as sensible and felt positive about how things transpired.

APPLETREE
Saturday 6 February 2021

Tier 4 … yes we took pudding up to our family and ate it on a cold garden bench. They changed their plans to keep to Christmas Day with the other parents so we had to change ours. Weary resignation.

CLARA
Thursday 11 February 2021

This area was in top tier. I did not change any plans. I had a lovely walk in the morning with my son, then my other son and two grandsons came into my garden. We all kept our distance and gave each other our presents. I had my roast chicken meal on my own, but joined a Skype call with my daughter (at present in Vancouver) and my younger son. Good fun. In the evening I went for another walk with a friend.

JACCA
Monday 8 March 2021

Having said all of that and thoroughly depressed myself I really enjoyed Christmas in lockdown and felt the relief of being able to consider only myself and my partner. I generally feel completely torn in two or three directions and it was wonderful to be able to stay at home and do exactly as we pleased without guilt or recrimination.

PANGOLIN
Monday 1 March 2021

Yes we had planned for an indoor meal with no overnight stays but this was even less fun. My son cycled over on Christmas Eve so I threw his stocking to him and at arm's length we pulled a cracker tied to a 1-metre walking stick. My daughter and her partner came to go for a distanced walk with me on Christmas Day, so I had a lovely time. I thought it was sensible to have a lockdown from before October half-term but as we'd had inept decisions at the top, to mess up our Christmas was necessary.

SARDOMIKE
Thursday 4 March 2021

Christmas was the same as any other day, just different food and presents to each other. It was obvious what was going to happen, I read only yesterday of two families who met up to celebrate, they all went down with Covid, two died. Could you live with yourself knowing that because of your selfish behaviour two people are dead, not especially old, a mother in her late 50s and her daughter.

TOPPER
Thursday 18 February 2021

We had to cancel our family Christmas meal as we moved into Tier 3. My neighbours very kindly gave us some of their meal (over the garden fence) as they were entertaining friends on the day.

A few, however, were less happy.

JESSIE
Friday 12 February 2021

This was the biggest hardship for my husband and I. The planned family Christmas with our oldest son in Devon to celebrate their move into their new home, with his brothers and families, had to be cancelled. It was really disappointing for all of us and we all had to make alternative arrangements, including having to cancel our hotel booking. For the first time in our marriage of 46 years, my husband and I had Christmas on our own. We decided that we would still make it special, ordered the turkey (far too much for us as there were only big turkeys left!) and set the table in the traditional way with my grandmother's lace tablecloth, the table decorations, candles, etc. We had family Zoom sessions before and after our meal and in the end it felt we had made the most of it though we did miss everyone.

TARANAKI
Sunday 7 February 2021
We had planned to spend a few hours only on Christmas Sunday in our house with our son, daughter-in-law and two little granddaughters. This obviously was no longer allowed. So on the 20th we drove to their home (20 miles away) and delivered cards and presents to the doorstep. The ensuing ten minutes were awful … instead of this being an acceptable alternative, it was nightmarish. The oldest granddaughter (8) started sobbing which made the younger one (3) start wailing and screaming. My daughter-in-law and I then began to weep and my husband and son welled up tears. Truly dreadful – we left very quickly and phoned later to see if they were okay. We certainly were *not* okay.

The pandemic and lockdowns restricted get-togethers between families and friends. Many diarists nonetheless found ways to enjoy birthday, anniversary and Christmas celebrations. They were pragmatic and adaptable.

Personal mood

The uncertainties and contradictions inherent in the pandemic, and particularly the lockdowns, inevitably gave rise to mixed emotions. As evident from the diary entries throughout this book, there was anxiety and concern about COVID-19 at an individual and societal level, but also much positivity on other scores. Sometimes the co-existence of these contrasting emotions could be unsettling and lead to a sense of cognitive dissonance (Festinger, 1957).

HATTIE
Sunday 17 May 2020
My feelings at the moment are fairly mixed. At our book group the other evening I felt very irritated by people talking about how well they were feeling enjoying doing things at a relaxed pace, and generally to my mind sounding a bit self-indulgent. This of course is exactly how I feel a lot of the

time, and I am equally guilty of being self-indulgent. It just takes half an hour of catching up from the papers with the chaos that seems to be surrounding any decisions made by government, to reduce me to a snarling mess.

HOLLY
Tuesday 19 May 2020

I haven't written a diary entry for a few days. The truth is that I've been feeling pretty bad about a whole range of things that are totally beyond my control – or that of anyone else I know, for that matter. One of my neighbours put it very well when she said that we're quite privileged compared with many others and we're also quite resilient and good at getting on with managing stuff that is to some degree at least, within our control. Then, from time to time, you look at the terrible things that are happening that you can seemingly do nothing about and it really hits you just how bad things are and what a mess is being made. I know a number of people who say that it takes them like that. Like lots of others, I keep up as well as I can with the bigger picture and think and write about it, too. Sometimes, though, it just jumps up and bites me.

ROB
Wednesday 10 June 2020

I get on the green ... and the pathways are strimmed and some muscari bulbs are planted. A calming sane ordinary moment in what are quite bewildering times.

SQUEALS
Friday 25 April 2020

I alternate between happy at all the family WhatsApps, etc. but also sadness at not even being able to contemplate trips to see family, let alone visit all the other places on my bucket list. I think that train trip across Russia will never happen. Not getting any younger.

This unsettling feeling might lead to a sense of unreality, as if the situation were being viewed from a distance. This could act as a coping mechanism.

KATJA
Sunday 13 April 2020

After speaking and face timing various friends during this Easter we all remarked how very odd this all was, it was as if we were watching this whole drama unfolding and we were just bystanders. Then going back to the diary I had written so far I noticed that my diary was written as if I was giving a little synopsis of events. There were no personal thoughts involved.

That in turn reminded me of that sentence I read in *Island* where this Mynah bird repeatedly screamed 'Here and now boys' reminding you to get involved in the 'here and now'. Although this here and now is not our choice, it has always helped me through sticky patches.

According to one large study, those in their 70s and 80s showed a 60 per cent increase in their anxiety score after the initial lockdown in March 2020 compared to just before (Robb et al, 2020). Inevitably the abrupt cessation to normal life brought its stresses as already outlined in earlier chapters. Decisions had to be made quickly, there were reports of escalating illness and death, and there was the invisible threat from a virus about which little was known. Nonetheless, as diarists adapted to the new order, they appeared very variable in their reporting of symptoms. Some wrote about considerable anxieties, on occasion at least, while others appeared largely relaxed and contented as they isolated themselves from immediate danger. All, however, described ways in which they thought the pandemic was affecting them as the lockdowns continued. The following few diary excerpts illustrate some of the ways in which it had an impact on mood and behaviour.

FRANCIA
Wednesday 29 April 2020

Our telephone rang at 1.15 am. So worrying when the telephone rings at such an unearthly hour. After I found it was a wrong number, I could not get back to sleep. At around 3.30 am. I decided to get up but what should I do? Reading, making coffee, using the computer would probably stimulate my brain and I would not be able to sleep so I decided to do a few pilates exercises. When the clock struck 4 am. I realised the absurdity of this. I am sure that it is my intention to keep fit during these times which lead me to such peculiar actions!

HELGA
Retrospective: Monday 27 April 2020

Staying healthy is, of course, of great importance. One doesn't want to have to go out to seek medical attention. Now that we've been out of circulation for so long, fear of catching the virus has disappeared. But there are so many other things that could befall one: heart attacks, strokes, appendicitis, dental emergencies, to name just a few.

And then there are accidents. Fear of accidents has become something of an obsession. The home, we all know, is one of the most dangerous places known to man, and the last thing any of us wants is to end up in A&E under the present circumstances. So I'm being very careful, especially in the kitchen where hot, and sharp, things abound. And the stairs are a major cause for concern. ... So ... coming downstairs these days is as much a mental as a physical exercise – concentrating fiercely at the beginning of the descent, then a few seconds respite in the middle, before taking extreme care on the last few steps.

LOUISE
Saturday 18 April 2020

I have described my state as lethargy, but that's not quite right as I am, for example, keeping up with all the news on the pandemic and the internecine struggles of the Labour Party. I think the right word is detachment. I am living a life like a hermit, shut away from the world and it brings a kind of calm with it. I care about what is going on out there, but I can't touch it or affect it. I don't feel sure that I will ever emerge from this isolation again and it doesn't worry me too much. It sounds rather dramatic but it is even a kind of endgame. The loss of my two planned holidays and the threat to my small amount of savings which worried me so much at first now seem unimportant. In this state of detachment the worries float away like soap bubbles.

SUSIEQ
Sunday 31 May 2020

While hanging out the washing, I note – not for the first time – my preference for pairing up pegs from our wide-ranging collection of colours and types and my tendency to do this more at times of stress. Daughter tends to do this as well and I wonder why we do it/why I do it. Is it a love of symmetry? Is it my way of exerting just a degree of control when I feel in control of so little else? Is it a trait that she has inherited?

On balance, nonetheless, there was more positivity than negativity among the diarists as apparent from much that has been reported in this and other chapters. Most were quick to adapt to the restrictions and devise new routines and interests. Stoicism was much in evidence.

Summary

The pandemic brought clouds but these could also have silver linings. Things that were missed might give rise to unexpected benefits. Thus being compelled to stay at home most of the time meant spending more time with partners, which could be rewarding. Not being allowed to meet families and friends led to much Zooming, which inspired creative and enjoyable activities. And the spare time some diarists acquired allowed them to engage in new activities that could provide interest and joy. Becoming greater environmental citizens, enjoying walking and gardening and the unaccustomed peace, and paying more attention to flora and fauna, were commonly mentioned as high spots of lockdown. Celebrations also often turned out to be much more enjoyable than had been anticipated. Lockdown life could give rise to cognitive dissonance and personal moods were up and down.

Despite the adaptations to new patterns of daily life, the restrictions imposed by the pandemic were not to last for ever. The next chapter considers the slow journey back to a greater normality.

8

The gradual return

At the time of the initial lockdown, there was a sudden change to the way of life, with a new symbolic universe and many taken-for-granted aspects abandoned. Unprecedented rules had been imposed and everybody was urged to fall in line. Diarists, as most others, adapted to this unusual situation as new routines and practices were developed. They were prepared to conform to the extent that it seemed sensible in keeping the virus at bay but did not want to give up everything that was important to them. They were pragmatists in the sense described by Dewey (Dewey, 1929; Campbell, 1995). They acted to maintain the equilibrium in their lives and defuse tensions. They were adaptable and resourceful.

The pandemic was bedevilled by uncertainty. This concerned the nature and operation of the virus as much as the likely duration of risk and restrictions. The continuing lack of knowledge about the virus and its mutations contributed to the question marks attached to daily life. When could one be sure that it was safe to resume close contact with family and friends and mingle in public places?

Indeed, the abandonment of restrictions was essentially a case of managing uncertainty. More was known as time went on but gaps in knowledge undeniably remained. The instructions early on were absolutely clear. For most people there was to be no face-to-face contact without social distancing with anyone from another household. But once certain meetings and activities became allowed again, personal agency came back into its own and with it an increase in uncertainty (Rutter et al, 2020). There were new questions to answer, such as should I visit my family, should I go to the hairdresser, and should I go on holiday? There was a return to responsibility for one's own actions.

At issue was whether it would be as easy to return to the 'old' normal as it had been to leave it behind. There were, indeed, important differences. First, going into the initial lockdown was mandated whereas coming out of a restricted life was voluntary. Second, becoming locked down was sudden whereas leaving restrictions behind was gradual. Third, the persisting fear and anxiety engendered by COVID-19 (see Chapter 3) encouraged a restricted life but discouraged a return to previous patterns of daily life.

This chapter examines reactions to the loosening of restrictions and the return, or otherwise, to old patterns of behaviour over the year or so following the initial lockdown in March 2020. Did the vaccine make a difference, and was the 'new new' normal the same as the 'old' normal? Was the pandemic likely to have a lasting impact on the diarists?

Changing rules and restrictions

The lessening of restrictions, and the return to some semblance of a former life, was a gradual process with reopenings occurring in stages. Of particular significance to diarists was the re-establishment of face-to-face contact with family and friends. It was, however, a roller coaster of a journey as rules and restrictions were constantly changing and causing confusion.

Following the initial lockdown in March 2020, it was in May 2020 when things began to change. The first significant easing of restrictions was on 10 May when it became lawful to meet one other person outside one's household if social distancing was observed. Diarists expressed their joy at the possibility of long-awaited reunions, and most took up the opportunity, some continuing to be cautious but many succumbing to the temptations of a cuddle.

ANNA
Monday 25 May 2020

My daughter's birthday. This is the first day I have strayed from the straight and narrow of social distancing. I had physical hugs! I drove about an hour to a rendezvous half that distance from them, and we considered ourselves as safe as we could be to hug. So so nice. And my granddaughter wanted to be carried by me and we certainly didn't keep two metres apart all the time. None of us did.

FRANCIA
Saturday 30 May 2020

I had coffee in a friend's garden this week. I entered her garden by a gate and did not go through her house. No hug on meeting, I took my own mug and we sat a good distance apart. It was good to see her but seemed strange to have this wary distance between us.

GATZOU
Thursday 14 May 2020

We have had visitors in the garden and, sitting at more than 2 m from each other, we don't wear masks. They arrive through the side gate and touch nothing, except the chairs in the garden. My friend was saying she disinfects the chairs in her garden after a visit. I must confess, I have not done this ... maybe I should.

SUSIEQ
Wednesday 27 May 2020
A brilliant day. We left here just after 10 and arrived just on midday. Children weren't expecting us, and the first thing they both did was come round to my side of the car for a cuddle. They were on excellent form throughout (and parents were very well-behaved too!). ... Hard to say what my favourite bit of the day was, but it was probably being in the hammock with both children snuggled up.

It was June 2020, however, that brought the most monumental change to date. From the beginning of that month up to six people from different households were able to meet outdoors, including in private gardens, provided they kept two metres apart from anyone not in their household. Barbeques were to make a comeback! Nonetheless, there were rules and expectations. So, for instance, anybody going into the house to use the loo was supposed to be very alert and take care to clean everything after them. Members of eating parties were also not to share cutlery or plates and regularly to wash their hands even if, presumably, this meant going indoors. According to *The Daily Mail*, 'It's Happy Monday!' Diarists took advantage of these new freedoms, despite differing levels of adherence to the rules, and differing levels of enthusiasm. And, even if weather conditions were not optimal, they were willing to endure some discomfort to manage the encounters.

ARAMINTA
Thursday 4 June 2020
Today the weather was fine in the morning as forecast. Another friend was coming round this afternoon and I suggested moving the event to the morning. However, she wanted to put out her washing and get it dry, which she did, so she came this afternoon. But immediately we had a very heavy downpour and it hailed too. After a while it stopped and I turned over the cushions which I had put out on the garden chairs to the dry side. But it wasn't too long before it started again. We both had waterproof jackets and she had a golf umbrella. Eventually the rain started to roll down the cushions and wet our trousers. I leapt up. I was quite grateful when she decided she should go home again! I came in and changed my trousers for warmer dry ones.

HATTIE
Thursday 4 June 2020
Our daughter and granddaughter came for lunch on Thursday and we sat out in the garden – with coats on as there was a very chilly wind and not a lot of sunshine. I did two trays of food to keep everything separate, and my daughter

piled up all of their dishes onto their tray at the end so it was simple to put it all straight into the dishwasher. It was lovely to see them and catch up a bit, though our granddaughter found it very difficult to keep her distance.

HOLGATE
Friday 26 June 2020

The highlight of my week was the day trip I made on Sunday to see my son, my daughter-in-law, and my two lovely grandchildren who live in Dorset. It was the first time I had seen them since 29th January. We were all a tad emotional at first when we hugged. We then got down to having some great fun. Both the children were for the very first time able to ride their bikes without assistance. A real milestone day in their short lives.

HUMPHREY
Sunday 28 June 2020

One of our children and his family are arriving shortly for the day. I hope the weather bucks up so we can all enjoy ourselves in the garden. If it gets too cold or starts to rain, I am happy to welcome them in the house. I fear the parents will be anxious to protect us and not so keen. We shall have to see.

TARANAKI
Wednesday 10 June 2020

We have seen my son and his family: in their garden for about one hour. It felt really strange, most notably at the times of arrival and departure. My granddaughter (7) clearly did not know how to greet us! We are so used to hugs and kisses. On the way to their house I went briefly into a Morrisons supermarket to buy gifts: prosecco and flowers for the grown-ups, duplo bricks for the youngest granddaughter (2) and a craft piece for the older one. Having the new toys gave us a starting point but of course we didn't sit close by them at the garden table. Perhaps we will see them again next week and it being a second time, it will be easier.

Not everyone, however, yearned for more social contact. Many enjoyed what they felt was a state of relaxation, while others had grown used to being on their own more of the time.

CAMPBELL
Saturday 13 June 2020

I'm invited to a small – and the hosts insist – socially distanced garden party which I'm not sure I really want to go to. Part of that no doubt is a residual fear about whether it will really be 'safe' but more I think it's to do with – despite being a decidedly social being in normal times – not necessarily being ready to be in a larger group at all.

JULES
Wednesday 10 June 2020

This week I've been starting to feel as if I'm in a bit of a rut. Too comfortable, so that my comfort zone is decreasing to a little circle around my house. I am becoming aware of a certain amount of fear about going out – not for walks but for socialising: I don't want to see the world as it is now but how it was before the lockdown, which I know is impossible.

SIMON
Sunday 14 June 2020

My friend from upstairs invited L and N round to the garden. Lovely to see them but I've become rather desocialised and although really pleased to see them was rather grumpy and combatative. Very odd. Took an anti-inflammatory before bed in the hope that it would ease the discomfort (and my irascibility!).

By the end of June 2020, there was an awareness of greater relaxations to come very shortly, and indeed Boris Johnson made his much anticipated statement about the further easing of the lockdown on 23 June 2020. All manner of changes were to come into effect from 4 July. Social distancing was to be reduced from two metres to one metre plus (which meant with the use of masks and other preventative measures), and hotels, B&Bs, restaurants, pubs, campsites, caravan parks, libraries, places of worship, cinemas, theatres and concert halls (but not live performances), museums, hairdressers, funfairs, model villages, indoor attractions at zoos, and other venues were set to open subject to provisos still to be fully elaborated. Indoor gyms would not yet be permitted. Also to be allowed were two households meeting indoors, although social distancing was to be maintained. The *Daily Express* headline that preceded the announcement said 'Freedom Pass for Millions' and there was a general impression from the press that the lockdown was essentially over. Many dubbed 4 July 2020 as Independence Day. However, it was not to be so for everyone, as the same day also saw the first local lockdown come into force in Leicester and parts of Leicestershire.

Reactions to the easing of restrictions were again variable and not always positive. The taken-for-granted aspects of daily life were continually changing and an overarching fear of the invisible virus lingered.

ARAMINTA
Friday 17 July 2020

In the evening my daughter and her family arrived for an overnight before going off to Colonsay. It was so good to see them. And the hugs! No hugs or physical contact for 17 weeks since we were effectively locked down – everything was cancelled for several days before lockdown was official.

The gradual return

BARKLEY
Thursday 25 June 2020

I have no confidence whatsoever in the 4 July relaxation of lockdown. It's a huge gamble purely for short-term gain – political and economic. I think a second wave probably kicking off in early autumn is highly likely, if not inevitable. We will, though, at some point soon – not 4 July – check out the pub.

BONIVARD
Wednesday 1 July 2020

On Wednesday afternoon my wife hosted her monthly book group. Rather than arrange a Zoom meeting, she took a chance with the weather to organise a gathering in the garden. Some of the other members were initially dubious – would they be able to enter via the back gate and avoid coming through the house, would they be adequately socially distanced, should they bring their own chairs and glasses, was it safe to handle next month's book choices, should they be handed around, and would sanitising spray and paper towels be available? Despite the earlier showers, the meeting was held outside and was a success. Anxiety levels were kept in check.

But with only a few days to go before the easing of lockdown, it was concerning that all the club members were so risk averse. Perhaps we have been more risk willing than most for our generation. So far, touch wood, we have kept out of trouble but other people we know appear to show classic signs of cabin fever – feelings of boredom, impatience, irritability, restlessness and anxiety. I've heard some people on the radio saying that they are now too afraid to go out even if they haven't been ill or having to self-isolate.

HOLLY
Thursday 2 July 2020

As I've been a bit remiss over diary writing, I'm including a shot of a piece by the master himself. The entry from the diary of Samuel Pepys (below) just about sums up where we're at right now as far as I'm concerned.

'The taverns are full of gadabouts making merry this eve. And though I may press my face against the window like an urchin at a confectioner's, I am tempted not by the sweetmeats within.

A dram in exchange for the pox is an ill bargain indeed.'
Diary of Samuel Pepys, Great Plague of 1665.

HUMPHREY
Monday 6 July 2020

Our grandchildren are getting closer to us all the time though their parents are watchful. The four-year-old said that he couldn't hug me 'till coronavirus has gone away'.

PETER
Saturday 25 July 2020

Just back from five days in a log cabin at a country hotel. With son, daughter-in-law and grandson in nearby cabin. So jolly good on separation or whatever it's called. Social distancing was easily maintained – for the first nanosecond. Then 14-month-old raised his arms to be lifted, and do you know what happened? His grandmother lifted him up for the first time since Feb 23.

I challenge anyone to resist.

We were ten miles from home but it still felt really holidayish.

Terrible dissonances just now. Life felt wonderfully normal for the last five days.

Despite the positivity of the media, Independence Day did not remove all uncertainty. It was but one more step in the long journey the country had been on since the initial lockdown in the previous March. Normality had not been restored and many diarists remained unsure of what the future held. There had been change but life was still on hold.

Diarists did, however, mention forays out to eat, something many of them had not done for several months. Reactions were mixed.

FISHERMAN
Wednesday 8 July 2020

That evening my partner drove us to our nearest pub for an evening meal. The drizzle was continuing and it was a grey evening, so we went inside and were shown to a table in an alcove. There were four other couples in the dining area, all spaced out and mainly silent, with the usual mix of eating or toying with their smartphones. Our drinks were brought to us, then, after ordering, our meals. The food was no more than acceptable. I chatted to the licensee and her brother when leaving, wishing them all the best for the future, but we won't go there again until the weather is finer and we can dine outside. Our experience seemed like being at a poorly attended funeral reception where the mourners didn't know the deceased, or each other.

OTTOLIE
Friday 10 July 2020

Went out to lunch with friend and had such a laugh. First restaurant meal for four months. Bloody brilliant. Bbq steak, rare and bloody, and garlicky salad, plus good bread and lovely wine.

Dining out was nonetheless encouraged with the announcement by Rishi Sunak, then Chancellor of the Exchequer, that an Eat Out to Help Out scheme would operate from Mondays to Wednesdays throughout August 2020. The initiative, which gave customers up to a £10 discount on eligible meals at participating outlets during this period, was ostensibly to support the hospitality industry. However, it was also an encouragement for diners to return to restaurants and other venues and led to some 160 million subsidised meals. There was subsequent controversy, nonetheless, about the impact on the industry as well as some suggestion that the scheme had inadvertently contributed to a later spike in COVID-19. Diarists were not all of similar mind when it came to either eating out or taking part in this scheme.

In addition, and apart from the Eat Out to Help Out scheme, August 2020 had seen more reopenings including indoor theatres and bowling alleys. September had also seen the introduction of the 'rule of six' in England (with a similar rule in Scotland) whereby up to six people could meet in either indoor or outdoor settings under socially distanced conditions. That month also saw a return to working from home where feasible and, for a brief period, a 10 pm curfew for the hospitality sector.

Further changes were still to come. Among these were two more national lockdowns in England, the first from 5 November 2020 for four weeks, and the second from January to March 2021, some local lockdowns, and the introduction of a three tier system from October 2020 whereby different rules applied in different parts of the country and, perhaps notably, the disruption of Christmas 2020 (see Chapter 7).

Nationally it appeared that people's responses to subsequent lockdowns were different from their reactions to the initial lockdown in March 2020. Research in Scotland, conducted by Edinburgh University, found that many more middle-class Scots were fined for breaking rules during the second than the first lockdown (Gorton et al, 2022). It seemed that compliance had waned over time among these groups. On another front, a survey of around 70,000 people had suggested that, in general, people reported spending less time on exercise, hobbies and volunteering, and more time watching television, during the third lockdown than they had during the spring of 2020 (Fancourt et al, 2021). There were fewer restrictions, more emphasis on police enforcement, and the weather was worse. It also seemed that the novelty of having extra time to spare had worn off. Pandemic burnout was on the rise (Marsh, 2021). Something akin to this was apparent among the diarists who responded to the second follow-up at the beginning of 2021.

AMBER
Tuesday 16 February 2021

In many ways, it is a good thing that we didn't know, way back in the very beginning last March, that a year later we would still be deep in the pandemic with no sure exit date or even strategy. Then it was a shock, it was frightening but I think most of us imagined it was a case of a few difficult months and then life would revert back to normal. So I think that then, we coped in a different way to the way we are now coping with the second, deeper, more frightening wave. It's not so much a form of resignation, more of familiarity and much reduced expectations. Before, as each day passed, it was as if we were ticking off that day and moving towards 'The End'. This time, it is as if each day is a carbon copy to be meandered through without too much analysis – a sort of 'groundhog day' effect. Life is not really either boring or bad, it is just ... happening, over and over again until the days are warmer and longer and outside living can start up again when it is so, so much easier.

JACCA
Monday 8 March 2021

I am struck by the fact that when we first went into lockdown there was a sense of energy and spark as people rallied trying to find ways to exist and to make it bearable. This last lockdown and indeed the prospect of coming out of lockdown has an entirely different feel. So many people have exacerbated mental health problems and I, who have never been depressed in my life, feel really flat and down. I have been wondering why. I think it's probably a chemical thing. The first round of lockdown stress induced the typical adrenaline surge and the fight or flight response. Many of us opted for fight and were jettisoned into action. I work really well under those conditions. However long-term stress produces a different response. You can't fight and fly forever.

ROB
Tuesday 9 February 2021

I think there was actually some feeling of novelty last time around but clearly that is long gone. And the best to be said this time is that it feels much more of a burden.

Restrictions continued well into 2021. In May, for instance, outdoor gatherings were still limited to 30 people and indoor meetings to six people or two households. And despite the so-called Freedom Day in August 2021 (see later), face masks were back in most public places on 10 December 2021. It was not until Thursday 24 February 2022 that guidance replaced legal restriction and the country was back to 'normal'.

Bubbles

Re-establishing contact with families and friends was also aided by the support and childcare bubbles introduced amid all the other changes. On Wednesday 10 June 2020 had come the announcement that single-person households could join a support bubble with one other household. This meant that households could visit one another and need not observe social distancing. And on Monday 12 October 2020 a further announcement saw the introduction of childcare bubbles which enabled someone in one household to provide unpaid childcare to a child aged 13 or under in another household. Only one childcare bubble with one other household was permitted. If eligible it was possible to have both a support bubble and a childcare bubble and they did not have to be with the same household. Support bubbles, but not childcare bubbles, counted as a single household. Accordingly, it was within the rules to meet indoors with a support bubble and a childcare bubble at the same time.

Understandably, many diarists said they had never really understood the finer details about bubbles and, as in other areas, they tended to act in the spirit rather than the letter of the law. Nonetheless, these provided an opportunity to widen their contacts and were often seized upon with enthusiasm. Sometimes, however, the children of the diarists had chosen to be bubbled within friendship rather than family groups. And in other cases they presented dilemmas. Which set of grandparents should families bubble with?

ANNA
Tuesday 16 June 2020

Getting ready for Thursday/Friday in my 'support-bubble'. My daughter and I have spent some time unpicking the complexities of the 'rules' which could have been written exactly for a lonely version of me. However, if I had two daughters with children how would I decide which to nominate, and show favouritism? Does staying 'overnight' allow two or three nights (which I might have to do on D-Day) and how is that policed? My daughter's husband, as a barrister, is very exercised with the niceties of it all, pouncing on how he would defend a prosecution because of inexact terminologies, or of the status of the instruction at the time of the offence (advice, a rule, a law?). I realise through him how contorted the procedures are for enacting a law under exceptional conditions – they are complicated enough without this emergency – and how many lacunae and loopholes will not have been identified.

FRANCES
Monday 20 July 2020

This entry is very late, I'm afraid! I am just coming down from a lovely but busy weekend. My son and his wife and their two teenager children were visiting (my support bubble), and yesterday my daughter, my other son and his wife and his son joined us in the garden. Stretching the rules a bit, but it *so great* to see them – all my children together for the first time since Christmas.

JESSIE
Saturday 27 June 2020
Today we put our family bubble to the test and suggested that our daughter-in-law bring her mother to lunch on their way to the airport. Our son, daughter-in-law, grandson and his mother-in-law came to lunch and unexpectedly our daughter-in-law's aunt. It was really good to see them and the plan had been for a lunch in the garden but the weather was not kind to us so we ate inside. ... We really enjoyed the day and while it was hard for our daughter-in-law we had the joy of our grandson most of the day.

In the main, diarists who formed bubbles did so with family members, often to enable them to see their children and look after grandchildren. Some, however, had linked up with friends. Nonetheless, there was again a considerable amount of confusion about what exactly bubbles were. Others were not forming bubbles because of the risks or because they were waiting until they might really need them.

KATJA
Thursday 18 June 2020
It all seemed to be happening, an increase in social contacts, I must say I am getting quite confused into which category to put myself. My social bubble consists of all my friends, family is out of bounds as that involves flying, so we carry on the contacts by FaceTime, email, phone, etc. How wonderful to have all this.

WILL
Thursday 16 July 2020
But a friend is coming over tomorrow to stay overnight and have a meal with us before going for a walk on Saturday. We've decided to make ourselves an honorary bubble as we all practise safe distancing and have very limited contacts.

Broadly speaking, it seemed that there was considerable confusion about what was meant by bubbles and how they could be formed. This lack of clarity was, in many ways, an advantage in that it enabled people to construct their own bubbles in accord with their own choices. Bubbles thus provided an additional route back to greater 'normality'.

The vaccine: a cause for optimism

There is little doubt that the return to an unrestricted life was aided by the rapid development of a vaccine for COVID-19 which, by September 2020, appeared to be on the horizon. Trials were under way and first signs were promising. Nonetheless, it was not seen as a total panacea. Asked at the first follow-up about whether they would be in the queue once it became available, most diarists said yes although with an element of caution. They mentioned how there was as yet little information on the level of protection the vaccine might offer as well as possible drawbacks and side-effects. There was also a recognition among many diarists that they might not be those most in need and that they would be willing to await their turn. Their views were comparable to those of participants in an interview study carried out in mid-July 2020 where only just over one in ten of the 55- to 75-year-olds said they would be unlikely to, or definitely would not, accept a vaccine (Allington et al, 2020).

The earlier promise was borne out and December 2020 saw the first vaccine being licensed in the UK and Margaret Keenan, aged 90 years, becoming the first to be inoculated. She was given the Pfizer/BioNTech vaccine. In the following month, 82-year-old Brian Pinker became the first person to receive the AstraZeneca vaccine. And then the roll-out began. By May 2021 some 60 million doses had been administered.

The otherwise healthy over-70s were formally offered the vaccine from Monday 18 January 2021. By the time of the second follow-up in early 2021, it appeared that all diarists offered vaccination had taken it up, even if they had previously been cautious or had misgivings. They had received either the Pfizer or AstraZeneca vaccine and few reported side-effects. A few did say they had felt unwell (hot sweats, headache, high temperature, muscle aches, sore arm, fatigue, nausea) but regarded this as a small price to pay. They were generally impressed and praised the efficiency of the vaccine programme and the enthusiastic volunteers helping it to run smoothly. They did, however, have concerns about when they would have their second dose and the change of policy to extend the interval between doses from three to 12 weeks. Furthermore, they did not think that a dose of vaccine would mean an overnight change in their behaviour.

APPLETREE
Saturday 6 February 2021

Just glad to get a jag ... we have to trust the scientists and medics on this one. We value Dr Chris on Radio 5 for his clear answers to medical questions.

... All was very well organised and well-disciplined (we are over 70!) but cheerless ... just like a bottling plant. Since all the age band from our GP practice were called on the same day I quite looked forward to it in the hope of meeting real people. But ... we were a lot of mask-muffled oldies shuffling in line from spot to spot then chair to chair in a dimly lit conference centre. We were barked at by conference centre staff if you turned round in the hope of chatting. This is what we have come to. The actual jagger was lovely but it was not the Big Day Out I was hoping for. However, we're done! Hallelujah. Freedom is in sight.

The vaccine heralded optimism even if most diarists were not about to change their behaviour in any dramatic way. The road back to normality continued to be slow and winding, and it was well understood that the effectiveness of the vaccine increased over time and did not peak until after a second dose. It was, however, a step in the right direction and widely welcomed.

ELEANOR
Monday 1 February 2021

Get a grip! Get a life! Get me the vaccine!

And lo and behold, the phone call came at 10.30 on Saturday 23rd January. Could I go for my jab at the local surgery at 6.10 pm that evening? Whoopee!

Amazing buzz of anticipation and positivity in the queue in the dark. Fast moving and cheerful, the mood continued inside the surgery with every corner seemingly used for something or somebody. It was rather like being on a station concourse with the hustle and bustle of masked helpers passing to and fro. Quick questions and then the jab and 15 minutes resting in an empty room while an oven timer marked my 'cooking' time! A cheery goodbye and off home. I felt that I was part of an important moment in history. Half an hour and a new world opening up. There is light at the end of the tunnel and despite initial scepticism that it was achievable, it seems that it really is.

FRANCIA
Friday 5 February 2021

Now that I have had my first jab, I suppose I feel less at risk from catching the virus but I am still being very cautious and abiding by the rules. I have had my concerns that there could be some at present unknown danger in taking the vaccine but life has it risks and contracting Covid is a known danger to be avoided.

JACCA
Monday 8 March 2021

Well I had my first vaccination. Just a week short of a year since I went into my own lockdown. I probably should be rejoicing and feel some sort of relief but, actually, I don't. I think vaccine or no vaccine we are in for a long haul and it will be a long time before I feel the confidence to mingle at close quarters with other people. For me that's more of an inconvenience than a real hardship. I am not a great social animal but there are a few things I would like to do and I do miss being able to travel.

JULES
Sunday 14 February 2021

Mine (followed a week later) and was the Pfizer version. ... It hasn't affected our activities at all so far. It reminds me of a Buddhist saying: 'Before enlightenment, chopping wood, carrying water. After enlightenment, chopping wood, carrying water'.

PERSIA
Wednesday 3 March 2021

My mother was called by text from the GP to have a jab on January 9th at Southall. I took her armed with brother and my NHS numbers, birthdates and GP practice details. There was no queue at Southall and my mother was duly vaccinated very efficiently. I gave the vaccinator our details and asked if there was any chance there would be any remaining vaccine as I had heard that they often got six jabs out of a vial and not five as planned. She very kindly took our details and put us on the reserve list but said we could be contacted quite late that evening. We heard nothing and I was really disappointed and decided my selling and negotiating skills had definitely left me. Next day was Sunday and I was really depressed until a doctor phoned at 11 am and invited us if we could still make it to go at 4 pm for the vaccine. I was ecstatic. As a result all three of us had the Pfizer jab that weekend. It really felt as though some weight had been lifted from our shoulders. Although it hasn't changed our behaviour at all it just felt as though there really was light at the end of the tunnel.

ROB
Tuesday 9 February 2021

Vaccine ... jabbed ... at Ludlow racecourse Tuesday 2nd Feb. No choice of carrot or sugar lump on completion. ... I had quite a short sharp initial immune reaction after about 24 hrs. chills and sweats ... I am advised that that is a positive thing ... but am not changing my habits/isolation any time soon ... 2nd jab due April 21st.

Many diarists hailed the vaccine roll-out as one of the greatest successes in the management of the pandemic.

JENNIFER
Wednesday 17 February 2021

The vaccination programme has proved to be the only detectable success story of the whole pandemic – thanks to the NHS and the many volunteers who have given their time and expertise to the programme. I was very cynical about the February 15th deadline, but, lo and behold, it has been achieved.

SARDOMIKE
Thursday 4 March 2021

Had our first vaccine, Pfizer. As a dentist, happy with the gap between doses, impossible that you have immunity for 21 days, then on day 22 it stops. Vaccination was well organised, priority lists were right, start with those most likely to die. The one success of this government.

Nationally, however, the availability of a vaccine did not appear to increase optimism for a rapid end to the pandemic. Indeed, survey data suggested that, towards the end of 2021, just over a third of those questioned thought it would take more than a further year for life to return to how it had been in pre-pandemic times (Dorling, 2021).

Emerging slowly

Indeed most diarists did make a slow return to the once taken-for-granted aspects of their daily lives they had left behind in March 2020 or even sooner. Some were anxious to get going and did not look back. For the majority, however, the way forward was characterised by caution. There was still much uncertainty and precautions remained sensible.

So while the removal of most remaining restrictions in England on Monday 19 July 2021 (tougher measures remained longer in Scotland and Wales), some 17 months after the initial lockdown and when anybody over 70 had been offered the vaccine, might have been considered a cause for celebration, in many quarters it was not. Both the PM and the chancellor were in self-isolation due to the virus, the national press did not appear sympathetic to the policy change, and around half the general population, according to the Office for National Statistics (2021f), was worried about the move. In addition, official statistics indicated that infection rates were showing a slightly upward trend. The Office for National Statistics data also suggested that around two thirds of people planned to continue wearing face coverings and practise social distancing.

Just under four in ten of the diarists responded to a call for diary entries in early August 2021 to chart their reactions to this so-called Freedom Day. A number were very displeased at the new apparent freedoms.

ANNA
Tuesday 31 August 2021

The (very good) Data not Dates slogan they claimed to be following was totally turned on its head by the designation of a Freedom Day. The data in mid-July didn't warrant widespread slackening of preventative measures; it wasn't even clear what was still required, and certainly not why certain things were relaxed and others not. Leaving it up to individuals to determine what they thought was safe or responsible may absolutely be Conservative 'laissez-faire' policy but is so wrong in this crisis. The switch from strict lockdown measures to 'decide for yourself' is a green light for all of us to breach safe behaviour. We are all able to argue we are the exception to the rule. There was so little emphasis on everybody's collective responsibility.

HOLLY
Tuesday 24 August 2021

So, how did I react to the announcement by the government about the changes to take place on 19th July 2021? Well, my lack of confidence in Johnson and his cabinet persists as strongly as ever. I felt livid (and helpless as usual) about the 'Freedom Day' labelling which I saw as basically a cheap and risky trick designed to boost Johnson's popularity.

JENNIFER
Tuesday 31 August 2021

When 'Freedom Day' was announced for England, my anxiety level went up a lot. I was waking up in the morning feeling sick and initially wondering what was wrong with me. At that time, we did not know whether Wales would join the free for all. Happily that did not take place. Gradually, my anxiety level has gone down but it is still there. So I agree with those who have labelled it 'Anxiety Day'.

Whether or not these changes would make a difference to them led to mixed reactions among the diarists. Many hoped to be able to make a reasonably speedy return to doing the things they enjoyed, and indeed may already have re-engaged with their former life.

BONIVARD
Thursday 14 October 2021

As Margaret Thatcher said, 'It's a funny old world'. We have experienced a period of nearly two years when there has been so much disruption to daily life and now we are emerging from it. Is it too much to compare this to the aftermath of a mini-war with deaths, lockdowns and travel restrictions? Life has changed in a few respects but I think that we (my family, relations and friends) will get back to a pre-pandemic way of life very soon. There is a positive feeling about the future and as restrictions are removed, everyday life will resume to a state very much as before.

HOLGATE
Sunday 12 September 2021

Life is short and I feel invigorated in the return to daily/weekly/yearly life with all its high and low spots. While it's been important to remain vigilant and careful, it's been great to travel within the UK, to see friends and family and to reconnect with the lifeblood of life!

JANWIG
Wednesday 8 September 2021

I behave as if no COVID exists. Have been to pub music, Ronnie Scott's, Soho Pizza Express for basement jazz. It's been wonderful. People think we are reckless. Maybe we are. All I can say is so far so good. Have drawn the line at 'abroad' though.

Others, however, remained more cautious.

APPLETREE
Tuesday 31 August 2021

Timidity seems to have set in. Fear of the contagious delta has put me off buses and the uncertainty of testing and quarantine has put me off travel to our grandchildren in France. ... It will take time and energy for all of us to get back to where we were in terms of social interaction and activity. Society, for our age group, has to be remade. If we have the energy.

BENCHMAN
Monday 2 August 2021

July 19 ('Freedom Day') was something of a damp squib. Not much has changed: most people are still wearing masks in shops and observing social distancing. On 13 July I went with friends to the one day international at Edgbaston (England v Pakistan). We had to provide proof of double vaccination in order to gain admission to the ground. We went by train, and everyone was wearing masks.

HATTIE
Friday 20 August 2021

In general, things are a good deal busier than they were last year, though Covid regulations are very few now, we continue to keep our distance from people, avoid very crowded places and wear masks. I have noticed that our age group still check out what visitors feel comfortable with – such as whether they would prefer a chilly cup of coffee in the garden or are happy to come inside – while the younger generation, whether or not fully vaccinated, seem to assume that life is back to normal.

I don't foresee huge changes in the way I do things in the future. It will take quite a lot to stop me from wearing a mask (still my very home-made but sturdy three-layer efforts, with elastic round my head because my ears just flap over with a loop round them) and I'm much happier at any time not to be in crowded places. Apart from my regular walks and gardening

> I don't think I have made any very improving changes to my way of living in the last year and a half, and I'm certainly not a nicer person!

Diarists were retreating from the restrictions of the pandemic at their own pace. It was, for many, a much slower process than the original adaptation to the new social order brought in by COVID-19. They were continuing to be pragmatic in taking precautions and continuing to take account of the uncertainty of the situation. Indeed a YouGov (2022) poll in February of that year found that almost half the respondents thought that anyone ever testing positive for COVID-19 should self-isolate. For some, nonetheless, the pandemic had been a fairly enjoyable experience that they were in no hurry to abandon.

The personal toll

Since becoming aware of the existence of COVID-19, and from the time of the first lockdown, diarists wrote copiously about the impact of the pandemic on them personally. Some six months later, but still in the throes of the pandemic, they told of any personal changes or adaptations they thought were likely to last. Did they expect these to affect them in any permanent way? The following diary entries from the first follow-up are illustrative of the wide variety of ways in which they thought the pandemic might take its toll.

ARAMINTA
Saturday 4 September 2020
The pandemic has certainly completely changed my life style. Now that things are opening up I am not sure I really want to go back to my very busy life I had before. I think I have become lazy. I'm not sure it has changed me as a person. I have had some very traumatic periods in my life but this is not one of them. I think I am taking it in my stride. I am concerned about the state of the country and the economy but I have not endured hardships such as others have.

AUSTEN
Friday 3 September 2020
The biggest effect of the pandemic has been to confirm that this is not our favourite town. I don't know whether it's the lockdown and feeling shut in around the narrow Victorian streets, or the stay with a daughter in the town where we used to live, but we have been thinking of going back there. … So far we have only received valuations on the house but I do think we will move. Funnily enough the estate agent said many people were moving because of the pandemic, either because working from home was easier and they wanted more room or they were also fed up with the situation and a move would possibly change that. Who knows?

BENCHMAN

Tuesday 1 September 2020

The main impact on me personally, as I have mentioned before, is that it has brought forward the decision to retire fully. Prior to the pandemic, I was seeking out lecturing work, partly to promote the book that I co-wrote which was published in October last year. I did have lecturing commitments in May, June and July, all of which were cancelled as a result of the pandemic. I have decided not to seek to reinstate those commitments. By the time face to face teaching can safely resume, the book will be old news and my legal and professional expertise increasingly outdated. The other impact is that I have rediscovered the art – and pleasure – of baking my own bread!

DEMPSEY

Saturday 12 September 2020

Obviously, it has made me anxious and worried about the safety of family and friends and, indeed, the effect on the country's economy in the future. I do suffer from depression, but I do not think that it has got worse as a result of the pandemic. Lockdown meant that there were fewer choices and less pressure. I have been reasonably happy to stay at home, albeit a very comfortable home and garden and feel lucky that all my family have remained well and in employment. I do not mean to sound smug, just grateful.

I think it will be a long time before I feel it is safe to go to the theatre, cinema, opera, etc. and I miss these activities. I will probably continue to do most of my shopping online.

EDGAR

Monday 6 September 2020

I like to think that it may have made me a bit more thoughtful of others and more patient but I am not confident about either of these.

ELISABETH

Thursday 3 September 2020

[I]t certainly has made me reassess my life, appreciate what I have more, value my friends even more than I already did and try to be kinder and less judgemental, even of the ones I consider overly cautious. I think sanitising my hands and washing them more frequently will stay with me!

JACCA

Wednesday 14 October 2020

As above the financial worries are a part of the impact but mostly it's deeper than that. I am certainly much more aware of my own mortality. I think both the pandemic and my age have contributed to the feeling that there is just not much time left. I am constantly trying to create some sort of meaning but don't even know what I mean by that. I am not a religious person. I have no real guidelines to fall back on. My philosophy has always been that it's a miracle to be alive and that creates an obligation to make the most of it. I don't need to be useful particularly or even benevolent to feel ok about myself. For me it's enough to try consciously not to act with disregard for others, to help people who need it who come into my life but primarily to make the most of life.

JANWIG
Wednesday 2 September 2020

It's made me think that I will never abuse my carbon footprint again, that I'd like to cycle everywhere locally I go, that protecting nature and biodiversity really matters to me.

LYNNE
Wednesday 9 September 2020

No great impact that I could discern. Possibly even a strange sort of relief at the beginning, and an appreciation of ordinary life. That is something that may well endure. If and when it is safe to do all the things we used to do that involved crowds and closer contact I may well be slow out of the starting blocks.

PANGOLIN
Monday 31 August 2020

I am sorry to say there is less spontaneity, e.g. I don't know if I'll ever swim in the ladies' pond again as you have to book a week in advance. I may continue with online shopping.

TERESA
Saturday 19 September 2020

I feel my horizons narrowing as a result of the pandemic. But I am a bit surprised that I have coped reasonably well with it so far. Can this possibly last? There's no telling. I must have been anxious about it at the outset because I spent so much time doing easy jobs and gardening. And I failed to tackle the clutter in our house that arose from clearing my aunt's house and the housing of her papers in our hall. Before lockdown I had been beginning to climb out of a lengthy trough where my life felt restricted by having responsibility for elderly members of my family. Now of course there are new restrictions.

TOPPER
Friday 11 September 2020

I feel that the pandemic has put my life on hold so I am living from day to day. I suspect it will have a permanent effect.

Almost two years further on, and according to some of the few who submitted additional diary entries at the time, it seemed that there could still be a lasting impact of the pandemic on daily lives. However, new lockdown habits might also have been abandoned.

BEA
Tuesday 2 August 2022

Yesterday I read my lockdown diary. ... I was shocked to realise that I took much more exercise during lockdown than I take now when I can go out whenever I want ... shocking!

CHARLES
Sunday 17 July 2022

I am now very conscious of railings in public places. Where possible I see if I can negotiate the steps or stairs without touching the railings! I wash my hands more than I have ever done before!

EVE
Thursday 21 July 2022

I have become more cautious as a result of the pandemic especially in avoiding holidays abroad (we have instead had some great walking holidays in the UK) and minimising my time in crowded indoor spaces. This may change if Covid disappears but I can't see that happening any time soon. I've also continued to use and enjoy video conferencing (mainly via Zoom) as a way of keeping in touch with family and friends that doesn't involve a lot of travelling.

HOLGATE
Thursday 21 July 2022

On a personal level the pandemic reminded me how important my friends and family are to my well-being. I have enjoyed the period post-pandemic visiting friends I haven't seen for some time and spending time with my family.

Finally, Covid made us realise the importance of positive personal contact, of small supportive groups, of time for reflection and meditation, and the joy of being outside whether in gardens, the countryside, in parks or at the seaside.

While the legislation had run its course, and there were no longer pandemic-related restrictions on behaviour, COVID-19 had not disappeared and was probably likely to be around in some form for years to come. Nonetheless, the general public had become more accustomed to its presence, those considered most vulnerable were to be regularly vaccinated, and the supremacy of personal agency was restored. This was not to say that the pandemic had not left an enduring mark.

Summary

The lockdowns had been imposed with little notice and were accompanied by clear directives. Life as it had been known was on hold while new rules and restrictions held sway. Diarists had been quick to adapt to the new order but found it more difficult to return to some semblance of their former life. Restrictions and permissions were continually changing and, increasingly, they had to make their own pragmatic decisions on the adaptations they would continue to make. The availability of a vaccine to protect against COVID-19 was an important factor in the return to a semblance of former normality but did not immediately reduce a sense of caution among the diarists. Some anticipated that the pandemic would, in some way or another, leave them changed forever.

The messages from this and earlier chapters provide pointers for issues to discuss and debate should there be a similar pandemic in the foreseeable future. These are considered in the next chapter.

9

Was anything learned?

It will take time and distance to gain the best understanding of exactly what transpired over the period of the pandemic, as well as what was done well and what was not. Blumer (1971) suggested that the fourth and fifth stages in the evolution of a social problem and its management are the development of a plan and the implementation of that plan. The issue is complicated in the case of the COVID-19 pandemic as these two latter stages were, in effect, largely merged into one. Moreover, as discussed in Chapter 8, these stages were fluid and rewritten many times over the duration of the period of restrictions.

Social policies cannot expect to remain uncontested. Blumer (1978) himself discussed how there can be collective protest and change and, as a result of social interactions, direct observation, new interpretations of the nature of the social problem, and perceptions of the validity of the plan and its execution, there was much to be said. Diarists showed a keen interest in the reality and rhetoric of events and were quick to give their verdicts on the unfolding situation. While there was, generally speaking, support for the lockdowns and the implementation of measures such as social distancing and mask wearing, there was also considerable criticism of the government on aspects including the timing and duration of lockdowns, the science and politics of decision-making, priorities of public health and the economy, the impact on children and young people, the availability of PPE and hospital beds, the situation in care homes, comparisons between policies in England, Scotland and Wales, the clarity of directives, and much more. There was, however, also a considerable number of diarists who acknowledged the unprecedented circumstances and felt the government was doing as well as could be expected.

Taking stock after the event, it is important that attention turns to pointers for the future, should a similar situation arise. There is currently an ongoing inquiry into the management and course of the pandemic chaired by Lady Hallett, and investigations announced so far (by May 2023) include: pandemic preparedness; decision-making and the impact of the pandemic on health systems; vaccines, therapeutics and anti-viral treatment; government procurement across the UK; the care sector across the UK; NHS test and trace; the effect of lockdowns on education, and the effect on children and young people; financial support for business; additional funding of public services; benefits and support for vulnerable people; and the impact of pandemic policies on inequalities in the context of public services, including key workers. Nonetheless, the final public hearings are not expected until summer 2026 and many conclusions will not be published before 2025. By the end of May 2023, the inquiry had already cost more than £116 million.

Beyond this, however, there are many wise words spoken by individuals, groups, organisations and others who had first-hand experience of the pandemic, its management and its impact, that deserve a hearing. The voices of the diarists, often issuing strong and vociferous comments on a wide range of issues such as those listed earlier, are among these. The rest of this chapter does not reiterate concerns with all these matters but instead identifies issues and implications meriting discussion that emerge from this project and the participants' diary entries. It is beyond the remit to detail very specific policies, partly because these were not suggested by the diarists and partly because these always need to be developed within the prevailing context. The focus here is, instead, on areas for consideration and debate. Although these highlight the particular case of relatively advantaged older adults, most have much wider applicability.

Deciding for the nation

Becker (1973) argued that social problems exist because they have been constructed as such, and the coronavirus pandemic is no exception. There is no denial that COVID-19 was making its way around the world, and that illness and death were being left in its wake. It is also not controversial to say that something had to be done. As outlined in other chapters, the British government followed many other countries in adopting a public health model that led to lockdowns and legally enforced restrictions. Whether or not this was the best response is more controversial and remains open to evidence, discussion and debate. Some contributory observations, however, can be made.

The starting point is to ask whether a public health model was the most appropriate. Best (2021) discussed how the construction of social problems depends on competing claimsmakers and the case that attracts the most concern and support. In this instance, the medical model predominated, as witnessed by the daily briefings led by the prime minister and public health advisers. Rarely was an economist, a social scientist, a representative of business, or indeed anybody else seen. It seems that their voices went largely unheard. Many diarists were critical of this and concerned that priorities were too narrow. They pointed to the heavy reliance on a few 'experts', with their priorities and models, to the neglect of the economy, business, education, health services other than for COVID-19, and other sectors of society.

The government's position was indeed not without its controversies and opponents. It differed both from more and less libertarian approaches, such as those in Sweden and New Zealand, respectively, and it rejected alternative positions, such as that put forward by the Great Barrington Declaration (Kulldorff et al, 2020) that called for a strategy placing greater emphasis on individual agency. The *Lockdown Files* (The Telegraph, 2023), containing many thousands of WhatsApp messages during the pandemic, also suggested a lack of consensus between ministers and officials, an often political rather than scientific rationale for policy, and discouragement of discussion and debate.

The main lesson is that, in future, policy in the event of a national crisis should be developed with greater national (and international) involvement and consensus, from experts in different fields as well as anybody else who is informed and interested. This includes the general public, who should not be underestimated. This project and others with different population groups demonstrate that individuals are in the best position to portray their experiences, needs and views. Diarists were a relatively educated and advantaged section of society but not the only ones with sensible opinions. However, their considered and pertinent observations throughout the pandemic demonstrate how any kind of national emergency needs to develop an official forum to tap into diverse experiences and views – and take them into account.

The question of lockdowns

The public health model, with its mantra of 'protect the NHS', aimed to put the prevention of illness and death at its heart. The virus was contagious, and a principal strategy was accordingly to isolate people from one another by means of lockdowns. An important question to be addressed in readiness for the possible arrival of another pandemic is whether these lockdowns were too early or too late, or indeed whether they were necessary at all.

Lockdowns curtailed individual liberty in a totally unprecedented manner, and led to considerable disadvantage to children and young people, those of all ages with health conditions other than COVID-19, and threatened the livelihoods of those in a wide variety of spheres. Whether or not they led to a significant reduction in deaths from the virus is not clear, and it does not seem that Sweden fared worse in this respect despite their more libertarian approach. So were the lockdowns timely and worthwhile? There are those on both sides of the fence. It was purportedly primarily the older members of society that were considered at greatest risk and in the most need of protection, so how did the lockdowns impact on the diarists?

Significantly, many diarists had begun to isolate themselves before the first formal lockdown. Even if they were not pleased to be singled out as at risk from the virus in an official and formal sense, they recognised that they might be vulnerable and did not want to become ill. Throughout the course of the project, most diarists continued to maintain their distance from others and conducted their daily lives in the spirit of the restrictions, even if diverging now and then when they deemed it safe enough to do so. The suggestion is that, even without legislated lockdowns, they would do what they could to avoid the virus.

Nonetheless, there were few diary entries that specifically challenged the existence of the lockdowns. There was a general acceptance of these measures and, indeed, considerable anxiety on the part of many whenever there was suggestion that restrictions would be lessened. This was not, however, simply for diarists' own protection, but also for that of others. They were worried for family and friends, and for the country more generally. For their own part they kept themselves safe.

Whether or not lockdowns should ever be repeated in the case of another pandemic is an open question that would need to take account of the characteristics of any such subsequent event. What is apparent is that lockdowns should not be undertaken lightly, and without a clear understanding and consideration of their impact on all sectors in society. Information, experiences and attitudes should be gathered widely and transparently, and the focus should be not only on illness and deaths, from both COVID-19 and other causes, but on inequalities, the economy, mental health, and much else too. The diarists were clear on this matter and so, as already iterated, input from the full range of national and international perspectives should be sought, examined and debated should there be another such occurrence.

Keeping everyone informed

The diarists clamoured for information as the pandemic unfolded. They were avidly reading the newspapers, and listening to and watching public broadcasts and other programmes, in order to understand what was happening and what was to be done. In the early weeks and months when few people, diarists included, had come into close contact with COVID-19, understandings were heavily dependent on what they were told. Key for the imparting of information, especially at the onset of the pandemic, were the daily briefings fronted by the prime minister and usually attended by medical and public health representatives. The government was responsible for the messages directed at the general population, with other perspectives largely sidelined.

Nonetheless, the government was in charge and diarists wished to be aware of their perspective and of any new restrictions that might be imposed or lifted. They were generally appreciative of the daily briefings even if they could feel bombarded with repetitive detail. Many wrote about how they assembled in front of their TV screens at 5 pm every weekday to be given the latest figures on hospitalisations and deaths, and to be updated on rules and restrictions and other key policy changes. It seemed that such regular televised events were welcomed and were an important aspect of any strategy to keep the nation in step with official thought and practice.

However, the message was more than the medium, and there was considerable dissatisfaction with the format and content of the briefings. Diarists were a literate and well-informed group who sought balanced and evidenced coverage of unfolding events. To be kept on board with the new policies, and compliant with instructions, they called for up-to-date, accurate and convincing information. Not everyone thought this was what they received.

First, they wanted a rational set of objectives when rules were changing all the time. What were the policy priorities and what were they hoping to achieve? There were many potential aims, such as reducing illness and death, protecting the most vulnerable, reducing the toll on children and young people, protecting the NHS, and reducing the burden on business and the economy. Was there a single priority or was it a matter of compromise?

ROSEMARY
Monday 27 April 2020

Every evening, as we listen and watch the daily press conference from politicians, medics and scientists, we hang on every word and try to comprehend the graphs which show whether or not our government's strategies are better or worse than the rest of the world. The unmentionable question which is not voiced directly is 'which is more important lives or livelihoods?'. We had hoped for some reprieve from this unnatural isolation.

Complaints were also forthcoming about the evidence base for policies and restrictions, and an over-reliance on a few perspectives as well as claims that policy was 'following the science'. Diarists called for greater honesty in policy briefings as some felt, for example, that conclusions drawn from complicated epidemiological modelling procedures were portrayed as factual rather than conjectural.

CAMPBELL
Saturday 13 June 2020

Today, a few phrases/words I wouldn't mind never hearing again: ...
Following the science as if 'the science' was some monolithic thing that you chose to follow or not follow. In fact (1) the science on the

pandemic – whether medical or in an epidemiological modelling sense has, because so little was known in advance of COVID-19, been (wholly forgivably) tentative, and often contradictory, depending on who the scientist is and (2) 'following the science' is a rather disingenuous politician's gloss on making a decision which may (or may not) take scientific advice into account, among a host of other factors.

ELEANOR
Sunday 2 August 2020
We seem to inhabit a surreal world where common sense plays no part in any government decisions. 'Follow the science', they said. I'm beginning to feel like a juggernaut led down a narrow lane by a faulty satnav with no possibility of reversing out or moving forward.

HOLLY
Saturday 11 April 2020
If they are being 'led by the science at every stage,' please will they publish what their sources are because I for one am still puzzled by some of it and I like a good read.

TARANAKI
Wednesday 3 June 2020
This week we have seen the actions of the government to be more politically based than scientifically based … despite repeated insistence by Johnson and co that they were 'following the science'. I think this mantra was preparation for a transfer of blame at some future enquiry.

There was also criticism of the use of statistics.

CARACTACUS
Saturday 18 July 2020
I see from today's *Times* that the officially published figures for coronavirus deaths have been over-estimated, as they include, as a coronavirus death, deaths of anyone who has once been diagnosed with the virus, even if death was actually caused by, say, a traffic accident. This is another example of poor administration by the government.

TERESA
Tuesday 14 April 2020
How come other countries were counting all the deaths that had occurred in 24 hours and the UK ignores the deaths in the community and only counts what happens in hospitals? This sounds heartless and cheating the statistics.

To have confidence in the messages that were being conveyed daily, it was also necessary that these were consensual among the proclaimed experts. Moreover, they were more convincing if they applied across Britain and did not differ between constituent countries.

CAMPBELL
Monday 20 July 2020
But this all illustrates the conflicting feelings I suspect many have now, that a fairly clear divergence has opened up between Johnson and the scientific advisers about the timing of the lockdown-ending/easing measures.

ELEANOR
Sunday 12 July 2020
It is interesting to notice that Scotland and Wales in particular, seem to wait for England to make its pronouncements and then follow a few days later with more measured and precise instructions. I often wish it was the other way round! Slow and steady wins the race.

KATJA
Friday 1 May 2020
It is all very confusing. I do wish the medics and scientific advisers plus the government could present a more united front to reassure the public.

Above all, diarists wanted honesty and transparency. They were well aware that knowledge about the COVID-19 virus was scant, particularly at the time of the initial lockdown, and clear that nobody, including politicians and public health officials, fully understood the situation and its prognosis. It was important that this was clearly acknowledged.

APPLETREE
Wednesday 3 June 2020
UK governments pronouncements that they made the right decisions at the right times look even more ridiculous. Why don't they admit it's just possible they might have made mistakes and that we're learning all the time about the virus and how to deal with it? We can't get rid of it for over four years … what a folly that fixed term Parliaments Act was.

HUMPHREY
Saturday 2 May 2020
As for the future, who knows? The government evidently doesn't have much of a clue either and I don't wholly blame them. There will be plenty of opportunities for re-assessment, and perhaps recriminations, at a later stage but it seems too early to know for sure whether they screwed up or

not. I'm sure glad I didn't have to take the decisions they had to take. My only worry is that I may be beginning to suffer from Stockholm syndrome. I'm beginning to sympathise with my jailors!

Providing transparent information on the progress of the pandemic, the rationale and evidence for policies, and clear information on how the nation should respond, was what the diarists called for. This provides a clear message from the experience of the recent pandemic.

Encouraging compliance

Individuals in positions of institutional authority become what Prus (1999) called 'targets of influence' noting 'the success of people's attempts to shape the behaviours of others generally depends on the target's willingness to cooperate with the agent or tactician in the situation at hand'. In this instance the government was the target of influence.

In this capacity, the government put out the daily briefings and other messages purportedly to inform and update but, importantly, also to encourage compliance. The coronavirus restrictions curtailed many taken-for-granted aspects of daily life across the nation and, as already suggested, the basis for these restrictions needed to be grounded. Beyond this, instructions had to be clear and they needed to make sense. While diarists were generally in favour of the lockdowns, they wanted to be told exactly what they were expected to do and why. Nonetheless, there was copious reference to misunderstandings and confusion. Indeed the UCL COVID-19 Social Study suggested that less than a third of people understood the prevailing rules (University College London News, 2021).

> ATHELSTANA
> *Friday 26 June 2020*
> Lockdown was simple. STAY AT HOME. Now all the lines are blurred and things no longer make sense. How does keeping children in small bubbles when at school equate to them mixing freely with everyone and anyone if they are on a crowded beach somewhere? Why is it necessary for footballers to arrive at a match in two coaches so they can be socially distanced when, once on the pitch, they are in close contact most of the time not just with their teammates and officials but the opposition too?

Diarists were quick to pick up on anomalies. It may be understandable that the rapidly changing nature and rules of the pandemic gave rise to confusion and a lack of clarity at all levels, but they nonetheless raised many unanswered questions for which they would have liked the best possible answers. Why, for example, did pubs reopen before schools? Why did the 'rule of six' allow the presence of additional infants in Scotland but not in England? Anomalies are inevitable but keeping them to a minimum is essential if the messages are to retain credibility.

> SIMON
> *Wednesday 16 July 2020*
> Re our library, it's 'open' to the extent that you can drop off books in the book bin outside and pick up books from the socially distanced counter but that's it. No browsing, etc. etc. Bit odd really when almost next door is a Waterstone's which has books piled high and theoretically if you pick one up and don't purchase it you are meant to put it on a trolley but no one seems to bother about it. Charity shops are open and one can browse the books and CDs (though our local music shop doesn't allow any browsing of music, CDs or instruments, only click and collect orders, which doesn't make much sense given that they have a very effective online site). Ah, the vagaries of post-lockdown transition.

Confusing messages had both serious and more frivolous implications. On the serious side, a poll undertaken by the charity Independent Age (2020) found that up to half the over-70s in their sample could be self-isolating unnecessarily as they thought this was what they had been told to do. On a much lighter note was the prolonged discussion about the definition of a 'substantial meal' towards the end of 2020. At the time, pubs in Tier 2 areas were allowed to serve drinks only if they accompanied a proper meal. The issue was whether or not a scotch egg would count. Although George Eustice, then Environment Secretary, suggested that it probably would, David Laing, co-owner of North Yorkshire-based specialists The Clucking Pig retorted that 'It depends on how they're made'.

As a key purpose of messages from the government was to encourage compliance with the rules, it was important that they were reasonable and convincingly linked to risk. Diarists were pragmatic in their adherence to the restrictions imposed by the pandemic. They conformed in the main, but would on occasion make their own decisions about acceptable and safe behaviour. A clear message is that all legally imposed restrictions need to be clear and justifiable.

Keeping spirits up

Compliance with the COVID-19 restrictions may also have been sought in more emotive ways. Despite some suggestion that *The Lockdown Files* (The Telegraph, 2023) revealed a government strategy to oversee 'project fear', overt accusations that this had been the case were rare among the diarists. What was clear, however, is that there was a considerable amount of anxiety in play, and that most people were exercising due caution. The virus was intangible and nobody really knew exactly where the dangers lay. As several diarists wrote, it was better to be safe than sorry.

Whether or not the official pandemic messages did, intentionally or unintentionally, instil a measure of fear, it is unquestionably true that for many months the official strategy was to err on the side of caution. The public health message appeared to be that lockdowns should continue until it was presumed safe to release people from protection. This approach had its supporters as well as its opponents, and it took precedence until 24 February 2022 when the message changed to one of living with the virus. The transition was not straightforward after such a prolonged period of restrictions. It had been much easier to lock people down than to unlock them again, and it took time for many diarists to fully embrace their former lives. Covid anxiety syndrome (Nikčević and Spada, 2020) could become a reality.

EDGAR
Monday 8 June 2020

Getting into lockdown now seems to have been the easy part; getting back to normality feels as though it's going to be hard. Living with uncertainty will take, I feel, a lot of time from which to recover. We were wondering about how people managed in previous pandemics and I mentioned the Spanish flu. My wife said that she didn't remember how that had been. I said, 'Well it did happen in 1918'. 'Oh yes,' she said, 'no wonder I don't remember it', and laughed. It was another nice moment which we enjoyed together.

Perhaps the lesson is that any strategy for the pandemic should include consideration of the mood of the nation. It is evidently impossible to be overly positive when in the throes of a crisis, but it is also beneficial not to induce a large measure of fear. This is important not only for the duration of the pandemic but also in enabling the population to emerge, without undue anxiety, from restrictions when it is safe to do so. It may be easy to take freedom away but it is also important to be able to give it back.

The role of the police

Compliance with the rules was overseen by the involvement of the police. The diarists were good at restricting their own activities, except in cases where their pragmatic reasoning suggested that strict compliance with the rules was not necessary, and few had had contact with the police, either directly or vicariously. Nonetheless, those who had were not necessarily impressed. It was no doubt difficult for the police to keep up with changing regulations and the message here is again a call for greater clarity about the rules as well as consistent treatment of those found to have flouted them.

It is also a call for understanding and reasonableness, and for restricting policing to only particularly serious breaches of the law that put others in danger. These messages are in line with the recommendations of a report on policing the pandemic from The Police Foundation and Crest Advisory (Aitkenhead et al, 2022) which stressed how the rules imposed in a national crisis must be clear and clearly communicated. The report also pointed to the difficulties caused by the grey area between the law and government guidance. The number of people fined by the courts during the pandemic were in the thousands, often for misdemeanours such as attending gatherings, not wearing a mask, or leaving home during the lockdowns. Did these all deserve criminal convictions or should they instead have been simply issued with a caution or word of advice? The criminalisation of what, in normal times, is perfectly lawful behaviour, is a decision not to be taken lightly.

Accountability all round

The lockdowns and new restrictions were endorsed in principle by almost all diarists who, in turn, adopted the new morality during the pandemic and, generally speaking, issued considerable condemnation of those who did not. They were especially incensed when public figures broke the rules they had helped to create. Double standards were not appreciated. Although not all followed all the rules to the letter themselves, they were generally law-abiding. Most also had children, grandchildren, friends and acquaintances who were making their own sacrifices to follow the rules, and there was general agreement that it was up to everybody to conform to the spirit of the law.

The new morality covered behaviour, but also the prudent use of money. Everyone was made aware that the pandemic would make a dent in the economy and, when there was clear evidence of hardship all around, spending millions on equipment that was never used, hospitals that were never populated, tracing procedures that had serious failings, and so on, was severely criticised. Even during a pandemic and lockdowns, the government is accountable for how money from the public purse is spent. Again, this comes back to transparency and the messages and information provided for public consumption.

The internet for all

The internet provided an invaluable lifeline for the millions of people confined to their homes during the lockdowns. It helped them to work, fulfil commitments of many kinds and, importantly, stay in touch with family and friends. The diarists were no exception. They wrote thousands of words describing the very many ways in which Zoom and other comparable programmes were central in their lives and used for myriad purposes. New forms of sociability developed rapidly, from virtual dinner dates to quiz nights, and from activities with grandchildren to family celebrations. The internet also facilitated social activities including exercise and painting classes, singing, participation in interest groups, attendance at religious services, ordering food and other items, and much more besides. Being able to go online was an important resource during the pandemic for almost all diarists.

There can be little doubt that a lockdown without the means to stay in touch with others would have led to much more loneliness and distress. This was indeed suggested by information gathered by the Covid-19 Social Study for which over 70,000 UK adults completed weekly questionnaires between March and August 2020 (Sommerlad et al, 2022). The main findings were that supportive relationships with others greatly reduced the risk of depression, and that phone and video calls could help in the absence of face-to-face interaction.

While the internet was used creatively throughout the lockdowns, it is unlikely to have reached its full potential. It has, for instance, been suggested that online technologies could be used to deliver cognitive behaviour therapies to counter isolation and loneliness (Käll et al, 2019). As a resource within most homes, a key message is to continue to develop means for support for individuals should they again be isolated and unable to make social contacts by other means.

Most diarists were adequately equipped to participate in online activities. Others, though, whether or not in their age group, were not so fortunate. The message is that it is important to ensure that everybody who wants it can have good access to the internet and working mobile phone connections. During a pandemic or other time when access to assistance for technical advice or problems is difficult, a national support service to help older people learn basic skills, and to assist those without alternative help, would also be invaluable.

Protection where protection is needed

Diarists had their fair share of worries and anxieties during the pandemic but, generally speaking, expressed more concern for others than for themselves. At a societal level, they mentioned the disproportionate risk experienced by essential workers and by those living in much more disadvantaged circumstances than themselves. There were many groups within the population that they felt needed more protection and assistance than they did. According to one diarist, it was perhaps only the over-70s who did not deserve a clap at the Thursday evening turnouts.

Among their own age group there were also many others far less advantaged than them, whether by dint of their economic circumstances, geographical location, race, ethnicity or ill-health. Diarists also acknowledged that social isolation and loneliness among the elderly could be concerning (Santini et al, 2020) and discussed how the most vulnerable, including the shielders, might best be protected and supported.

BETTYMAC
Thursday 8 May 2020

I like many others have a husband with serious underlying health conditions. I have gone to great lengths to shield him and would like to continue to do so. Most people I know have adopted a common sense approach to this and will be prepared to be very careful, and keep to a regime involving social distancing of some sort. … I can take risk for myself, can I take it for my husband? What is the balance however between that and seeing grandchildren, resuming sport and meeting friends face to face, albeit at a social distance? Is it a choice between grandchildren and husband for example. Apart from personal considerations many over 70s, myself included, provide vital childcare on which the economy depends. Without an economy we are blighting future generations. … I would therefore like a clear policy for 'shielders of the shielded'.

ROSA
Sunday 16 August 2020

I cannot say I have worked out how to do it, but if there is a re-imposition of social distancing the position of people who live on their own should be borne in mind by those working out the rules, otherwise I think the severe loneliness factor could be fatal to some and very challenging to many.

SKYE
Friday 16 May 2020

As time goes on it's not so much social isolation that is affecting people but lack of touch, hugs and cuddles. We can phone people, Skype and face time but not hug. I support an elderly lady who lives on her own. I'm unable to visit her but phone regularly. She is struggling both physically and mentally. Her son visited yesterday and the small act of him making her a cup of coffee cheered her up. It was a small thing but meant a lot to her. Food for thought.

Where resources are finite, the clear message is a call for a triage of need to ensure that these are allocated in the best possible way.

Seventy somethings as a resource

As a group of seventy somethings living in comfortable conditions, diarists were able to protect themselves from the risk of becoming ill during the pandemic. The fact that no diarist appeared to contract the virus between the time of the first lockdown and the easing of restrictions testifies to this ability. Three diarists believed they contracted the virus during the early months before lockdown, and one mentioned being unwell some months later when restrictions were eased, but these cases are somewhat different. This group was, generally speaking, at low risk. They made their own assessments of risk and were capable of looking after themselves. They also tended to be active and energetic.

> ROSEMARY
> *Wednesday 20 May 2020*
> From my point of view, I would like to get some maintenance done on my house but it doesn't look as though I can organise trades people to come any time soon. I would also like to buy a new laptop but will need assistance transferring files and setting up a new system. This is very frustrating when one is getting older and as a GP nurse said to me the other day not having met me, 'Well you may be sprightly but you are 77'. We over-70s don't want to hang about. We need to get on with things.

So, rather than needing support and protection, many diarists felt frustrated at not being able to help out as much as they might like. They mentioned how they wished they could do something useful other than giving money to charities or donations to food banks. Volunteering did not seem to be easy to sign up for, and some diarists were told they were too old. Those that made enquiries often seemed not to be asked to do anything. Apart from personal and community initiatives, there did not appear to be much that they could do to help. Several wrote about how they were making masks or bags for nurses to wash their uniforms in, or were on a list to sew medical gowns, but many wanted to be of greater assistance.

> OLIVE
> *Friday 1 May 2020*
> Agency – the ability to take some control is empowering even in difficult circumstances. Making donations and volunteering to help others in respectful ways, clapping the NHS etc., are important forms of agency at this time.

> RAIN
> *Thursday 23 April 2020*
> At the Zoom meeting for our monthly breakfast group one person talked about feeling so useless being confined to self-isolation when she knew

there would be contributions she could make. Another person feeling the same felt reduced to just donating money. The theme of what social contribution we can make, other than staying at home and keeping our distance, is becoming more pressing. Gestures like clapping, gestures of thoughtful kindness to friends is another, but there is such need and no way yet of finding out what we can do from home with the materials we have. I am going to ask the younger generation, particularly the teachers, if they have any ideas or suggestions.

This was a missed opportunity. Healthy, fit and enterprising citizens of 70 and over were a neglected national asset. They may have put energies into enhanced activity within the community, but more should have been done to give them the chance to do more for those less fortunate and less able than themselves. They had both time and motivation to help, and indeed a study commissioned by the Centre for Ageing Better (Addario et al, 2022b) found that the over-70s were more likely than other age groups to continue volunteering over the period of the pandemic. The diarists commonly regarded themselves as belonging to a particularly advantaged demographic. They wanted to help.

The pandemic as an opportunity for change

Parker (2020) and co-authors argued that, besides recommendations for the course and content of policies should there be another comparable pandemic, there should be a rethink of the state of the nation more generally. They regarded the crisis of the pandemic as a turning point, or a non-linear moment (Kashtan, 2020) when something out of the ordinary happens and the anticipated trajectory of daily life becomes disrupted and creates a 'sudden enhancement of possibilities'.

Many diarists had also considered whether the pandemic might effect lasting change. On the one hand, and around the time of the first lockdown, there had been concerns for a toll on the economy, social unrest and a possible breakdown in law and order, a shortage of jobs for young people, an increase in public surveillance, and lowered standards in public services. On the other hand, however, there had been hopes that the crisis of the pandemic, and in particular the inequalities it had underlined, would lead to more beneficial changes once some normality was restored.

BAREFOOT DOC
Saturday 17 May 2020
Seeing women's responses (in this evening's news) to the challenges of the next phase of un-lockdown-ing, I was aware of something else gendered in what will unroll over the coming period – of years, I think. The enormous

importance and centrality of care work – typically marginalised and low paid – is blatantly now on the surface: in acute medicine, in nursing homes, in primary schools. There will be arguments and recriminations, and powerful pressures to revalue, reward and re-invest these sectors of contribution to our 'living economy', as well as the pragmatic re-organisations that will not just vanish when 'normality' has been resumed.

WILL
Wednesday 8 April 2020

If anything good is to come out of this crisis perhaps it will be the need to rethink, from first principles, the way we live, the things we value and the way we reward people for the work they do. The level of inequality, even within our own country, is obscene and we cannot let the rich come out of it unscathed as we did with the 2008 financial crash, while the Tory government claimed we were 'all in this together'. The massive debts we will have amassed when we emerge must be paid for predominantly by those who can most afford to carry the financial burden, not those who can least afford it. We need the sort of rethink that followed WW2 which created the welfare state, the NHS and a better education system. But will it happen?

Here endeth the lesson – till I become angry again.

It is too early to make any definitive statement about permanent societal changes consequent on the pandemic, but Kirk et al (2022) provided some evidence on how COVID-19 had changed lives in the UK nearly two years on from the first lockdown. The picture regarding inequalities was not encouraging: there seemed to be a growing divide between the most and least advantaged, with higher income households most likely to have managed to save during the pandemic. On other matters, it was concluded that working from home, at least part of the time, seemed set to stay, and that there had been some population movement from urban to rural areas, although whether this would continue was not clear. The evidence was more equivocal for the impact on foreign travel, staycations, and the use of video technologies such as Zoom. Online shopping had increased but companies such as Ocado were facing significant challenges. The future of cash, partly because money could be seen as dirty, was also in question (Tischer et al, 2020).

At the more personal level, Office for National Statistics (2022) data collected in March of that year, suggested that lockdown behaviours had subsided to a considerable extent. People appeared to be getting up earlier but were engaging in DIY, gardening, reading and watching TV much less. It seemed, however, that the over-60s were still keeping up with keeping fit and exercise. The People and Nature Survey (Natural England, 2022) further found that in March 2022 almost half the adults surveyed were spending more time outdoors than they had before the pandemic, with a slightly smaller proportion saying that nature and wildlife had become more important for their well-being. People from higher income households were most likely to contribute to these trends.

From what the diarists wrote in the follow-ups, it seemed that there had also been some lasting impact within communities. At the time of the third lockdown in early 2021, there was not much enthusiasm for the revived Thursday night clapping, and the level of community activity was generally down, but WhatsApp groups were often still thriving, and many diarists knew a few more people in their neighbourhoods. The poorer weather was no doubt in part responsible for the diminished community spirit, but so too was the novelty factor of the original lockdown. This picture was corroborated by an Opinium poll of 7,000 Britons in January 2021 which suggested that over a third of people felt more a part of their local community due to the pandemic (Press Association, 2021). Moreover, a survey of 2,000 adults by Pro Bono Economics (2020) indicated that community spirit had waned in the second compared to the first lockdown. According to participants, far fewer people had helped or supported their neighbours at the later date. Research commissioned by Ageing Better also confirmed some decline overall in community spirit and support as time went on (Addario et al, 2022a).

The picture is mixed. Britain is unlikely to be quite the same after the pandemic as before, but the evidence is still being gathered. In general, most people's behaviour has returned to its previous state, although new habits developed during the lockdowns may be sustained at some level. The lesson would seem to be to seek to encourage the continuation of any silver linings arising from the pandemic once the crisis has subsided. This is true at both societal and personal levels.

Being prepared for next time

Britain, as other countries, was largely unprepared for the arrival of COVID-19 on its shores. Had it learned from previous or previously threatened pandemics? Perhaps the greatest lesson of all is that the country needs to be ready in case there is a next time. *Sperate parati* or go forward prepared.

CHARLES
Sunday 17 July 2022
When I hear radio commentary on scientific research relating to the last or a future pandemic I remind myself that funding for this research is so important, and how woefully our previous governments fell short in this respect.

> **MABEL**
> *Monday 1 August 2022*
> We know now that pandemics are possible, and we need to be vigilant and prepared. For instance we need to be alert for warning signs, support relevant scientific, medical and research programmes, maintain stocks of essential equipment, and have an emergency action plan at the ready. I'm sure there is much more that should also be done, but this would be a start.

There are many ways to prepare for any future pandemic, and many voices that need to be taken into account. Apart from the issues already discussed, there are economic considerations. There was considerable criticism from the diarists about how money was spent during the main phases of the pandemic on contracts issued, support provided, equipment bought and not used, and the test and trace system. Indeed, a report in October 2021 suggested that this in itself cost £37 million. The arguments on all these matters are, however, complex and beyond the scope of this chapter. Nonetheless, they do suggest the necessity of accountability in spending patterns.

Being prepared for next time means repeating the successes as well as avoiding the failures. The heightened sense of community and altruism, for instance, arose spontaneously and, it would be hoped, could do so again. And, despite some question marks over the safety and effectiveness of all forms of the vaccine, there is little doubt that its speedy development was an enormous high spot that gave the nation hope that the end to the pandemic was in sight. The creativity and imagination demonstrated by so many people in their activities via Zoom, and the sense of humour that endured the pandemic, are other positives to be drawn from the situation.

Maybe the ultimate thought is not to forget. Spinney (2017) described the 'collective forgetting' that occurred after the 1918 pandemic, suggesting it was remembered as millions of private tragedies rather than a national crisis. It is to be hoped that the coronavirus pandemic will not be subject to a similar fate.

Summary

Discussion and debate on the management of the pandemic, and the policies and restrictions put in place, will continue for many years to come. It is unlikely there will ever be complete consensus as to what 'worked' and what did not. This chapter outlines a few areas for consideration, arising from this diary project, should a comparable situation recur. These relate to participation in decision-making, the issue of lockdowns, communications from government as the pandemic appeared and progressed, and the encouragement of compliance from the government and the police. The mood of the nation is also discussed. Other issues raised include the internet as an invaluable lifeline when people are confined to their homes, the need to focus resources where they are most needed, the potential for crises to provide opportunities for social change, and older people as a neglected resource. It is also important that memories of the pandemic are kept alive so that the nation is prepared should there be a comparable occurrence. COVID-19 affected the nation and not simply the lives of countless people.

10

Conclusion

The COVID-19 pandemic was a period of historic importance. Not only did it signify a universal and global health issue, but it also brought in unprecedented restrictions on personal freedom across the world. As Jarvis et al (2020) discussed, it was a state of exception, a concept developed by the German philosopher Schmitt in the 1920s. It was a time when the government overturned the prevailing rule of law in the name of the public good. Legislation was enacted in new areas of daily life and citizens were expected to toe the line and accept the status quo.

How did citizens react to this novel situation? Previous chapters in this book have addressed this question from the perspective of a group of older diarists in Britain, and predominantly living in England. Through their regular diary entries during the period when the pandemic was at its height, they provide an interesting and contemporaneous case study that illustrates how these seventy somethings developed their understandings of what was happening, and the impact this had on their behaviour and attitudes. It shows how, in the main, they acted in accordance with the restrictions, but also how they used their own human agency to do so pragmatically. They adapted quickly to the changing circumstances but did so according to their own interpretations of what was required and what was safe. As well as recounting their own activities, they looked beyond their own situations to the circumstances of others and the management of the pandemic. They also reminisced, told funny stories, shared recipes and much more. Despite the domination of an invisible virus, life went on.

Information on the nature and potency of the virus was in short supply, and diarists – as indeed the government, institutions and everyone else – gleaned their understandings from informal as well as formal sources. Although traditional social interactionists, such as Berger and Luckmann, Blumer, Goffman and others, based their theories of knowledge on more gradual and incremental social change, their interpretations and explanations remain relevant to the much more sudden and rapid transformations that occurred in response to the arrival of COVID-19 on Britain's shores. This interactionist approach examines how people acquire knowledge about their social universes, or their sets of beliefs that give meaning and legitimacy to the institutional structure of which they are a part. This type of knowledge or, more strictly speaking, understanding, is different from the knowledge of less controversial factual aspects, such as today is Wednesday or there are

100 pence in a pound. Social universes are determined through interactions, and traditionally face-to-face interactions, with others. In current times, however, and in the case of the pandemic, these are extended to include virtual interactions with both others and the media, as well as with modern technology, place, space and time.

The pandemic as a social problem

The coronavirus pandemic was characterised by uncertainty. It had arisen with little warning and brought with it scant indication of how the virus could be identified, and where and how it could be contracted. There was also an absence of knowledge on its likely impact on both the nation and its citizens, and on how long it would remain a problem. In the early stages of the pandemic there were few diarists who had any first-hand, or even second-hand, experience of it. Indeed, and throughout the course of the project, only four diarists thought they had had the virus, although in three cases this was early on in the development of the pandemic and there had been no confirmatory tests. Perhaps the event that afforded the most public, albeit indirect, experience of the virus was the early hospitalisation of the then prime minister, Boris Johnson. Generally speaking, however, government and citizens alike relied on vicarious knowledge that was, at best, patchy. There was an intangible threat.

Uncertainty is a central concept in the analysis of risk. In earlier times, people had turned to astrologers, seers and religion for answers to the unknowable. Currently, however, the emphasis is much more on what is often termed scientific evidence. As Zinn (2021) discussed, there is a tendency to regard societal risks as largely manageable by identifying the risk factors and then assessing their impact. Such risk analysis is nowadays fundamental in many spheres from the costing of insurance premiums to the likelihood of a hot summer or an economic crash. In other words, uncertainty is reformulated as knowledge.

Whatever the spin, the pandemic brought uncertainty coupled with a lack of experience of comparable situations. There was also an imperative to act quickly to manage the crisis. Becker (1973) argued that social issues do not simply exist but are constructed as problematic and, accordingly, enforced through new social rules. This seems to be what happened in this instance. A constructionist perspective gains support from the varied responses to the pandemic internationally. Although it was a global phenomenon, different nation states dealt with it differently. For instance, while Sweden minimised regulation and avoided mandatory lockdowns, New Zealand was among countries to impose long-standing and severe restrictions. In the event, Britain went with most other countries and introduced legislation that curbed individual freedoms in previously unknown ways.

Dealing with the pandemic and the uncertainty indeed demanded a considerable amount of social construction on everyone's part. The nation was confronted daily with graphs and statistics regarding illness and deaths, and epidemiologists presented their models that purported to make predictions about the likely course of the crisis. In addition, politicians chanted their mantra of 'following the science' in the absence of definitive information, shops were reorganised to maintain, possibly somewhat randomly, at least two metres distance between customers, and all manner of activity was curtailed in a somewhat arbitrary fashion. The restrictions sometimes defied logic and anomalies abounded. Amid these claims and measures, citizens themselves were also doing their best to remain safe. Nobody quite knew what would lead to the best outcome, but almost everybody was acting in accordance with the new rules as interpreted by their own constructions of risk and danger.

Pragmatic adaptation

Uncertainty is a form of knowledge, but it is not grounded in the sense that knowing it has been raining all day, or that a dentist appointment is at ten o'clock, might be. It does not prescribe specific behaviour other than perhaps seeking out interactions to gain more information, or acting with caution in a context engendering fear and anxiety. Most diarists did both these things. They watched and listened to government and news briefings in the hope of understanding more, and shared their understandings through their face-to-face and virtual interactions with others. They also largely obeyed the imposed restrictions.

They did not, however, conform with the new legislation to the letter, but acted pragmatically. Diarists were generally law-abiding and did not want to contract COVID-19 and face the possibility of illness or death, but they also did not abandon their own cognitive powers or a sense of personal agency. They were generally supportive of the lockdowns, for both their own and others' safety but, as time went on, and rules became confusing, they became more likely to bend them to a degree if they deemed their actions to be safe. They were not always supportive of police activity to caution behaviours that did not strictly follow the law of the day, and nor did they always want to do what they were told by their children. They could, nonetheless, be censorious of others' behaviour seen as risky. It was a complex mix.

It is often said that social interactionists fail to take account of social structure and power. Hannem (2021) countered this assertion by demonstrating how, in the case of the pandemic, the government exerted its influence on social interactions. The ability to talk to whoever one liked wherever one liked was curtailed, and interactions in the physical presence of another were severely restricted. Social interactionists also assert that individual agency operates within social constraints, and this was clearly demonstrated by diarists who made pragmatic adaptations to enable them to approximate the taken-for-granted aspects of their previous lives. They were generally stoic and wanted to be able to carry on doing the things that were important to them.

Family and friends were particularly significant and, accordingly, almost everybody became (if they were not already) adept at participating in Zoom or other video messaging platforms. Not only did this enable them to keep in touch with those close to them, and often grandchildren in particular, but provided opportunities to communicate with colleagues, participate in activities such as exercise classes, quizzes, social events, religious meetings, and much more.

They also sought out new opportunities for social contacts, in part to compensate for the missed interactions with family and friends. Increased contact with neighbours and greater involvement in the local community were aspects of this adaptation, reflecting stronger 'bonding' within peer groups as well as more 'bridging' between groups not usually in touch (Putnam, 2000). Following the initial forays for the Thursday evening clap for essential workers, localities developed their own WhatsApp neighbourhood groups as well as other initiatives to support one another. Many diarists also commented on how they had got to know neighbours and others better, and that people they encountered on their daily walks seemed friendlier than before. There was a sense of mutualism and commonality induced by the pandemic.

Adaptations were also required for many household tasks. A considerable number of diary entries charted the new chores of cleaning and gardening, as outside help was outlawed. Sourcing food also called for new tactics. A preoccupation for many at the start of the pandemic was arranging a food delivery or a 'click and collect'. This seemed a monumental task and success brought a sense of achievement.

Simply touching everyday objects also called for new strategies. Diarists wrote about washing food, isolating items until they were deemed safe, leaving post unopened, manipulating country gates with sticks, and generally avoiding the handling of anything that might possibly transmit the virus. Keeping it at bay was a key priority.

In all these ways diarists were diverging from their taken-for-granted lives (Schutz, 1945). The pandemic encouraged them to restructure living spaces and rules. Substitutions were being made, such as Zoom for face-to-face contact, flowers for hugs, the local community for friends and family, and perhaps flora and fauna for friends. Adaptations were made pragmatically to satisfy practical, cognitive and emotional needs.

New interactions and meanings

Early symbolic interactionists developed their theories of knowledge in the early to mid-twentieth century when life was rather different from how it is now. There was radio and the beginnings of television, but everybody did not have a personal computer or mobile phone, and there were no such things as video calling or social media. The interactions the early theorists described were essentially face-to-face communications between individuals. Their pronouncements, nonetheless, continue to have validity with the advent of new technologies and ways of life. During the pandemic, as outlined above, social interaction with those outside households was maintained via Zoom or other similar platforms. Diarists had become what Gottschalk (2021) termed 'terminal selves'. Social encounters were virtual although no less real. While participants might meet others in their pyjama bottoms, they were still able to discern body language and facial expressions.

Recent interactionists have added more types of encounter to the list of those facilitating interactions and knowledge. Puddephatt (2021), for example, cited the natural environment as a context of interest for symbolic interactionists as citizens engage in dialogue with their surroundings. This was very much the case for the diarists for whom the first visible signs of the national emergency were the absence of traffic and aeroplanes, the peace and quiet, and perhaps the long-since-heard sound of birdsong. They passed much time outside during the hot months of 2020, spending time in their gardens as well as taking daily walks and exploring their neighbourhoods with much greater interest than before. They also engaged with the natural environment and diary entries included copious writings on their observations. Sightings of many types of flora and fauna were recorded with considerable enthusiasm and excitement.

Place and space took on new meanings. Large sections of the population were spending much more time at home than usual, and this could mean significant change. Many diarists, for example, were used to being out and about and often eating away from home. This was now off the agenda. They might also have started to use their staircases and gardens for exercise in a way they had not done before, transformed rooms for new projects, and organised a comfortable place with a suitable backcloth for the considerable amount of time they would be spending on their computers. Paradoxically, while not permitted to allow the physical presence of others in their homes, they were now becoming accustomed to opening up their homes to acquaintances as well as strangers via Zoom. Private spaces had, in a sense, become public, and the presentation of self on the front stage was now taking place in settings previously regarded as back stage (Goffman, 1959).

Other spaces too changed their meaning. The streets were peaceful and almost free of vehicles, shops that remained open were potentially risky places, playgrounds were areas where children were no longer welcome, and hospital and other car parks were all but empty. The outward signs were a daily confirmation of the national emergency.

Time too was viewed and used differently. There were new things to do, and new timetables. Many diarists, especially in the early days following the first lockdown, adapted quickly to the absence of any prior structure to the day and reported getting up later as there was nowhere to go. New routines were then to be established, or not. There seemed to be much more time and many diarists wrote about their good intentions which may, or may not, have materialised. There were few constraints in the early stages of the pandemic, but this changed as timetabled events, such as Zoom meetings, increased. Many diarists commented on how the pace of life instantly slowed down as the first lockdown was announced, but how that feeling did not necessarily last for very long.

When one day could seem much like any other, there was also an emphasis on keeping weekends and holidays special, and often putting a special effort into ensuring that occasions such as birthdays and wedding anniversaries were memorable. The greater significance of food also led some diarists to treat meals and mealtimes with heightened reverence. These pragmatic adaptations went some way to preserving old habits and priorities as well as injecting something 'special' into the new regimen.

An emphasis on altruism

Despite some stories of selfishness, such as those clearing the supermarket shelves of pasta and loo rolls, or scamming for profit, the pandemic was characterised by endless examples of altruism and prosocial behaviour. Earlier chapters have detailed the general respect for restrictions and measures to keep both self and others safe, greater friendliness in neighbourhoods, the overt appreciation for essential workers and the wish for them to be properly remunerated and not just clapped, the countless initiatives and activities within communities to assist both strangers and acquaintances, the provision of free food and goods by restaurants and other outlets, and the production of pandemic-related materials and equipment by individuals and businesses.

It seemed that circles of altruism (Singer, 1981) had not only expanded as a consequence of the pandemic, but also shifted. This appeared to be the case for the diarists. First, they were not always able to support their family and friends in accustomed ways. They could communicate remotely, as almost all did, but they were frequently prevented from maintaining their normal patterns of face-to-face interaction. It was perhaps as a form of compensation that many then turned to nearby and further neighbours for more direct contact. This contact, in turn, promoted mutual support and aid within communities. There was a heightened level of 'bonding' and 'bridging' within localities (Putnam, 2000) and a shift in focus for acts of altruism. Second, they were generally subject to a bombardment of news stories, many of which presented the tragic side of the pandemic. Awareness of the dire conditions of many others was brought to the fore and engendered concern. This also could spark empathy and altruism. Third, and as most diarists were retired, the pandemic brought spare time and a wish to be useful. This also encouraged activities to help others, especially where there were evident gaps in state provision. Pragmatic adaptation was again in evidence.

For social interactionists, and particularly stemming from the work of Mead, altruism is explained by an understanding of the generalised other (Callero, 1985–86). As well as the influences of moral laws and other people's expectations, prosocial behaviour is influenced by the ability to put oneself in the situation of others. This ability is developed with maturity through interactions with multiple perspectives that have been identified, organised, and used as a basis for action (Miller, 1982).

CAMPBELL
Friday 1 May 2020

On the one hand I hardly think I am more fearful than the next person. With some reason since I have been in fairly dangerous situations from time to time over the last two decades of my professional life – rather more I suspect than Mr Gloves; but then it had a *purpose* – doing my job. Of course I don't want to wind up in ICU, let alone die, fighting for every breath. But up to now at least it's been possible to see my obedience to the social distancing guidelines as partly – maybe only a small part, I don't know – as altruistic. First because anyone who is infected risks infecting someone else. And secondly because if you were to get infected with an underlying condition you have been at risk of taking a hospital bed that could be occupied by someone who certainly hasn't been infected because of their own irresponsibility – an NHS worker for example; it might be a doctor or nurse, it might be a hospital porter or an ambulance driver, or a bus driver or a supermarket employee, or any one of a dozen categories of people who have no choice but to expose themselves to danger. Perhaps the second argument has partly abated because the NHS, as the government keeps proclaiming, has not been overwhelmed. But I'd still be a little – well more than a little actually – embarrassed – especially once contact tracing starts in earnest as it should, if it ever does – to wind up in hospital and have to list all the people I have mingled with in contravention of the guidelines.

Diarists tended to follow the rules, or their personal interpretations of the rules, both to keep themselves safe but also with a concern for others. They did not want to feel guilty for somebody else's ill-health, and they also did not want to be the object of negative regard. This reflected what Cooley (1902) termed 'the looking glass self'. Personal identity is not simply a matter of how a person regards themselves but also how they are perceived by everybody else. Social interaction is an important determinant of self-identification.

Empathy is a key constituent of altruism and there was much evidence of prosocial attitudes and behaviour towards the less fortunate. For the diarists' part, they usually had spare time and regarded themselves as luckier than most. Many were keen to help where they could, and to this end established food banks in their communities, delivered food to others who were homebound, and helped neighbours in both practical and emotional ways. The early setting up of WhatsApp groups in many localities often had the initial purpose of offering shopping and other services to others in the community. Diarists were also busy maintaining contact with family and friends, and particularly those who might be feeling isolated. They were worrying about their families and children just as their children were worrying about them.

AUSTEN
Friday 24 July 2020

I feel so sorry for my friend suffering with Parkinsons, at 78 and with no family other than an older brother, her only regular contacts are carers a couple of times a week, and then me and another friend visit on separate days for a chat. Her health has deteriorated badly, and although it is a degenerative disease I can't help thinking that lockdown hasn't helped. She is so depressed, it is hard work to get a smile now, and we used to have really quite jolly coffee mornings.

I'm so sorry for my grandchildren, between 18 and 29. The younger boys worrying about the cost of university, accommodation etc. when they are not getting the education they expected. The older girls at work worrying about their career futures, job security etc.

Many diarists wanted to be able to do more (see Chapters 4 and 9). Increased concern for others was not surprising in the face of an uncertain but major social threat and, in the main, they wanted to be active and, probably, to have a sense of purpose and control. It is not suggested that all actions were pure altruism in the sense of complete selflessness in that being helpful can be rewarding. Nonetheless, whatever the motive, an evident rise in mutuality, reciprocity and concern for others was a positive note in an otherwise out-of-the-ordinary situation. Although physical horizons had contracted, social horizons had expanded.

Varieties of experience

The pandemic, the lockdowns and other restrictions, and the changes to daily life, were new experiences for all. Among the diarists they came with a growing recognition, as their interactions with others and the media increased, of their own fortune in comparison with most other people.

While they had their disappointments and anxieties, they could, in the main, remain in comfort and hide away out of danger. They regularly expressed concern for doctors, nurses, care home assistants and all the other essential workers that daily faced the risk of contracting COVID-19, for those losing their jobs, businesses and income, and for the young people whose education, career and social activities had been derailed. They also wrote about the disparities in outcome experienced by those living in richer and poorer locations, those with pre-existing health conditions that made them particularly vulnerable, and those in certain ethnic and racial groups. It was also a very different experience for those who became ill and for those who did not, as it was for those living alone and those in happy and unhappy relationships. Worries extended to friends and families who might be putting themselves at risk or who were lonely and isolated. Everyone was affected by the pandemic but not everyone was affected equally.

There is not, and never will be, a definitive account of the pandemic in Britain or indeed in the world. It was experienced very differently by different people. Even within families there could be a wide variety of experiences.

BEA
Wednesday 8 April 2020

I have been doing a mental 'roll call' of all the members of the wider family to work out how the Coronavirus is affecting them all.

The Oldies – aged in their 70s (two of us) and 60s (five others). Six, including we two, are at home. We all have gardens, thank goodness. Two of the six are in France. They are in serious lockdown. Two others are in quarantine having returned from Australia after their stay there was cut short. The final one is working in our local community hospital. She is on the desk in the Minor Injury Unit but because it is very quiet, she might be transferred to a ward as a clerk. She lives with a cat who is not self-isolating.

The Mid-lifers – aged in their 40s (seven members). The nurse is back to work in the Surgical Department but has been 'upskilled' to work on Critical Care if necessary. Her husband, a quantity surveyor is furloughed from his job. The supply teacher has no work. Her self-employed roofer husband has some emergency work but is struggling to get materials. The reviewing officer (child protection) is working mainly from home. She holds conference phone calls and says that though the professionals struggle, the young clients are often more forthcoming than face to face. Her husband is being 'shielded' as he is disabled with multiple health issues. The dockyard worker is working from home, which seems very bizarre. (I have not noticed many submarines parked up in the yard.) The recruiter is working from home. His wife, who has her own business on-line, is busier than ever.

The Youngsters – aged in their 20s (five members, including one in Australia). The administrator is working from home. The hotel management trainee has been furloughed. The student is studying back in the family home. The buyer has taken a cut in hours (and pay) and is working from home. The Australian sales rep. has also taken a cut in hours and pay.

The Teenagers – (six members) are all at home with their families.

Because of this diversity of experience, there were also strong contrasts in reactions to the pandemic. While pleasurable for some, it was not for most. The UCL Covid-19 Social Study found that, on balance, about one in three people in the UK said they had enjoyed the first months of the pandemic while almost half had not enjoyed them and just over one in five had mixed feelings (University College London News, 2020b). Most, but not all, of the diarists could be said to fall within the first of these groups.

Dominance and preoccupation

COVID-19 was dominant in most lives during the early months of the pandemic and lockdown. Indeed, diarists reported how media outlets gave priority to the crisis to the exclusion of much else, even if there was nothing new to say. Other things, however, were going on too. Diarists were also aware of notable dates in the calendar, issues and controversies in the country and the wider world. Probably the most significant date in the early months of the pandemic was 8 May 2020 and VE (Victory in Europe) Day. This marked the 75th anniversary of the end of the Second World War in 1945 and was celebrated by many diarists in their own localities.

A wide range of other dates and events were mentioned in diaries, including the death and funeral of Dame Vera Lynn who had died at the age of 103, and the anniversaries of the deaths of Billie Holiday 61 years earlier and Martin Luther King who had been assassinated in 1968. Birthdays mentioned included Captain Tom's centenary, and the NHS which celebrated 72 years. The birth of Boris Johnson's son Wilf got several mentions. Also recorded by diarists were Easter and April Fool's Day.

The majority of diarists also showed a keen interest in other non-pandemic news stories of the day. Of predominance during this period were the election of Sir Keir Starmer to the leadership of the Labour Party and, most notably, the issues surrounding Black Lives Matter and the death of George Floyd in Minneapolis on 25 May 2020. In the UK, protests included the toppling or defacing of statues of white men, such as Edward Colston in Bristol, said to have links to the slave trade. To a lesser extent, diarists also touched on other prevailing issues such as the transgender debate and space travel. The diarists had mixed views on most of these issues.

Conclusion

Aside from matters in the news, diarists had their own personal dramas and excitements to report (see Chapter 7). Time and again, however, these were linked to COVID-19 in some way. Everyday happenings, such as losing a pair of scissors or forgetting to put the bins out, gave rise to new meanings and understandings that could somehow be attributed to the pandemic. It seemed that the virus was always there in the background.

ROSEMARY
Wednesday 20 May 2020

My own horticultural adventure last week was to buy some pelargoniums from a man called Fred, who turned up with a white van packed with crimson plants. I turned him away saying that I am going for pale pink this year so if he could find some, he was to call back later. I didn't expect a return visit as he was cagey about where the plants had come from and hesitant about a return visit. So when I was in the shower a few days later I was surprised to hear the letter box rattle, then the door bell urgently thumped and a voice from directly below the bathroom window shouting 'Are you there?'. Well, of course, I didn't go down immediately but when he called an hour later I bought 12 pale pink pelargoniums and thanked him for coming back. I still don't know where the plants came from but I was grateful I didn't have to go to a newly opened garden centre wearing protective mask and gloves.

The dominance of the pandemic, and the constant awareness of the restrictions, gave rise to a new world view which, when disregarded, could lead to some cognitive dissonance (Festinger, 1957). For example, more than one diarist commented on how they could feel anxious when people got too close to one another on television. *The Archers* also provoked comments from a number of diarists.

EDGAR
Saturday 3 May 2020

Now to something important – the Archers! As we all know, Ambridge has been coronavirus-free during lockdown. I read in the paper that some islands in the Outer Hebrides have managed to escape but Ambridge in the heart of the Midlands, one of the worst affected areas – how can that be? For the next three weeks they will be broadcasting 'themed' episodes over the past two decades from the archives whilst they sort how to deal with COVID-19. It will be interesting to see how they do it. From listening to this first episode today, I don't think I will be tuning in much over the next three weeks unless they feature 'the episode' with Helen and Rob!

Not only the population at large, but also fictional characters on radio and television, were compelled to conform to the law.

An evolving story

Perhaps a defining feature of the pandemic was that it was a continually evolving story. Throughout the diaries there are vivid illustrations of how life was constantly changing throughout the period as restrictions were modified and COVID-19 became closer to home. From an immediate cessation of activity, with quiet roads, empty skies and the lull of birdsong one moment, to the rush of traffic to the beach and staycation destinations at another. From dinner parties and birthday celebrations on Zoom to tentative forays into other people's gardens armed with one's own cup and tea bag to wholesale reunions around the dinner table. Life was a merry-go-round with stops here and there. Indeed, just when it was thought safe to get off, plans could be thwarted by new restrictions. What was permissible one week might not be the next. Pragmatic adaptations were continually called for. Even after the first lockdown came to an end, there were two more to come. Tiers, bubbles, local lockdowns, and different rules across the country borders in Britain, were confusing. The last-minute alteration to what was permitted for Christmas 2020 was disappointing for many.

Diarists were nonetheless stoic and adapted to the changing landscape, whether by growing their hair because hairdressers and barbers were closed, learning new intricacies of the internet and social media, or turning attention to gardens rather than going out. No doubt the feelings of self-preservation, anxiety, caution and uncertainty they variously reported played some part in influencing their behaviour. It has been argued that, in Britain and probably in many other places too, such compliance may also have been encouraged by an induced state of fear. This is, indeed, the thrust of a book by Dodsworth (2021) who suggested that the government generated a climate of fear in the population which, in her view, undermined democracy and reason. Whether this was the case, or whether apprehension reflected a sensible reaction in the circumstances, an Ipsos Mori survey in April 2020 found that people in the UK seemed very cautious about relaxing restrictions. At this stage, 70 per cent of respondents admitted to feeling 'very nervous about leaving my home' (Woodcock, 2020). A majority of the diarists echoed this sentiment. They had adapted fairly easily to the lockdowns but were not always sure that they would so readily re-adapt to their old routines and behaviours.

The pandemic has not had a finite end as, indeed, COVID-19 remains present in some form some three years after the initial lockdown in March 2020. Its dominance over daily lives has had peaks and troughs but has nonetheless declined over the intervening years. One notable turning point was the development and distribution of a vaccine. This was a moment eagerly awaited by most diarists, and reinforces how the increasing medicalisation of human problems means that people look to medical technology to keep them safe and well (Moore and Khan, 2021). Although some diarists were unsure whether or not they would accept the vaccine once it was available, no diarist wrote that they had turned it down once it had been offered.

The vaccine was, however, not enough to instil full confidence. It was much easier to respond to the edict to stay at home than to decide for oneself that it was safe to re-engage with former activities. The virus remained invisible and intractable, and it continued to be constructed as a threat to many for some time after all restrictions were lifted. It was easier to adapt to the lockdowns than it was to adapt to their ending.

Messages and lessons

COVID-19 presented the world with a global crisis threatening health and well-being quite unlike anything that had gone before. There are lessons to be learned should there be a similar recurrence, and it is hoped these will emerge and be taken to heart when the public enquiry on the management of the pandemic in Britain concludes. While necessarily narrow in scope, this project does also give rise to some of its own suggestions for issues to be taken into consideration.

Discussion and debate are two keywords that frame the broader messages. COVID-19 descended on the nation with little warning, and inevitably decisions had to be made quickly. Drastic measures were, however, devised by, apparently, a small coterie of people with predominantly political or public health credentials. These dictated unprecedented steps, such as the lockdowns, which deprived the population of their personal liberty for an unspecified period of time and had consequences for many sectors of society. Diarists demonstrated the capacity for rational thought on pandemic-related issues, and an important message is that a wide range of stakeholders, including both professional and lay representatives, should be included in any future decision-making should there be a comparable occurrence.

Another call from this project is for more and better information in a context of confusion. Diarists pointed to the competing priorities, a lack of clarity in pronouncements, unclear statistics, poor support for specific groups, issues of timing, the consensus between science and politics, and contrasting policies across the UK. There was also mention of the differing policies across the world. Diarists and others adapt pragmatically and can do so most effectively if they are in possession of a clear but authoritative account of what is being done and why. If good information is not available, this should be transmitted as well. Honesty and transparency are most likely to encourage compliance with restrictions deemed in the general interest.

Other pointers for the future include ensuring opportunities for anyone (whatever their age) who wishes to play a supporting rather than supported role, making sure that everybody who wants to use the internet is able to do so, and paying attention to the mood of the nation – important both for the duration of the pandemic and the subsequent return to greater normality. Last, but certainly not least, there is a call to be prepared should the nation face a similar crisis in the future.

Contribution to social history

The diary entries assembled for this project tell about a certain period in social history. They are eyewitness and participatory accounts of an unprecedented event in their authors' lifetimes, comprising a total of around a million and a half words reflecting their daily lives. Interestingly, Malcolmson and Malcolmson (2012) noted how Nella Last devoted most space in her diaries overall to the four topics of the weather, ill-health, preparing meals and shopping. These diarists too provided considerable coverage of the same four areas despite writing extensively on many other subjects. Their entries were informative and often amusing and always a pleasure to read. Writing them was a performative act (Goffman, 1959) and a presentation of self in that diarists knew that any entries might be made public, albeit anonymously.

These accounts make an important contribution to social history. Malcolmson and Malcolmson (2012) wrote how on 16 February 1941 Nella Last had written, 'It's impossible for me to grasp that diaries and what people – people like me, for instance – think about things are much use'. But personal thoughts and experiences are what keep events in the moment and in the memory. The pandemic was such an important and unusual occurrence that its impact on the population, and different groups within the population, should be recorded and remembered. It also calls for lessons to be learned as, to repeat Santayana's proclamation from the introductory chapter, 'Those who cannot remember the past are condemned to repeat it' (Santayana, 1905).

The accounts were also important from a more personal perspective, both in providing an activity that gave some structure to the extraordinary circumstances of the time, and in helping to manage a difficult period in daily lives. Many wrote how they would not have thought to keep a diary of events until it was too late, and so had been pleased to have been prompted to keep a record of their own personal experiences and thoughts.

Towards the completion of the main and initial stage of the project at the end of July 2020, diarists were asked whether they had enjoyed taking part and contributing to social history. Not surprisingly, views were mixed. First, and fortunately, there were many who said that they were.

HOLLY
Thursday 30 July 2020
So, this is the last diary entry for a while. I've been very pleased to take part in the project. I think that at the start of lockdown particularly, writing the

diary helped me to structure my thoughts about what was happening to us all and to look in some detail at our changed way of living. I found it quite a reflexive process and as such, very absorbing and helpful. The idea of there being a stash of people's personal narratives on their lives at this time is quite a pleasing one to me! During my time as a researcher, I've often asked people to trust me with personal information and with their observations about things that were very important to them. Taking part in this project is one way of putting something back into that collective pot which aims to help us gain a better understanding of who we are, and what we all get up to.

TARANAKI
Friday 31 July 2020

Dear Diary,

I shall miss you! Today will be my last entry of this long-haul monologue about my life during the 2020 pandemic of the COVID-19 virus. It has really helped me to organise and rationalise my thoughts and feelings during this truly ghastly period.

I decided to look back over some of my entries and I detect a common theme: my deep frustration and anger at the Johnson government. Again today I have a catalogue of misdemeanours that he and his ministers have perpetrated.

I want to finish with a word of thanks to you, Nicola, for your encouraging messages, useful guidelines and unfailing impartiality in your messaging. As I said above, I shall miss these sessions in front of my computer screen and thank you again for giving me the opportunity to be in some small way associated with this stressful period of our history.

WILL
Sunday 2 August 2020

The last day of the diary. It feels almost like a bereavement, having seen the diary as a part of my life for the last few months and as a way of encapsulating what I feel about the pandemic, the government's lamentable handling of it and about everything else that's going on in this country and more widely.

Will in fact went on to write a few more entries on overtime! Other diarists, however, found the task more of a chore, especially as time went on and they felt they had nothing new to say.

ARAMINTA
Friday 24 July 2020

Another week gone. Where does the time go? I am glad this duty is coming to an end. At the beginning of lockdown I felt it was important to keep a diary and I have kept my own private one going, but now, as with your diary, I find I am not making many entries.

SARDOMIKE
Monday 27 July 2020

Here we are, writing the final entry, it's been like the Sword of Damocles hanging over one's head, the thought 'Oh yes, I have a diary entry to do' but, once started – no problem, enjoyable to let the words flow.

SQUEALS
Saturday 25 July 2020

Filled with guilt for yet again being such a dilatory diarist. ... No excuse really except for laziness and perhaps a feeling that there's been nothing interesting going on in my life.

Although the focus of the project was on the reactions, understandings and adaptations of the diarists to COVID-19 and the restrictions it brought in its wake, there was no prior knowledge of the key themes to emerge. The content of the diaries evolved as the pandemic progressed.

The accounts drawn from these diary entries and relayed in this book narrate the circumstances of a group that considered itself one of the luckiest. Diarists were older, white, comfortably-off men and women who, in the main, could happily isolate themselves from risk. Their experiences and views complement those portrayed in other reports where the perspectives of professional authors, such as a doctor, a politician or an actor, or groups far more disadvantaged than the diarists, were the focus. The greater the number and variety of population groups examined, the better will be the understanding of what transpired.

All forms of information gathering have their limitations, and the analysis of diaries is no exception. As John Madge (1953) (the author's father) described, there is some inevitable distortion on the part of both diarists and investigator. Regarding the former, diarists were aware that what they wrote might be reproduced in a publication, and they may have tailored what they wrote for an audience rather than simply for themselves. According to Crowther (1999), 'The sense of a diary's audience, however nebulous or unacknowledged, is bound to have some bearing on the writer's selection and focus'. Even though their anonymity was guaranteed, there may have been confidential matters left out but also additional observations, perhaps particularly if they were humorous, included. Also as Madge (1953) discussed, 'every contributor is a prisoner of his own particular culture'.

The author inevitably also contributed to some distortion, even if unintentionally. The introduction of suggested topics to include in diary entries, for instance, may have refocused diarists, giving significance to aspects that might otherwise have been overlooked. Also, as it was only possible to include a small fraction of the diary entries in this book, the choice of topics and illustrations for inclusion, and the subsequent discussion, is of course selective. For example, documentation of films and books frequently mentioned and discussed by diarists has been marginalised, as have accounts of politics and world events other than the pandemic. The author's interest was in the diarists' responses and adaptation to the daily order imposed by the pandemic, and herein lies the focus of this book.

It is important to stress that the diarists were not a representative sample, either of the country or their age group, and findings for other groups may well be different. They were a specific demographic who were living comfortable lives and who were willing and able to produce regular written diary entries. There was, nonetheless, a lack of uniformity among their contributions. They largely chose their own topics to write about, adopted their own style of writing, and decided how often they wanted to produce and submit entries. They were documenting events but also charting understandings and reactions. The data are rich but they tell an incomplete story.

How would the pandemic be remembered?

Diarists appreciated that they were living through a period in history that would be remembered variously for the deaths and illness, for the lockdowns, for the speedy development of vaccines, for the deprivation and disadvantage it spread, for the sunshine and tranquillity, for the new recipes they had tried, and for much more. They have the penultimate word in remarking on how they think it might be remembered in the future.

ANNA
Wednesday 29 July 2020

So – in the future: What did you do in the Covid-lockdown, Granny? Or: How Was It For You?

ARAMINTA
Friday 31 July 2020

I think that in the future we will talk about 'the year of the lockdown', and possibly use it as a marker. 'Before the lockdown' we did things this way, in the same way as my mother used to say 'Before the war …'. And we may say, 'During lockdown we could not do …' as my mother used to say, 'During the war this or that was not able to be done'. I remember her saying how lucky I was to be able to go to my choirs and enjoy singing, because none of that could be done during the war and she'd missed it. She never did get back to singing as by the time choirs started up again, she was bringing up three young children and two older boys.

BONIVARD
Saturday 25 July 2020

Looking back on lockdown a few years hence, I think it will be seen as a one-off event (I hope). I assume that an all-purpose vaccine will be developed which will take care of future mutations. Will this period be seen as the equivalent of a lost weekend when people will have few memories of this year, assuming they haven't lost family or friends?

HOLGATE
Friday 25 July 2020

The pandemic and the resultant lockdown was undoubtedly psychologically difficult, something I can now see but at the time I just felt was bad and I tried hard to remain positive. This is something to reflect on in the coming months. There were positives from the very different period of April and May when things felt dark and unknown. Thank goodness the weather then was so beautiful. The impact of the lockdown will remain with me for the rest of my life.

JULES
Friday 22 May 2020

One thing I always pull myself up on when I find myself doing it is 'wishing my life away'. I want to look back on this period of time without regret, or the feeling that I wasted the many opportunities it has afforded me. This includes, alas, the massive de-cluttering operation that I promised myself would take place.

PEN
Wednesday 5 August 2020

My memories of lockdown and how it has affected us will be very positive. We have worked hard and have a glut of veg to show for it. The garden looks great. We have muddled along together pretty well. We have had some excellent meals and watched some amazing screenings. The family have all been fine. We aren't gagging to do anything else. But these good memories are bound to be tempered by how the next year or two play out for the country and everyone else here and in the wider world. One good outcome might be seeing the back of Donald Trump. Maybe there will be less air travel and more cycling ... a slower pace. I think many people have had the opportunity to mull over what they want from life and might be able to tweak some changes. But who is making the decisions and will they guess right? What has the virus in store for us? What about the Third World? It does feel as though the future is in the lap of the gods.

Memories were very varied, and might be quite practical or rather emotional. Just as nobody had known quite what the pandemic would entail, nobody could be sure what it would leave in its wake.

A final word

It is impossible to sum up the pandemic and its impact on a group of relatively advantaged seventy somethings in a few sentences, and even the preceding chapters fail to tell the whole story. Suffice it to say that it was a unique experience that overtook individual lives for one, two or maybe more years. It curtailed freedoms in unknown ways but yet evoked pragmatism, stoicism and initiative. There was anxiety and a concern for self and others, but diarists nonetheless adapted to the new situation. They were well aware that they were among the most fortunate both in their personal circumstances and in their ability to hide away and remain safe. Everyone's situation was, however, different as were their perceptions. While some described the pandemic as a horrific time in their lives, others went as far as saying that they would miss it when it came to an end. Whatever their view, there was much to say. The one and a half million words they wrote in their diaries are, accordingly, testament to the significance of the pandemic as an unprecedented event in modern history.

References

Addario, G., Sivathasan, C. and Taylor, I. (2022a) *Community connectedness in the COVID-19 outbreak*, Centre for Ageing Better in partnership with NatCen. Available from: https://ageing-better.org.uk/sites/default/files/2022-03/community-connectedness-in-the-COVID-19-outbreak-report.pdf

Addario, G., Sivathasan, C. and Taylor, I. (2022b) *Volunteering and helping out in the COVID-19 outbreak*, Centre for Ageing Better in partnership with NatCen. Available from: https://ageing-better.org.uk/sites/default/files/2022-03/Volunteering-and-helping-out-in-the-covid-19-outbreak.pdf

Age UK (2020) *The impact of COVID-19 to date on older people's mental and physical health*. Available from: www.ageuk.org.uk/globalassets/age-uk/documents/reports-and-publications/reports-and-briefings/health--wellbeing/the-impact-of-covid-19-on-older-people_age-uk.pdf

Aitkenhead, E., Clements, J., Lumley, J., Muir, R., Redgrave, H. and Skidmore, M. (2022) *Policing the Pandemic*, The Police Foundation and Crest Advisory.

Allington, D., Beaver, K., Duffy, B., Meyer, C., Moxham-Hall, V., Murkin, G., et al (2020) *Coronavirus Uncertainties: Vaccines, symptoms and contested claims*, The Policy Institute, King's College London. Available from: www.kcl.ac.uk/policy-institute/assets/coronavirus-uncertainties.pdf

Altheide, D.L. (2002) *Creating Fear: News and the construction of crisis*. Hawthorne, NY: Aldine de Gruyter.

Altheide, D.L. (2016) *The Media Syndrome*. New York: Routledge.

Aragunde-Kohl, Ú.A., Gómez-Galán, J., Lázaro-Pérez, C. and Mantínez-López, J.Á. (2020) 'Interaction and emotional connection with pets: a descriptive analysis from Puerto Rico', *Animals*, 10(11): E2136.

Bambra, C., Lynch, J. and Smith, K.E. (2021) *The Unequal Pandemic: COVID-19 and health inequalities*. Bristol: Bristol University Press.

Barber, N. (2020) 'What the Pandemic Tells Us About Adaptation: Adaptive change can be much faster than most theorists assume', *Psychology Today*, 18 June.

BBC News (2021a) 'Households "buy 3.2 million pets in lockdown"', 12 March. Available from: www.bbc.co.uk/news/business-56362987

BBC News (2021b) 'Lockdown fashion: "People are back in their pyjamas"', 8 January. Available from: www.bbc.co.uk/news/business-55584843

Beck, U. (1992) *The Risk Society: Towards a new modernity*. London: Sage. First published in German in 1986.

Becker, H.S. (1963) *Outsiders: Studies in the sociology of deviance*. Glencoe, IL: Free Press.

References

Becker, H.S. (1973) 'Labeling theory reconsidered', in H.S. Becker (ed) *Outsiders: Studies in the sociology of deviance* (2nd edn), New York: Free Press, pp 177–212.

Bellotti, E., D'Angelo, A., Ryan, L. and Vrain, E. (2021) *Life in lockdown: the impact on inter-personal relationships. Preliminary Report.* Available from: https://lockdownnetworks.files.wordpress.com/2021/02/life-in-lockdown-preliminary-report-february-2021-1.pdf

Bennett, A. (2022) *House Arrest: Pandemic diaries.* London: Faber and Faber Limited and Profile Books Ltd.

Berg-Weger, M. and Morley, J.E. (2020) 'Loneliness and social isolation in older adults during the COVID-19 pandemic: implications for gerontological social work', *Journal of Nutrition, Health and Ageing*, 24(5): 456–8.

Berger, P. and Luckmann, T. (1966) *The Social Construction of Reality: A treatise in the sociology of knowledge.* London: Allen Lane.

Best, J. (2021) 'Public fear and the media', in D. vom Lehn, N. Ruiz-Junco and W. Gibson (eds) *The Routledge International Handbook of Interactionism*, Abingdon, Oxon: Routledge, pp 288–97.

Binns, F. (2020) 'Final ADEPT waste survey reports continued disruption', *Resource.co*, 17 September. Available from: https://resource.co/article/final-adept-waste-survey-reports-continued-disruption

Blumer, H. (1969) *Symbolic Interactionism: Perspective and method.* Englewood Cliffs, NJ: Prentice Hall.

Blumer, H. (1971) 'Social problems as collective behavior', *Social Problems*, 18(Winter): 298–306.

Blumer, H. (1978) 'Social unrest and collective protest', in N. Denzin (ed) *Studies in Symbolic Interaction*, Greenwich, CT: JAI Press, pp 1–54.

BMA (2020) *The hidden impact of COVID-19 on patient care in the NHS in England.* Available from: www.bma.org.uk/media/2841/the-hidden-impact-of-covid_web-pdf.pdf

BMA (2023) *COVID-19: Impact of the pandemic on healthcare delivery.* Available from: www.bma.org.uk/advice-and-support/covid-19/what-the-bma-is-doing/covid-19-impact-of-the-pandemic-on-healthcare-delivery

Bourdieu, P. (1984) *Distinction: A social critique of the judgement of taste* (English translation). London: Routledge. First published in French in 1979.

Brewster, B.H. and Bell, M.M. (2010) 'The environmental Goffman: toward an environmental sociology of everyday life', *Society and Natural Resources*, 23: 45–57.

BritainThinks (2020) *Local Government Association Covid-19 Public Opinion Research. Final Report.* Available from: www.local.gov.uk/sites/default/files/documents/Covid19-Public-Opinion-Research-Report-BritainThinks.pdf

British Trust for Ornithology (2021) 'UK public embraces garden wildlife during coronavirus lockdown', 11 March. Available from: www.bto.org/press-releases/uk-public-embraces-garden-wildlife-during-coronavirus-lockdown

Bu, F., Bone, J.K., Mitchell, J.J., Steptoe, A. and Fancourt, D. (2021) 'Longitudinal changes in physical activity during and after the first national lockdown due to the COVID-19 pandemic in England', *Scientific Reports*, 11: 17723.

Buck, K. (2020) '73% say having a cleaner round during coronavirus lockdown is "unacceptable"', *LBC News*, 13 May. Available from: www.lbc.co.uk/news/uk/73-say-having-a-cleaner-round-during-coronavirus-l/

Bude, H. (2018) *Society of Fear*. Cambridge: Polity.

Calkins, K. (1970) 'Time: Perspectives, marking and styles of usage', *Social Problems*, 17: 487–501.

Callero, P.L. (1985–86) 'Putting the social in prosocial behavior: An interactions approach to altruism', *Humboldt Journal of Social Relations*, 13(1 & 2): 15–32.

Campbell, J. (1995) *Understanding John Dewey: Nature and cooperative intelligence*. Chicago and La Salle, IL: Open Court Publishing.

Cannadine, D. (1985) 'Social history is easier to defend than define', *History Today*, 35(3), March. Available from: https://www.historytoday.com/archive/what-social-history.

Carleton, R.N. (2016) 'Fear of the unknown: One fear to rule them all?', *Journal of Anxiety Disorders*, 41: 5–21.

Clarke, R. (2021) *Breathtaking: The UK's human story of Covid*, London: Little, Brown.

Clarke, N. (ed) (2024) *Everyday Life in the Covid-19 Pandemic. Mass Observation's 12th May Diaries*. London: Bloomsbury Publishing.

Cohen, S. (1973) *Folk Devils and Moral Panics: The creation of the Mods and Rockers*. London: Paladin.

Cooley, C.H. (1902) *Human Nature and the Social Order*. New York: Charles Scribner's Sons.

CrimeRate (2022) *Crime and Covid-19 lockdowns*. Available from: https://crimerate.co.uk/research/coronavirus-lockdown-trends

Crowther, B. (1999) 'Writing as performance', in R. Josselson and A. Lieblich (eds) *Making Meanings of Narratives*, London: Sage, pp 197–220.

Dalgleish, R. (2020) *How the COVID-19 Pandemic has accelerated the shift to online spending*, Office for National Statistics. Available from: https://blog.ons.gov.uk/2020/09/18/how-the-covid-19-pandemic-has-accelerated-the-shift-to-online-spending/

Dewey, J. (1929) *Experience and Nature*. New York: W. W. Norton.

Dingwall, R. (2023a) 'The sociology of epidemics and pandemics', in A. Petersen (ed) *Handbook on the Sociology of Health and Medicine*, Cheltenham, Glos: Edward Elgar Publishing, pp 455–473.

Dingwall, R. (2023b) 'The UK pandemic inquiry – missing the point?' *Social Science Space*, 9 August. Available from: www.socialsciencespace.com/2023/08/the-uk-pandemic-inquiry-missing-the-point/

Dodsworth, L. (2021) *A State of Fear: How the UK government weaponised fear during the Covid-19 pandemic*. London: Pinter & Martin.

Dorling, D. (2021) 'When will life return to normal after the pandemic?', *The Conversation*, 2 December. Available from: https://theconversation.com/when-will-life-return-to-normal-after-the-pandemic-172726

Durkheim, E. (1912) *The Elementary Forms of the Religious Life* (translated by Joseph Swain). London: George Allen & Unwin.

Durkheim, E. (1997) *The Division of Labour in Society* (translated by W.D. Halls). New York: Free Press. First published in French in 1893.

Fancourt, D., Bu, F., Mak, H.W. and Steptoe, A. (2021) *Covid-19 Social Study Results Release 29*, University College London. Available from: https://www.nuffieldfoundation.org/wp-content/uploads/2021/01/COVID-19-social-study-29-January-2021.pdf

Farewill (2021) *The Year in Wills Report 2020: How COVID-19 made us all face our mortality*. Available from: https://farewill.com/blog/the-year-in-wills-report-2020-how-covid-19-made-us-all-face-our-mortality

Ferguson, D. (2021) 'Quarter of English families plan to break Covid rules for a Mother's Day visit', *The Observer*, 13 March. Available from: www.theguardian.com/lifeandstyle/2021/mar/13/quarter-of-english-families-plan-to-break-covid-rules-for-a-mothers-day-visit

Festinger, L. (1957) *A Theory of Cognitive Dissonance*. Stanford, CA: Stanford University Press.

Flaherty, M.G. (2021) 'The social organization of time', in D. vom Lehn, N. Ruiz-Junco and W. Gibson (eds) *The Routledge International Handbook of Interactionism*, Abingdon, Oxon: Routledge, pp 254–63.

Food Standards Agency (2020) *Guidance for consumers on coronavirus (COVID-19) and food*, 25 April. Available from: www.gov.uk/government/publications/guidance-for-consumers-on-coronavirus-covid-19-and-food/guidance-for-consumers-on-coronavirus-covid-19-and-food

Frank, A. (1952: English version) *The Diary of a Young Girl*. Amsterdam, NL: Doubleday.

Furedi, F. (1997) *Culture of Fear: Risk and the morality of low expectation*. London: Cassell.

Furedi, F. (2018) *How Fear Works: Culture of fear in the twenty-first century*. London: Bloomsbury Publishing.

Giddens, A. (1984) *The Constitution of Society*. Oxford: Polity Press.

Giddens, A. (1991) *Modernity and Self-identity: Self and society in the late modern age*. Cambridge: Polity Press.

Gifford, C. (2020) 'Will-writing soars in lockdown: have you got your affairs in order?', *Which?*, 2 December. Available from: www.which.co.uk/news/article/will-writing-soars-in-lockdown-have-you-got-your-affairs-in-order-aA3o87S8iCTl

Gilman, S.L. (2010) 'Moral panic and pandemics', *The Lancet*, 375(9729): 1866–7.

Glaser, B. and Strauss, A. (1971) *Status Passage: A formal theory*. Chicago, IL: Aldine-Atherton.

Goffman, E. (1959) *The Presentation of Self in Everyday Life*. Garden City, NY: Doubleday.

Goffman, E. (1967) *Interaction Ritual: Essays on face-to-face behavior*. New York: Routledge.

Gorton, V., Matthews, B., McVie, S. and Murray, K. (2022) *Police Use of Covid-19 Fixed Penalty Notices in Scotland. Trends in enforcement from March 2020 to May 2021*, Edinburgh: University of Edinburgh.

Gottschalk, S. (2018) *The Terminal Self: Everyday life in hypermodern times*. London: Routledge.

Gottschalk, S. (2021) 'Click, validate and reply: three paradoxes of the terminal self', in D. vom Lehn, N. Ruiz-Junco and W. Gibson (eds) *The Routledge International Handbook of Interactionism*, Abingdon, Oxon: Routledge, pp 99–111.

Gray, J.A. (1987) *The Psychology of Fear and Stress*. Cambridge: Cambridge University Press.

Hall, S., Critcher, C., Jefferson, T., Clarke, J. and Roberts, B. (2013) 'The social history of a "moral panic"', in *Policing the Crisis: Mugging, the state and law & order* (35th anniversary edn), London: Macmillan, pp 7–31.

Hampson, L. (2020) '64% of weddings expected to be postponed or cancelled this year, new study shows', *The Standard*, 9 April. Available from: www.standard.co.uk/lifestyle/weddings/wedding-industry-coronavirus-statistics-a4410426.html

Hancock, M. and Oakeshott, I. (2022) *Pandemic Diaries: The inside story of Britain's battle against Covid*. Hull: Biteback Publishing.

Hannem, S. (2021) 'Symbolic interactionism, social structure, and social change: historical debates and contemporary challenges', in D. vom Lehn, N. Ruiz-Junco and W. Gibson (eds) *The Routledge International Handbook of Interactionism*, Abingdon, Oxon: Routledge, pp 194–204.

Harris, T. (2023) 'Ruling by fear is no way to govern', *The Telegraph*, 6 March. Available from: www.telegraph.co.uk/news/2023/03/06/project-fear-politics-will-ruin-britain/

Heidegger, M. (1996) *Being and Time* (translated by Joan Stambaugh). Albany, NY: State University of New York Press. Originally published in German in 1927.

Hooson, M. (2021) 'Will-writing surge reflects coronavirus fears', Forbes, 14 January. Available from: www.forbes.com/uk/advisor/personal-finance/2021/01/14/will-writing-surge-reflects-coronavirus-fears/

Horton, H. (2021) 'Urban walks replace rural strolls during pandemic data from Ordnance Survey shows', *The Telegraph*, 15 March. Available from: www.telegraph.co.uk/news/2021/03/15/urban-walks-replace-rural-strolls-pandemic-data-ordnance-survey/

Hume, S., John, P., Sanders, M. and Stockdale, E. (2021) 'Nudge in the time of coronavirus: compliance to behavioral messages during crisis', *Journal of Behavioral Public Administration*, 4(2): 1–12.

Iacobucci, G. (2021) 'How is the pandemic affecting non-covid services?', *British Medical Journal*, 372: n215.

Independent Age (2020) *Independent Age calls for clarity in government's COVID-19 messaging to over-70s ahead of lockdown easing.* Available from: www.independentage.org/news-media/press-releases/independent-age-calls-for-clarity-governments-covid-19-messaging-to-over

Inman, P. (2020) 'UK's richest 20% reduce spending by £23bn during lockdown', *The Guardian*, 31 May. Available from: www.theguardian.com/money/2020/may/31/uks-richest-20-reduce-spending-by-23bn-during--coronavirus-lockdown

International Federation of Red Cross and Red Crescent Societies (nd) *What is a disaster?* Available from: www.ifrc.org/our-work/disasters-climate-and-crises/what-disaster

James, W. (1949) *Pragmatism*. New York: Longmans.

Jarvis, C., Gaggiotti, H. and Kars-Unluoglu, S. (2020) 'Unleadership', in M. Parker (ed) *Life After Covid-19: The other side of crisis*. Bristol: Bristol University Press, pp 125–34.

Jennings, H. and Madge, C. (eds) (1987) *May the Twelfth: Mass-Observation Day-Surveys 1937 by over two hundred observers*. London: Faber & Faber.

John Lewis Partnership (2020) *How we shop, live and look 2020. 2020: The year that changed everything*. Available from: www.johnlewispartnership.co.uk/media/press/y2020/2020-the-year-that-changed-everything.html

Joyner, L. (2020) 'Lockdown sparked a rise in dog behaviour issues, a new study has found', *Country Living*, 27 August. Available from: www.countryliving.com/uk/wildlife/pets/a33814182/dog-behaviour-change-lockdown/

Julians, S. (2023) *Breakable*. London: New Generation Publishing.

Käll, A., Jägholm, S., Hesser, H., Andersson, F., Mathaldi, A., Norkvist, B.T., et al (2019) 'Internet-based cognitive behavior therapy for loneliness: a pilot randomized controlled trial', *Behavior Therapy*, 51(1): 54–68.

Kashtan, M. (2020) 'Together into a future', in M. Parker (ed) *Life After Covid-19: The other side of crisis*, Bristol: Bristol University Press, pp 165–73.

King's College London News Centre (2021) *Covid lockdown loneliness linked to more depressive symptoms in older adults*. Available from: www.kcl.ac.uk/news/covid-lockdown-loneliness-linked-to-more-depressive-symptoms-in-older-adults

Kirk, A., Duncan, P., Quach, G., Probyn, M., Gutiérrez, P., Blood, D. and Hall, R. (2022) 'Lockdown lifestyles: how has Covid changed lives in the UK?', *The Guardian*, 25 February. Available from: www.theguardian.com/lifeandstyle/ng-interactive/2022/feb/25/lockdown-lifestyles-how-lives-changed-covid-pandemic

Kulldorff, M., Gupta, S. and Bhattacharya, J. (2020) *Great Barrington Declaration*, 4 October, Great Barrington, US. Available from: https://gbdeclaration.org/

Kynaston, D. (2007) *Austerity Britain 1945–51*. London: Bloomsbury Publishing Plc.

Kynaston, D. (2009) *Family Britain, 1951–57*. London: Bloomsbury Publishing Plc.

Kynaston, D. (2013) *Modernity Britain: Opening the box, 1957–59*. London: Bloomsbury Publishing Plc.

Kynaston, D. (2014) *Modernity Britain: A shake of the dice, 1959–62*. London: Bloomsbury Publishing Plc.

Kynaston, D. (2021) *On the Cusp: Days of '62*. London: Bloomsbury Publishing Plc.

Kynaston, D. (2023) *A Northern Wind, Britain 1962–65*. London: Bloomsbury Publishing Plc.

Link (2021) 'Consumers still withdrew £1,500 per person in 2020, despite ATM transactions falling by 37%', 27 January. Available from: www.link.co.uk/about/news/consumer-usage-2020/

Loseke, D.R. (2016) *Methodological Thinking: Basic principles of social research design*. Thousand Oaks, CA: Sage Publications.

Madge, G. (2020) 'May 2020 becomes the sunniest calendar month on record', *Met Office*, 1 June. Available from: www.metoffice.gov.uk/about-us/press-office/news/weather-and-climate/2020/2020-spring-and-may-stats

Madge, J. (1953) *The Tools of Social Science*. London: Longmans.

Madge, N. and Hoggart, P. (2020) *Sixty Somethings: The lives of women who remember the Sixties*. London: Quartet Books.

Malcolmson, P. and Malcolmson, R. (eds) (2012) *The Diaries of Nella Last: Writing in war & peace*. London: Profile Books.

Marsh, S. (2021) '"Pandemic burnout" on rise as latest Covid lockdowns take toll', *The Guardian*, 5 February. Available from: www.theguardian.com/society/2021/feb/05/pandemic-burnout-rise-uk-latest-covid-lockdowns-take-toll

References

Martins Van Jaarsveld, G. (2020) 'The effects of COVID-19 among the elderly population: a case for closing the digital divide', *Frontiers in Psychiatry*, 11: 577427.

Mayhew, F. (2020) 'Five in every six BBC News articles devoted to Covid-19 while B2B coverage varies by sector, analysis shows', *Press Gazette*, 9 April. Available from: https://pressgazette.co.uk/news/five-in-every-six-bbc-news-articles-devoted-to-covid-19-while-b2b-coverage-varies-by-sector-analysis-shows/

McCarthy, H. (2024) 'Histories of Everyday Life in Britain during the Covid-19 Pandemic', *UCL Press*. Available from: https://ucldigitalpress.co.uk/BOOC/Article/3/144/

McKenzie, L. and The Working Class Directive (eds) (2022) *Lockdown Diaries of the Working Class*. London: The Working Class Collective.

McVie, S., Murray, K., Gorton, V. and Matthews, B. (2023) *Policing the Pandemic in England and Wales: Police use of Fixed Penalty Notices from 27 March 2020 to 31 May 2021*, Edinburgh: University of Edinburgh.

Mead, G.H. (1934) *Mind, Self, and Society from the Standpoint of a Social Behaviorist*. Chicago, IL: University of Chicago Press.

Melville, E. and Wilkinson, H. (2020) 'From conflict to collaboration', in M. Parker (ed) *Life After Covid-19: The other side of crisis*, Bristol: Bristol University Press, pp 31–42.

Miller, D.L. (1982) 'Introduction', in D.L. Miller (ed) *The Individual and the Social Self: Unpublished work of George Herbert Mead*, Chicago, IL: University of Chicago Press, pp 1–26.

Moore, L.J. and Khan, S. (2021) 'The (un)healthy body and the self', in D. vom Lehn, N. Ruiz-Junco and W. Gibson (eds) *The Routledge International Handbook of Interactionism*, Abingdon, Oxon: Routledge, pp 134–44.

Morales, S.R. and Ali, S.N. (2021) 'COVID-19 and disparities affecting ethnic minorities', *The Lancet*, 397(10286): 1684–5.

Murphy, S. (2020) 'Police in England warn rural vigilantes not to take law into own hands during lockdown', *The Guardian*, 26 April. Available from: www.theguardian.com/uk-news/2020/apr/26/police-in-england-warn-rural-vigilantes-not-to-take-law-into-own-hands-coronavirus-lockdown

Natural England (updated 2021) *The People and Nature Survey for England: Adult Data Y1Q1 (April–June 2020) (Experimental Statistics)*. Available from: www.gov.uk/government/statistics/the-people-and-nature-survey-for-england-adult-data-y1q1-april-june-2020-experimental-statistics/

Natural England (2022) *Indicators from the People and Nature Survey covering the month of March 2022 to understand how people use the natural environment in England and the impact of coronavirus (COVID-19)*. Available from: www.gov.uk/government/statistics/the-people-and-nature-survey-for-england-monthly-indicators-for-march-2022-official-statistics

Natural History Museum (2020) *Nature: liberated by lockdown?* 21 September. Available from: www.nhm.ac.uk/discover/nature-liberated-by-lockdown.html

Nazir, S. (2021) 'Brits sending flowers as "substitute hugs", Bloom & Wild says', *Retail Gazette*, 22 March. Available from: www.retailgazette.co.uk/blog/2021/03/brits-sending-flowers-as-substitute-hugs-bloom-wild-says/

Nguyen, H. (2020) 'How do masks make voters feel?' *YouGov*. Available from: https://today.yougov.com/politics/articles/30804-how-do-masks-make-voters-feel

Nikčević, A.V. and Spada, M.M. (2020) 'The COVID-19 anxiety syndrome scale: development and psychometric properties', *Psychiatry Research*, 292: 113322.

Nolsoe, E. (2020) *How are Brits spending money during COVID-19?*, YouGov, 4 June. Available from: https://d3nkl3psvxxpe9.cloudfront.net/documents/Spending_in_lockdown.pdf

Obrdlík, A. (1942) '"Gallows humor": a sociological phenomenon', *American Journal of Sociology*, 47: 709–16.

O'Connor, R.C., Wetherall, K., Cleare, S., McClelland, H., Melson, A.J., Niedzwiedz, C.L., et al (2021) 'Mental health and well-being during the COVID-19 pandemic: longitudinal analyses of adults in the UK COVID-19 mental health & wellbeing study', *British Journal of Psychiatry*, 218(6): 326–33.

Ofcom (2020a) *Lockdown leads to surge in TV screen time and streaming*, 5 August. Available from: www.ofcom.org.uk/news-centre/2020/lockdown-leads-to-surge-in-tv-screen-time-and-streaming

Ofcom (2020b) *UK's internet use surges to record levels*, 24 June. Available from: www.ofcom.org.uk/news-centre/2020/uk-internet-use-surges

Office for National Statistics (2021a) *Consumer price inflation basket of goods and services: 2021*. Available from: www.ons.gov.uk/economy/inflationandpriceindices/articles/ukconsumerpriceinflationbasketofgoodsandservices/2021

Office for National Statistics (2021b) *Coronavirus and the social impact on Great Britain: 30 July 2021*. Available from: www.ons.gov.uk/peoplepopulationandcommunity/healthandsocialcare/healthandwellbeing/bulletins/coronavirusandthesocialimpactsongreatbritain/30july2021

Office for National Statistics (2021c) *How has lockdown changed our relationship with nature?*, 26 April. Available from: www.ons.gov.uk/economy/environmentalaccounts/articles/howhaslockdownchangedourrelationshipwithnature/2021-04-26

Office for National Statistics (2021d) *Impact of the coronavirus (COVID-19) pandemic on retail sales in 2020*, 1 February. Available from: www.ons.gov.uk/economy/grossdomesticproductgdp/articles/impactofthecoronaviruscovid19pandemiconretailsalesin2020/2021-01-28

Office for National Statistics (2021e) *Personal and economic well-being in Great Britain: January 2021*, 21 January. Available from: www.ons.gov.uk/peoplepopulationandcommunity/wellbeing/bulletins/personalandeconomicwellbeingintheuk/january2021

Office for National Statistics (2021f) *Two-thirds of adults still plan to wear masks in shops and on public transport*, 16 July. Available from: www.ons.gov.uk/peoplepopulationandcommunity/healthandsocialcare/healthandwellbeing/articles/twothirdsofadultsstillplantowearmasksinshopsandonpublictransport/2021-07-16

Office for National Statistics (2022) *Coronavirus and the social impacts on Great Britain*, 1 April. Available from: www.ons.gov.uk/peoplepopulationandcommunity/healthandsocialcare/healthandwellbeing/bulletins/coronavirusandthesocialimpactsongreatbritain/1april2022

Osborne, H. (2021) 'More than half of UK households fear losing savings in Covid crisis', *The Guardian*, 23 January. Available from: www.theguardian.com/money/2021/jan/23/uk-savings-covid-crisis-bills

Palley, L.S., O'Rourke, P.P. and Niemi, S.M. (2010) 'Mainstreaming animal-assisted therapy', *Journal of the Institute for Laboratory Animal Research*, 51: 199–207.

Parker, M. (ed) (2020) *Life After Covid-19: The other side of crisis*. Bristol: Bristol University Press.

Parr, J. (2021) 'Consumer spending up on pre-pandemic levels, driven by online grocery surge', *Retail Gazette*, 31 December. Available from: www.retailgazette.co.uk/blog/2021/12/consumer-spending-up-on-pre-pandemic-levels/

Patrick, R., Power, M., Garthwaite, K., Kaufman, J., Page, G. and Pybus, K. (2022) *A Year Like No Other: Life on a low income during COVID-19*. Bristol: Policy Press.

Pensiero, N., Kelly, A. and Bokhove, C. (2020) *Learning Inequalities during the COVID-19 Pandemic: How families cope with home-schooling*. Southampton: University of Southampton.

Pierce, M., Hope, H., Ford, T., Hatch, S., Hotopf, M., John, A., et al (2020) 'Mental health before and during the COVID-19 pandemic: a longitudinal probability sample survey of the UK population', *Lancet Psychiatry*, 7(10): 883–92.

Piret, J. and Boivin, G. (2021) 'Pandemics throughout history', *Frontiers in Microbiology*, 11: 631736.

Portes, J. (2020) 'The important role of social scientists during the Covid-19 pandemic', Campaign for Social Science. Available from: www.kcl.ac.uk/news/the-important-role-of-social-scientists-during-the-covid-19-pandemic

Poulain, J.-P. (2017) *The Sociology of Food: Eating and the place of food in society* (translated by Augusta Dörr). London and New York: Bloomsbury Academic. First published in French in 2002.

Press Association (2021) *Coronavirus pandemic has brought local communities closer – survey*, 12 January. Available from: www.aol.co.uk/2021/01/12/coronavirus-pandemic-has-brought-local-communities-closer-a-su/

Pro Bono Economics (2020) *Press release: Community support falls by third at start of second lockdown*, 1 December. Available from: www.probonoeconomics.com/news/press-release-community-support-falls-by-third-at-start-of-second-lockdown

Prus, R. (1996) *Symbolic Interaction and Ethnographic Research: Intersubjectivity and the study of human lived experience*. New York: SUNY Press.

Prus, R. (1999) *Beyond the Power Mystique: Power as intersubjective accomplishment*. Albany: State University of New York Press.

Public Health England (2020) *Impact of COVID-19 pandemic on grocery shopping behaviours*, Public Health England. Available from: https://assets.publishing.service.gov.uk/government/uploads/system/uploads/attachment_data/file/932350/Grocery_Purchasing_Report.pdf

Puddephatt, A. (2021) 'Nature and the environment in interaction', in D. vom Lehn, N. Ruiz-Junco and W. Gibson (eds) *The Routledge International Handbook of Interactionism*, Abingdon, Oxon: Routledge, pp 242–53.

Putnam, R.D. (2000) *Bowling Alone: The collapse and revival of American community*. New York: Simon & Schuster.

Quinio, V. and Ramuni, L. (2020) 'How has spending recovered in our town and city centres?', *Centre for Cities*, 3 September. Available from: https://www.centreforcities.org/blog/how-has-spending-recovered-in-our-town-and-city-centres/

Rahman, M. (2020) 'The historical roots of your lockdown sourdough obsession', *The Conversation*, 12 May. Available from: https://theconversation.com/the-historical-roots-of-your-lockdown-sourdough-obsession-137528

Reiner, R. (2010) *The Politics of the Police* (4th edn). Oxford: Oxford University Press.

Robb, C.E., de Jager, C.A., Ahmadi-Abhari, S., Giannakopoulou, P., Udeh-Momoh, C., McKeand, J., et al (2020) 'Associations of social isolation with anxiety and depression during the early COVID-19 pandemic: a survey of older adults in London, UK', *Front Psychiatry*, 11: 591120.

Rock, P. (1979) 'Pragmatism and symbolic interactionism', in *The Making of Symbolic Interactionism*, London: Palgrave Macmillan, pp 59–101.

Rosen, M. (2021) *Many Different Types of Love: A story of life, death and the NHS*. London: Ebury Press.

Royal London (2020) *National Funeral Cost Index report 2020*, Royal London. Available from: www.royallondon.com/about-us/media/media-centre/research/national-funeral-cost-index-report-2020/

Rutter, H., Wolpert, M. and Greenhalgh, T. (2020) 'Managing uncertainty in the covid-19 era', *British Medical Journal*, 370: m3349.

Salzgeber, J. (2019) *The Little Book of Stoicism: Timeless wisdom to gain resilience, confidence, and calmness*, Jonas Salzgeber.

Sanders, M., Stockdale, E., Hume, S. and John, P. (2021) 'Loss aversion fails to replicate in the coronavirus pandemic: evidence from an online experiment', *Economics Letters*, 199: 109433.

Santayana, G. (1905) Volume 1 of *The Life of Reason, Or, The Phases of Human Progress: Introduction, and Reason in common sense*, C Scribner's Sons.

Santini, Z.I., Jose, P.E., Cornwell, E.Y., Koyanagi, A., Nielsen, L., Hinrichsen, C., et al (2020) 'Social disconnectedness, perceived isolation, and symptoms of depression and anxiety among older Americans (NSHAP): a longitudinal mediation analysis', *Lancet Public Health*, 5: e62–70.

Savage, M. (2020a) 'Poll reveals scale of "home alone" Christmas in the UK this year', *The Observer*, 5 December. Available from: www.theguardian.com/society/2020/dec/05/poll-reveals-scale-of-home-alone-christmas-in-the-uk-this-year

Savage, M. (2020b) 'Seven in 10 back mandatory use of masks in shops in England, poll finds', *The Observer*, 19 July. Available from: www.theguardian.com/world/2020/jul/19/three-quarters-uk-support-mandatory-masks-coronavirus

Schmitt, Carl (2014) *Dictatorship: From the origin of the modern concept of sovereignty to proletarian class struggle* (translated by M. Hoelzl and G. Ward). Cambridge: Polity Press.

Schneider, C.J. (2021) 'Policing and social media', in D. vom Lehn, N. Ruiz-Junco and W. Gibson (eds) *The Routledge International Handbook of Interactionism*, Abingdon, Oxon: Routledge, pp 298–309.

Schutz, A. (1945) 'On multiple realities', *Philosophy and Phenomenological Research*, 5: 533–76.

Sibony, A.-L. (2020) 'The UK COVID-19 response: a behavioural irony?' *European Journal of Risk Regulation*, 11(2): 350–7.

Singer, P. (1981) *The Expanding Circle: Ethics and sociobiology*. Oxford: Clarendon Press.

Smith, R.J. (2021) 'Space, mobility and interaction', in D. vom Lehn, N. Ruiz-Junco and W. Gibson (eds) *The Routledge International Handbook of Interactionism*, Abingdon, Oxon: Routledge, pp 231–41.

Sommerlad, A., Marston, L., Huntley, J., Livingston, G., Lewis, G., Steptoe, A. and Fancourt, D. (2022) 'Social relationships and depression during the COVID-19 lockdown: longitudinal analysis of the COVID-19 Social Study', *Psychological Medicine*, 52: 3381–90.

Spinney, L. (2017) *Pale Rider: The Spanish Flu of 1918 and how it changed the world*. London: Jonathan Cape.

Stenson, K. (2005) 'Sovereignty, biopolitics and the local government of crime in Britain', *Theoretical Criminology*, 9(3): 265–87.

Stewart, C. (2020) 'Activities missed most during the coronavirus lockdown in the UK as of May 2020', *Statista*, 20 May. Available from: www.statista.com/statistics/1119092/uk-activities-missed-most-during-lockdown/

Strauss, A.L. (1978) *Negotiations: Varieties, contexts, processes, and social order.* San Francisco, CA: Jossey-Bass.

Street-Porter, J. (2021) 'We are all drinking more – and government fear-mongering won't stop us', *Independent*, 16 July. Available from: www.independent.co.uk/independentpremium/voices/alcohol-rates-rise-world-health-organisation-b1885496.html

Sweney, M. and Butler, S. (2021) 'B&Q owner's profits soar as Covid creates "generation of DIYers"', *The Guardian*, 22 March. Available from: www.theguardian.com/business/2021/mar/22/b-and-q-owner-profits-soar-as-covid-creates-generation-of-diyers-kingfisher

Swerling, G. (2020) 'Older people more likely to break lockdown rules than young, ONS finds', *The Telegraph*, 13 November. Available from: www.telegraph.co.uk/news/2020/11/13/older-people-likely-break-lockdown-rules-young-ons-study-finds/

Swerling, G (2021) 'One in four adults has not been hugged for more than a year', *The Telegraph*, 28 July. Available from: www.telegraph.co.uk/news/2021/07/28/one-four-adults-has-not-hugged-year/

Swinford, S. and Courea, E. (2020) 'Coronavirus: don't keep over-70s indoors, Tories warn', *The Times*, 5 May. Available from: www.thetimes.co.uk/article/don-t-keep-over-70s-indoors-tories-warn-9nn3x3rzz

Syal, R. (2021) 'English Covid rules have changed 64 times since March, says barrister', *The Guardian*, 12 January. Available from: www.theguardian.com/world/2021/jan/12/england-covid-lockdown-rules-have-changed-64-times-says-barrister

The National Police Chiefs' Council and the College of Policing (2020) *Policing the pandemic: the Act, the Regulations and guidance.* Available from: www.police.uk/SysSiteAssets/media/downloads/central/advice/covid/policing-the-pandemic_-the-act-the-regulations-and-guidance.pdf

The Telegraph (2023) 'The Lockdown Files'. Available from: www.telegraph.co.uk/news/lockdown-files/

Tischer, D., Evans, J. and Davies, S. (2020) 'Cash', in M. Parker (ed) *Life After Covid-19: The other side of crisis*, Bristol: Bristol University Press, pp 83–94.

Trevelyan, G.M. (1944) *English Social History: A survey of six centuries: Chaucer to Queen Victoria.* New York: Longmans.

University College London News (2020a) 'Over 65s exercising more than before lockdown', 12 October. Available from: www.ucl.ac.uk/news/headlines/2020/oct/over-65s-exercising-more-lockdown

University College London News (2020b) 'Third of people report enjoying lockdown', 26 June. Available from: www.ucl.ac.uk/news/2020/jun/third-people-report-enjoying-lockdown

References

University College London News (2021) 'Less than a third completely understand Covid-19 rules', 21 May. Available from: www.ucl.ac.uk/news/2021/may/less-third-completely-understand-covid-19-rules

Ward, M. (2020) 'Lockdown diaries: the everyday voices of the coronavirus pandemic', *The Conversation*, 29 May. Available from: https://theconversation.com/lockdown-diaries-the-everyday-voices-of-the-coronavirus-pandemic-138631

Washtell, F. (2020) 'The Zoom boom: it's a company most people had never heard of before Covid, but now it's bigger than HSBC and Lloyds put together', *This Is Money*, 2 September. Available from: www.thisismoney.co.uk/money/markets/article-8686935/The-Zoom-BOOM-Company-bigger-HSBC-Lloyds-together.html

Webb, E. (2020) *Coronavirus risk for older people: the updated picture*, AgeUK. Available from: www.ageuk.org.uk/discover/2020/06/coronavirus-risk-for-older-people-updated/

Wilson, T. and Buzzeo, J. (2021) *Laid low: the impacts of the Covid-19 crisis on low-paid and insecure workers*, Institute for Employment Studies. Available from: www.employment-studies.co.uk/resource/laid-low

Wittgenstein, L. (1953) *Philosophical Investigations*. Oxford: Blackwell Publishing.

Woodcock, A. (2020) 'Coronavirus: almost three in four Britons "very nervous" about leaving homes after lockdown, poll finds', *Independent*, 28 April. Available from: www.independent.co.uk/news/uk/politics/coronavirus-lockdown-uk-us-italy-spain-germany-australia-opinion-poll-a9487756.html

YouGov (2022) 'Do you think people should or should not be legally required to self-isolate if they test positive for Covid-19?', 9 February. Available from: https://yougov.co.uk/topics/health/survey-results/daily/2022/02/09/7c596/1

Zilanawala, A., Chanfreau, J., Sironi, M. and Palma, M. (2020) *Household composition, couples' relationship quality, and social support during lockdown: initial findings from the COVID-19 Survey in five national longitudinal studies*. London: UCL Centre for Longitudinal Studies. Available from: https://cls.ucl.ac.uk/wp-content/uploads/2020/11/Household-composition-couples-relationship-quality-and-social-support-during-lockdown-%E2%80%93-Initial-findings-from-COVID.pdf

Zinn, J.O. (2021) 'Introduction: towards a sociology of pandemics', *Current Sociology*, 69(4): 435–52.

Index

Participants' pseudonyms are marked with * (e.g. Amber*).

A

adaptation 7, 31, 36–41, 44, 47, 55, 187–191
 Blumer's stages of 19, 20, 22, 192
 see also pragmatic adaptation
Addario, G. et al 206, 208
adult children 27, 61–63, 98, 145, 213
Age UK 74
air travel 23, 29–31, 77, 215
alcohol 65, 112, 113, 114–115, 117, 119, 133, 140
Ali, S.N. 73
altruism 85, 209, 216–218
Amber* 25, 85, 101, 159, 163, 177
anger 60–61, 65, 70, 132, 207, 225
Anna* 23, 37, 46, 64–65, 74, 93, 97–98, 131–132, 152, 171, 179, 184, 227
anxiety and fear
 compliance rates 52, 54–55, 56, 200, 222
 economic factors 76–77
 first lockdown 37–38, 39, 51–55
 of hospitals 134, 167–168
 Johnson's hospitalisation 45–46, 50
 media impact on 48, 49–51, 55, 123, 134, 166
 older adults, other studies 74, 167
 post-pandemic 188, 189
 pre-lockdown 20, 27–28, 29
 as restrictions eased 173–175, 184–186, 195, 200–201, 222
 of vaccinations 181, 182
 will-writing surge due to 97
Appletree* 9, 46, 70, 111, 137–138, 159, 162, 163, 181–182, 186, 198
April* 27–28, 150–151
Aragunde-Kohl, Ú.A. et al 86–87
Araminta* 9, 31, 38, 63, 71, 150, 172, 174, 187, 225–226, 227
AstraZeneca vaccine 181
Athelstana* 44, 45, 138, 199
Austen* 32, 37, 53, 187, 218
Australia 29–30, 219, 220

B

baking 83, 111–112, 161, 188
Bambra, C. et al 73
Barber, N. 44
Barefoot Doc* 61, 70, 138, 148, 160, 206–207
Barkley* 29, 32, 39, 56, 86, 89, 93, 114, 117, 120, 138–139, 147, 153, 175
BBC
 news 45, 49–50, 58, 86
 other output 62–63, 181, 221
Bea* 9, 27, 28, 98, 108, 125, 139, 152, 190, 219
beaches 59, 60, 63, 127, 141, 162
Becker, H.S. 55, 193, 212
Behavioural Insights Team 55
Bell, M.M. 158
Bellotti, E. et al 80, 146
Benchman* 9–10, 19, 97, 102, 104, 111, 153, 186, 188
Bennett, Alan 13
Berger, P. 14, 36, 69, 92, 123
Best, J. 51, 88, 89, 193
Bettymac* 49, 64, 84, 117, 129, 204
Binns, F. 100
birthdays 33, 61, 107, 108, 132, 161, 171, 216
Bloom & Wild 150
Blumer, H. 14, 45, 49, 52, 59, 123
 adaptation stages 19, 20, 22, 192
Bonanza Bill* 76, 121, 126, 139, 142, 155
Bonivard* 32, 53–54, 87, 115, 175, 185, 228
book groups 31, 32, 108, 165, 175
books 104, 139, 175, 200, 207
Bourdieu, P. 110
Brewster, B.H. 158
Brexit 20, 45, 54
Bridebook 28
BritainThinks 13–14, 76
British Medical Association (BMA) 34, 72, 73
British Trust for Ornithology 159
Bu, F. et al 118
bubbles 143, 162, 163, 178–180

C

cafés *see* restaurants/cafés
Calkins, K. 94
Campbell* 41, 71, 77–78, 99, 173, 196–197, 198, 217
cancer 34, 35, 43, 73, 135
Cannadine, D. 7
Caractacus* 24, 32, 58, 61, 83, 100, 124, 132, 156, 197
cardiovascular disease 43, 73

Index

care homes/staff 46, 72–73, 206–207
Carleton, R.N. 52
cars
  essential trips 134–135, 136
  maintenance 102, 139, 154–155
  purchasing 121
  restrictions 60, 140, 143, 145, 152, 157, 171
Centre for Ageing Better 206, 208
Centre for Cities thinktank 80
charity shops 100, 137, 200
Charles★ 10, 19–20, 24, 34, 38, 81, 108–109, 134, 139, 150, 155, 159, 190, 208
childcare 8, 108, 140, 148, 149, 178–180, 204
children 68, 119, 194
  see also adult children; grandchildren; schools
China 1, 2, 20, 21, 22, 29, 130
Christmas 162–165, 222
churches 110, 113, 139
clapping for NHS/essential workers 4, 78, 81, 96, 205–206, 208, 214
Clara★ 93, 131, 133, 163
class 8, 14, 43, 68, 72, 110, 177
cleaners 22, 99–100, 140, 154, 214
clothing 108, 115–117, 118, 121, 139, 215
cognitive dissonance 145, 165, 176, 221
Cohen, S. 52, 125
College of Policing 56
community spirit 22, 79–85, 145, 152, 205–206, 208–209, 216–218
  see also neighbourhoods
Comparethemarket 76
compliance rates
  adult children as rule enforcers 61–63, 213
  fear, role of 52, 54–55, 56, 200, 222
  Office for National Statistics 128, 140, 184
  personal agency 123, 137, 141–143, 213
concerts 21, 32, 82, 106, 119
Cooley, C.H. 217
Coronavirus Act 2020 42, 43, 55
couple households
  feel relatively fortunate 44, 74
  further discussion 8, 116, 117, 118, 147
  lockdown's impact on 145–147, 148
  newly formed 26–27
  sharing tasks 44, 101, 103, 114, 121, 137
courts 77, 155, 202
COVID-19 inquiry 192–193
crime figures 55–56, 58, 66
Crowther, B. 226
Cummings, Dominic 65, 140
cycling 25, 118, 126, 157, 173, 228

D

daily briefings 49–51, 96, 143, 193, 195–199, 213
Daily Express 174

The Daily Mail 172
daily routine 93–96, 105, 116, 147, 154, 216
  exercise 64, 94–95, 104, 118, 186, 215
de-cluttering 95, 96, 100, 102, 137–138, 189, 228
deaths, figures
  daily briefings 49, 196, 197, 213
  global 97
  Italy 18, 20
  local 133
  older adults 69
  rapid increase 1, 3, 18, 19, 37, 40, 41
Dempsey★ 99, 188
dental care 34, 35, 36, 117, 120
Department of Health and Social Care 18
depression 38, 57, 118, 178, 188, 203, 218
deprivation 14, 58, 73–74, 77, 203, 226
diaries 5–7, 9–14, 97–98, 211, 224–229
Dingwall, Robert 3, 55
disabled people 4, 74, 104, 219
disasters, definition 22
Do-It-Yourself (DIY) 56, 101, 102, 103, 146, 207
Dodsworth, L. 222
dog walking 38, 63, 86, 87, 138–139
Dogs Trust 87
Durkheim, E. 43

E

Easter 28, 30–31, 82, 84, 107, 120, 166
economy
  consumer spending 112, 115, 119–122, 176–177
  government spending 202, 209
  post-pandemic 207, 228
  vs. public health 2–3, 49, 68, 193–194, 196, 204
  see also deprivation; furlough system; unemployment
Edgar★ 32–33, 50–51, 83, 112, 188, 201, 221
Eleanor★ 38, 57, 74, 79, 101, 116, 131, 136, 158, 182, 197, 198
Elisabeth★ 57, 133, 151, 188
emails
  administrative tasks 31, 84, 98, 139
  friends and family 32, 53, 108, 150, 151, 156
emotions
  disagreements with friends 65, 126, 133
  first lockdown 38–39, 48, 63, 156, 165–168, 228
  later lockdowns 164, 178
  lessons learned 201, 223
  as restrictions eased 173–174
  vaccinations 182, 183, 184
  see also anger

245

England 1, 8, 18, 58, 97, 141
  Coronavirus Act 2020 42, 43, 55
  rules *cf.* other UK nations 47, 124, 128, 143, 162, 177, 184, 198, 199–200
essential workers
  children of 18, 83
  clapping for NHS/essential workers 4, 78, 81, 96, 205–206, 208, 214
  NHS 58–59, 78, 85, 217, 219
  other contexts 78, 140
  post-pandemic 206–207
  risk 4, 72, 78, 203, 219
ethnic minorities 58, 73, 74, 78, 219
Eustice, George 200
Eve★ 10, 20, 24–25, 26, 51, 64, 119, 142, 159, 190
exercise
  daily routine 64, 94–95, 104, 118, 186, 215
  equipment 120, 121
  further mentions 167, 177, 190, 207
  home/garden spaces 79, 157, 215
  online classes 106, 107, 118, 203
  restrictions 56, 59–60, 80, 157
  types 118–119, 134
  see also cycling; jogging; walking

F

face masks *see* mask wearing
face-to-face interactions 14–15, 89, 105, 125, 130, 212–215
FaceTime 107, 110, 180
families 99, 171–176, 178–180, 218–220
  see also adult children; couple households; grandchildren
Farewill 97
fear *see* anxiety and fear
Festinger, L. 145, 165, 221
fines 58, 60, 66, 128, 202
Fisherman★ 50, 59, 127, 137, 176
Flaherty, M.G. 92–93
food 110–115
  government-supplied 90
  growing 102, 103, 111, 113, 228
  Nella Last's focus on 224
  preparation 98, 111–112, 121, 146
  see also baking; grocery shopping; pubs, meals; restaurants/cafés; take-away food; weight gain
food banks 83, 84, 110, 113, 119, 205, 218
Food Standards Agency 130
France 19, 20, 21, 30, 128–129, 186
Frances★ 20, 47–48, 50, 64, 101, 131, 150, 179
Francia★ 37, 50, 62, 84, 101, 116, 121, 126, 146, 167, 171, 182
Frank, Anne 6, 9
Freedland, Jonathan 93

freedom 2, 3, 7, 59
  see also personal agency
Freedom Day (19 July 2021) 11, 178, 184–186
friendliness 79, 125, 126, 214, 216
friends
  anxiety for 150–151, 218
  disagreements with friends 65, 126, 133
  links to Covid cases 46–47
  living with 27, 56, 63
  new 85
  post-pandemic 190
  as restrictions eased 171–176, 204
  support between 32, 39, 43, 53, 105, 131, 150–151
funerals
  pre-planning 53, 98
  restrictions 28, 33, 42, 46, 47, 135–136
furlough system 3, 18, 219, 220

G

garden centres 102, 103, 121, 143, 221
gardening
  first lockdown 38, 53, 95, 100, 102–103, 129, 189
  growing food 102, 103, 111, 113, 228
  post-pandemic 186, 207
gardens, private
  access to 8, 38, 53, 74, 123, 146
  enjoyment of nature 158–159
  exercise space 79, 157, 215
  lack of 27, 74
  over-the-fence chats 58–59, 85
  see also outdoor gatherings
gates and stiles 45, 139–140, 214
Gatzou★ 20, 45–46, 109, 121, 132, 146, 171
General Practitioners (GPs) 34, 35, 36, 183
Giddens, A. 23, 36, 72
Gilman, S.L. 52
Glaser, B. 28, 94, 135
gloves 131, 132, 133, 136, 137, 221
Goffman, E. 14, 88, 115, 118, 125–126, 215, 224
Gorton, V. et al 177
Gottschalk, S. 105, 110, 149, 215
Gove, Michael 128
Grace★ 25, 41, 48, 56–57, 90, 125, 154, 157
grandchildren
  celebrations with 132, 141, 163, 165
  online calls 108–110, 214
  pain of separation 108, 148–149, 150, 165
  pre-pandemic childcare 8, 148
  as restrictions eased 171–173, 175–176, 179–180, 204
  social distancing 171–173, 175–176
  young adults 218
Gray, J.A. 52

Great Barrington Declaration 4, 43, 194
grocery shopping
  first lockdown 24–25, 44, 110, 135, 138
  frequency of 119, 120
  mask wearing 128–130, 137
  older adults, times/services 113–114
  online 107–108, 113–114, 161, 165, 203, 207, 214, 222
  for or by others 44, 62, 80, 82–83, 112–113, 218
  packaging, contamination fear 130–132, 137
  pre-pandemic 21, 30, 216
Guardian 93

H

hairdressing 115, 116, 117–118, 119, 138
Hallett, Heather, Baroness 192
Hancock, Matt 4, 13, 54
hand washing 130, 132–133, 135, 136, 137, 188, 190
Hannem, S. 15, 213
Harris, T. 54
Harrisson, Tom 6
Hastings, Max 77
Hattie★ 51, 59, 62, 87, 94, 109, 149, 165, 172, 186
Heidegger, M. 92
Helga★ 29–30, 167–168
herd immunity strategy 4, 43, 70
Hoggart, P. 8, 95, 111
Hold Still project 13
Holgate★ 39, 76–77, 79, 93, 148, 158, 173, 185–186, 190, 228
holidays
  Britons advised to return home 28
  cancellations 19, 29, 31–32, 101, 119, 161–162, 165, 168
  post-pandemic 186, 190
  pre-lockdown 21–22, 29–30, 40, 127
  pretend 109
  as restrictions eased 176, 186
  spending/refunds 31, 119, 120, 121, 154
Holly★ 10, 72, 83, 90, 107, 117, 120, 147, 157, 166, 175, 185, 197, 224–225
home ownership 44, 77, 98
home schooling 24, 108–109, 110
Hooson, M. 97
hospitalisations
  figures 3, 19, 41, 49, 133, 196, 213
  Johnson 45–46, 47, 50, 97, 212
hospitality industry 25, 31, 77, 174, 176–177
households 26–27, 145
  see also couple households; multi-person households; single-person households
Housewife 49 6
housework 38, 53, 94, 98, 132, 205
  see also cleaners; de-cluttering

housing market 26, 187
hugs
  footballers on TV 126
  missing hugs 74–75, 136, 149–150
  as restrictions eased 171–172, 174, 175–176, 204
humour
  coping strategy 88–91, 104, 132, 140, 209
  online 82, 89, 116
  self-presentation 226
Humphrey★ 33, 62–63, 89, 93–94, 106, 107, 147, 152, 163, 173, 175, 198–199

I

Iacobucci, G. 73
Imperial College 18
income 32, 76, 119, 120, 138, 207–208
  see also furlough system; low-paid employment; pensions
Independent Age 200
information
  lack of 45, 211, 212
  lessons learned 195–202, 223
  statistical presentation of 71, 123, 196, 197, 213, 223
  see also daily briefings; deaths, figures; hospitalisations, figures
Institute for Employment Studies 76
International Federation of Red Cross and Red Crescent Societies 22
Ipsos Mori 140, 222
Italy 18, 20, 49

J

Jacca★ 26, 37, 48, 71, 120, 127, 148–149, 151, 164, 178, 182, 188–189
James, Erwin 93
Janwig★ 40, 83, 116, 153, 160, 161, 186, 189
Jarvis, C. et al 80, 211
Jennifer★ 52–53, 75, 78, 98, 127, 136, 151, 183, 185
Jennings, Humphrey 6
Jessie★ 30, 46, 59–60, 82, 107, 109, 128–129, 162, 164–165, 180
jigsaws 95, 104, 109
Jimmy★ 27, 40, 44, 157
jogging 25, 126, 129
John Lewis Partnership 94
Johnson, Boris
  COVID-19 hospitalisation 45–46, 47, 50, 97, 212
  daily briefings 49, 193, 197, 198
  further mentions 128, 130, 174, 184, 185, 220
  lockdown announcement 1, 18, 23, 47, 124
Jojo★ 34, 46, 60, 87, 101, 109, 115, 116

Joyner, L. 87
Jules* 21, 48, 50, 70, 84, 152, 174, 183, 228

K

Katja* 40, 51, 166, 180, 198
key workers *see* essential workers
Kirk, A. et al 207
Kynaston, D. Foreword, 6

L

Laing, David 200
Last, Nella 6, 48, 224
legislation 3, 45, 211
  see also Coronavirus Act 2020; rules and restrictions
The Lockdown Files 13, 54, 55, 194, 200
lockdowns
  first announcement 1, 18, 23, 28, 47, 124
  international variations 2, 4, 43, 194, 212, 223
  later lockdowns 58, 97
  local 174, 177
  overview 3, 177–178
loneliness 74–75, 85–88, 118, 204
Louise* 25, 54, 65–66, 86, 102, 134–135, 168
low-paid employment 14, 76, 79, 110, 207
Luckmann, T. 14, 36, 69, 92, 123
Lynne* 82, 96, 98, 110, 129, 154, 189

M

Mabel* 33, 35, 57, 62, 116, 125, 139, 209
Madge, Charles 6
Madge, John 226
Madge, N. 8, 95, 111
maintenance (household) 205
  see also Do-It-Yourself (DIY)
Malaysia 29
Malcolmson, P. and R. 224
mask wearing 128–130
  Freedom Day 178, 186
  at funerals 136
  further discussion 45, 79, 181, 182, 184, 202
  in hospital 134, 135
  public transport 128, 129, 186
  shops and services 128–130, 137, 138, 139, 186
  Thailand 29, 30
Mass Observation 6, 13
McCarthy, Helen 14
McKenzie, Lisa 14
Mead, G.H. 26, 79, 92, 125, 217
media 5, 48, 49–51, 55, 58
  see also news coverage; television
medications 44, 82, 137
men 58, 69
Menand, Louis 15

mental health 43, 74, 86–87, 158, 178, 203, 204
  see also anxiety and fear; depression
Met Office 156
Microsoft Teams 139
middle class 8, 68, 72, 177
mobile phones 34, 80, 203
Moore, Captain Tom 76, 79, 220
moral panic 52, 55
Morales, S.R. 73
Mother's Day 41, 141
moving house 26, 27, 187
multi-person households
  living with adult children 27, 98, 145
  living with friends 27, 56, 63
  see also couple households
mutualism 69, 80, 126, 132, 214, 218

N

National Health Service (NHS)
  Captain Tom Moore's fundraising 76, 79
  core services (non-COVID-19) 34–35, 37, 73, 133–135
  essential workers 58–59, 78, 85, 217, 219
  protection of 68, 71, 123, 194, 217
  vaccination programme 183
National Police Chiefs' Council 56
National Portrait Gallery 13
National Rural Crime Network 66
National Trust 148
natural environment
  enjoyment of 61, 65, 156–160, 214
  lockdown's impact on 25, 39, 40, 88, 154, 215
  post-pandemic 189, 190, 207–208
neighbourhoods
  community spirit 22, 79–85, 145, 152, 205–206, 208–209, 216–218
  COVID-19 cases in 47
  improved knowledge of 157, 214, 215
  over-the-fence chats 58–59, 85
  rule-breaking reported 65–66
  WhatsApp groups 40, 66, 82, 83, 208, 214, 218
New Policy Institute 119
New Zealand 43, 194, 212
news coverage
  altruism as result of 216–217
  diarists' descriptions of 49–51, 58, 71, 73, 85, 166, 168
  lessons learned 195–196
  non-pandemic stories 220
  symbolic interactionism 49, 51, 52, 123
  see also daily briefings
newspapers
  delivering/buying 56, 82, 142
  reading 9, 12, 49–51, 132, 166, 195, 221
  see also The Lockdown Files

Index

NHS *see* National Health Service (NHS)
Nikčević, A.V. 201

O

Oakeshott, Isobel 13
Obrdlík, A. 89
The Observer 128, 141, 162
OECD (Organisation for Economic Co-operation and Development) 76–77
Ofcom 105
Office for National Statistics
  compliance rates 128, 140, 184
  economic factors 73, 76, 77
  other topics 158, 207
  shopping 113, 115, 120
older adults
  computer literacy 106, 203, 205, 223
  exercise statistics 157
  feel relatively fortunate 38, 44, 76–78, 84, 203–204, 218–219, 226
  mortality rates 69, 70–71
  other studies 74, 167
  as resource 205–206, 223
  rule-breaking rates 141
  self-isolation 142, 200, 205–206
  shop times/services 113–114
  special risk 4, 69–72, 194–195
  volunteering restrictions 84–85, 205–206, 218
Olive★ 23, 33, 44, 58, 60, 73–74, 154, 156, 161, 205
online activities 105–110
  celebrations 107–108, 161, 162, 163–164, 165, 222
  court hearings 77
  exercise classes 106, 107, 118, 203
  funerals 135–136
  grocery shopping 107–108, 113–114, 161, 165, 203, 207, 214, 222
  health care 34
  other shopping 121, 203
  social activities 82, 106–108, 148, 153, 161, 203, 205
  technology requirements 106, 110, 121, 139, 202–203, 214
  working from home 104
  see also Zoom
Opinions and Lifestyle Survey 128
Opinium 128, 162, 208
Ordnance Survey 80
Ottolie★ 33–34, 39, 47, 53, 65, 70, 84, 86, 90, 106, 116, 148, 176
outdoor gatherings
  gardens 75, 133, 140, 163, 171–175, 179
  permitted numbers 177, 178

P

pandemic, definition/term use 1, 52
Pangolin★ 64, 106–107, 164, 189

Parker, M. 206
parks
  benches 56, 59, 63, 64, 148, 159
  restriction enforcement 56–57, 59–60, 138–139
  usage rates 24, 127, 138
participants, demographics 1, 4–5, 7–8, 12, 227
Patel, Priti 65
Patrick, Ruth 14
Pen★ 40, 70, 96, 100, 103, 142, 149, 228–229
pensions 32, 44, 76, 77, 78, 120
People and Nature Survey 158, 207–208
Pepys, Samuel 5, 175
Persia★ 27, 39, 71, 112, 114, 117–118, 129, 157, 183
personal agency
  older adults 205
  pragmatic adaptation 14–15, 123, 130–133, 137, 140–143, 211, 213
  reduction of 42–44, 62–63, 68
  as restrictions eased 170, 185
Personal Protective Equipment (PPE) 72, 134, 135
Pet Food Manufacturers' Association 86
Peter★ 23–24, 39, 62, 96, 113, 114, 149, 176
pets 75, 85–88, 153
  see also dog walking
Pfizer/BioNTech vaccine 97, 181, 183, 184
  see also vaccinations
physical touch 74–75
  see also hugs; surface contamination
Plas, Annemarie 81
police 55–61, 65–66, 134, 177, 201–202, 213
Police Foundation and Crest Advisory 202
Portes, Jonathan 2
Poulain, J.-P. 110
pragmatic adaptation
  living arrangements 26–27, 145
  neighbourhoods 82–83
  personal agency 14–15, 123, 130–133, 137, 140–143, 211, 213
  research conclusions 211, 213–214, 216, 217, 222–223
pre-existing health conditions 4, 71, 73, 74, 142, 194, 204
Press Gazette 49
Pro Bono Economics 208
Prus, R. 199
Public Administration and Constitutional Affairs Committee 55
Public Health England 112
public health management model
  description of 2–3, 42–44
  lessons learned 193–199, 201, 223
  vs. wider focus 2–3, 49, 68, 193–194, 196, 204

public transport 23, 24, 30, 41, 63, 142
  mask wearing 128, 129, 186
pubs
  closure of 22
  meals 153, 162, 176, 200
  as restrictions eased 116, 153, 162, 175, 176, 186, 199
  spending patterns 112
  take-away food 24
Puddephatt, A. 17, 158, 215
Puerto Rico 86–87
Putnam, R.D. 80, 216
puzzles 95, 104, 109
pyjamas 115, 116, 139, 215

Q

quizzes 107, 108, 161

R

Raab, Dominic 28
race 8, 58, 73, 74, 78, 219
Rahman, M. 111
Rain* 95, 132, 153, 158–159, 205
Rashford, Marcus 79
reciprocity 79, 88, 125–126, 130, 132, 218
religious organisations 28, 83, 110, 113, 139, 174, 203
restaurants/cafés 19, 22, 24–25, 112, 153, 162, 176–177
restrictions *see* rules and restrictions
Retail Gazette 113
retirement 95, 123, 146, 188
  see also pensions
risk
  essential workers 4, 72, 78, 203, 219
  management of 42–44, 52, 71, 212–213
  older adults 4, 69–72, 194–195
  personal assessment of 61, 63, 130–133, 141–143, 175, 205
  unequal exposure to 72–76
  variability of 68
Rob* 54, 75, 82, 96, 102, 121, 129, 150, 166, 178, 183
Robb, C.E. et al 167
Rosa* 48, 66, 75, 143, 204
Rosemary* 38, 196, 205, 221
RSPB 158
rule of six 65, 124, 141, 177, 178, 199–200
rules and restrictions
  changes/confusion 49, 57, 143, 171, 179–180, 199–202, 213, 222–223
  daily briefings 143, 195–199
  differences by nation of UK 47, 75, 124, 128, 143, 162, 177, 184, 198–200
  easing of 170–177, 178, 180, 184–187
  see also compliance rates; courts; fines; police

S

Sachs, Albie 95
Salzgeber, J. 37
Santayana, G. 7, 224
Sardomike* 50, 85, 104, 135, 164, 184, 226
Schmitt, C. 3, 211
schools 18, 22, 43, 76, 77, 78, 83, 199
  see also home schooling
Schutz, A. 92
Scotland 1, 8, 18
  rules *cf.* other UK nations 124, 128, 162, 177, 184, 198, 199–200
second homes 26, 63, 64, 65, 120
Second World War 6, 37, 40, 89, 111
self-isolation
  first lockdown 22, 26, 44, 133, 168
  older adults 142, 200, 205–206
  as restrictions eased 3, 184, 187
self-presentation 112, 115, 118, 125, 217, 224, 226
Serious Acute Respiratory Syndrome (SARS) (2002–03) 2, 21
shielding 4, 72, 90, 204, 219
shopping
  clothing 115
  first lockdown 24–25, 42, 56
  hardware 56, 101, 102
  as leisure activity 141, 153–154
  mask wearing 128–130, 137
  Nella Last's focus on 224
  post-pandemic 188, 189
  as restrictions eased 173, 200
  staff 78
  see also economy, consumer spending; garden centres; grocery shopping; newspapers, delivering/buying
Simon* 63, 94, 159, 174, 200
Singapore 19, 20, 21
Singer, P. 85, 216
single-person households 8, 74–75, 86, 107, 145, 149–150, 162, 178
Skye* 88, 94, 104, 131, 157, 204
Skype 109, 163
sleep 39, 94, 101, 167
social activities
  cancellations 31–34, 37, 41, 44, 227–228
  neighbourhoods 80, 81–82
  online 82, 106–108, 148, 153, 161, 203, 205
  Zoom 82, 106–108, 148, 168, 205
social distancing
  Christmas 163–164, 165
  definition/time span 42, 124
  enforcement 56, 60

Index

first lockdown 38, 74, 97, 103, 124–127, 142, 217
grandchildren 171–173, 175–176
indoor public spaces 113, 135, 136, 153, 174
non-live-in partners 148
post-vaccination 184
pre-lockdown 18, 22, 25
as restrictions eased 170, 171–176, 178, 186, 204
rule-breaking 126–127, 129, 135, 141, 157
walking 64, 79, 87, 116, 123, 125–127
see also outdoor gatherings
social history, overview 5–7, 224–229
social media 3, 49, 101, 106, 126, 150
social order
 breakdown of old 36, 69, 124
 new 42–44, 55, 68, 88, 123–126, 187
Sommerlad, A. et al 203
Spada, M.M. 201
Spinney, L. 209
Squeals★ 47, 81, 166, 226
Stanley★ 129–130, 141
Statista 148
stoicism
 of Captain Tom Moore 79 Replace
 first lockdown 31, 36–37, 53, 149
 pragmatic adaptation 140, 168, 214, 222
Strathspey★ 35, 107, 127–128
Strauss, A.L. 28, 94, 124–125, 135
Street-Porter, Janet 115
Sumption, Jonathan, Lord 58
Sunak, Rishi 176, 184
surface contamination
 books 139, 175, 200
 food packaging 130–132, 137
 further examples 131, 171, 207
 gates 45, 139–140, 214
SusieQ★ 95, 103, 108, 118, 143, 168, 172
Sweden 2, 43, 136, 194, 212
Sweetpea★ 21, 71, 126–127
symbolic interactionism 14–15, 49, 51, 52, 87, 89, 92, 105, 110–112, 123, 125, 158, 212–215
see also adaptation; pragmatic adaptation
symbols
 first lockdown 44–46, 49, 55, 123, 130, 133
 pre-lockdown 20, 22–23

T

take-away food 24, 25, 128
Taranaki★ 10–11, 39, 95, 100, 110, 112, 114, 165, 173, 197, 225
The Telegraph 13, 54, 55, 194, 200
telephone calls
 first lockdown 53, 59, 65, 71, 100, 150–151
 further examples 77, 114, 132, 167, 180
 health care 34, 35–36, 37
 mobile phones 34, 80, 203
 volunteering 84, 204
television 50, 62–63, 105, 126, 177, 207, 221
see also daily briefings
Teresa★ 73, 108, 111, 189, 197
terminal self 105, 110, 149, 215
testing 51, 62, 72, 212
Thailand 29, 30, 127
time 92–96, 97, 100, 110, 154, 216
see also daily routine
The Times 69–70, 77, 142, 197
toilet rolls 21, 25, 29, 89, 107, 110, 111
Topper★ 27, 38, 54, 60, 117, 164, 189
touching *see* hugs; physical touch; surface contamination
tourist industry 25, 31, 77, 174
travel restrictions 28, 42, 55, 135, 136, 166, 186
see also cars, restrictions
Trevelyan, G.M. 7
Tweegy★ 46, 102, 113

U

UK COVID-19 Inquiry 192–193
unemployment 40, 76, 77, 78, 206
University College London (UCL) COVID-19 Social Study 199, 220

V

vaccinations
 childhood 43
 COVID-19 11, 45, 97, 180–184, 186, 209, 222–223
video calls *see* online/video calls
volunteering 177, 181
 grocery shopping 44, 62, 80, 82–83, 112–113, 218
 older adults, barriers to 84–85, 205–206, 218
 pre-pandemic 104, 107
 remotely 84, 107, 204

W

Wagner, Adam 49
Waite, Terry 116
Wales 1, 8, 18
 rules *cf.* other UK nations 75, 128, 143, 162, 184, 198
walking 157–159
 celebrations marked by 162, 164
 couples 146, 156, 162
 daily routine 64, 95, 104, 118, 186, 215
 rule-breaking 64, 139–140, 141, 142
 social distancing 64, 79, 116, 123, 125–127
 travel restrictions 60, 143, 157
 see also dog walking

Ward, Michael 13
Warrener* 21, 30, 36, 60, 103, 106, 112–113, 140
waste management 100, 140, 156
weather
  first lockdown 53, 100, 102–103, 127, 132, 138, 156–157, 228
  later lockdowns 81, 177
  non-pandemic diaries 9–10, 224
  outdoor gatherings 75, 163, 172–173
wedding anniversaries 161–162, 216
weddings 28, 42
weight gain 82, 119
WhatsApp
  friends and family 109–110, 148, 166
  government use of 13, 54, 194
  neighbourhood groups 40, 66, 82, 83, 208, 214, 218
Which? 97
Will* 11, 22, 88, 103, 132, 180, 207, 225
will-writing 96–97
window cleaning 46, 101, 154
Wittgenstein, L. 142
working class 14, 43, 68, 72
Working Class Collective 14
working from home 18, 104, 119, 177, 187, 207, 219

World Health Organization (WHO) 1, 2, 18, 22, 52

Y

YouGov 119, 128, 187
young people
  anxiety for 77, 78, 218–219, 220
  enforcement focus 58, 59–60
  lockdown's impact on 68, 77, 78, 97, 146, 194
YouTube 101, 106

Z

Zilanawala, A. et al 145–146
Zinn, J.O. 212
Zoom 105–110
  celebrations 107–108, 161, 165, 222
  daily routine 75, 96, 216
  family calls 59, 62, 108–110
  further examples 129, 136, 150, 151, 175, 190
  pragmatic adaptation 168, 209, 214–215, 216, 222
  self-presentation 118, 215
  social activities 82, 106–108, 148, 168, 205
  technology requirements 106, 110, 121, 203, 214

www.ingramcontent.com/pod-product-compliance
Lightning Source LLC
Chambersburg PA
CBHW051535020426
42333CB00016B/1937